Woodrow Wilson

American Presidents Series
Herbert S. Parmet, Series Editor

Woodrow Wilson,
Sigmund Freud and William C. Bullitt

Eisenhower and the American Crusades
Herbert S. Parmet

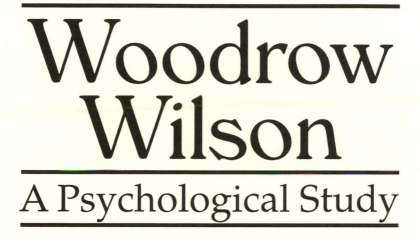

Woodrow Wilson

A Psychological Study

Sigmund Freud
William C. Bullitt

Transaction Publishers
New Brunswick (U.S.A.) and London (U.K.)

Transaction Publishers edition printed in 1999 by arrangement with the Houghton Mifflin Company, All Rights Reserved.
Copyright © 1966 by Sigmund Freud Copyrights Ltd. and William C. Bullitt.

This book is printed on acid-free paper that meets the American National Standard for Permanence of Paper for Printed Library Materials.

Library of Congress Catalog Number: 98-9392
ISBN: 0-7658-0426-3
Printed in the United States of America

Library of Congress Cataloging-in-Publication Data

Freud, Sigmund, 1856–1939.
    [Thomas Woodrow Wilson, twenty-eighth President of the United States]
    Woodrow Wilson : a psychological study / Sigmund Freud and William C. Bullitt.
        p. cm. — (American presidency series)
    Originally published: Thomas Woodrow Wilson, twenty-eighth President of the United States. Boston : Houghton Mifflin, 1967 [c1966].
    ISBN 0-7658-0426-3 (pbk. : alk. paper)
    1. Wilson, Woodrow, 1856–1924—Psychology. 2. Presidents—United States—Biography. I. Bullitt, William C. (William Christian), 1891–1967. II. Title. III. Series.
E767.F7   1998
937.91'3'092—dc21   98-9392
    [B]   CIP

FOREWORD

BY WILLIAM C. BULLITT

To FOLLOW FACTS wherever they may lead requires a courage that few men possess. Freud dared to follow facts to the depths of man's mind, and to describe the desires he discerned in the dark substrata of the unconscious. His descriptions threatened many of man's cherished beliefs. He was denounced; but he continued to rejoice whenever a theory —even one of his own — was slain by a refractory fact. Truth was his passion.

In the long run, only the insane can resist facts. Mankind now accepts without a trace of scandalized rage Galileo's proof that the earth moves around the sun, and the discoveries of Freud are beginning to be accepted calmly. Psychology was a branch of philosophy but not a science before Freud invented the method of investigation called psychoanalysis. Psychology has now become a science based on fact, and Freud is established among the benefactors of mankind.

He and I had been friends for some years before we decided to collaborate in writing this volume. He was in Berlin for a small operation. I called on him and found him depressed. Somberly he said that he had not long to live and that his death would be unimportant to him or to anyone else, because he had written everything he wished to write and his mind was emptied.

He asked what I was doing, and I told him I was working on a book about the Treaty of Versailles which would contain studies of Clemenceau, Orlando, Lloyd George, Lenin and Woodrow Wilson — all of whom I happened to know personally.

Freud's eyes brightened and he became very much alive. Rapidly he asked a number of questions, which I answered. Then he astonished me by saying he would like to collaborate with me in writing the Wilson chapter of my book.

I laughed and remarked that the idea was delightful but bizarre. My book would interest specialists in the field of foreign affairs. A study of Wilson by him might possess the permanent interest of an analysis of Plato by Aristotle. Every educated man would wish to read it. To bury Freud on Wilson in a chapter of my book would be to produce an impossible monstrosity; the part would be greater than the whole.

Freud persisted, saying that I might consider his proposal comic but it was intended to be serious. To collaborate with me would compel him to start writing again. That would give him new life. Moreover, he was dissatisfied by his studies of Leonardo da Vinci and of the Moses statue by Michelangelo because he had been obliged to draw large conclusions from few facts, and he had long wished to make a psychological study of a contemporary with regard to whom thousands of facts could be ascertained. He had been interested in Wilson ever since he had discovered that they were both born in 1856. He could not do the research necessary for an analysis of Wilson's character; but I could do it easily since I had worked with Wilson and knew all his close friends and associates. He hoped I would accept his proposal.

I replied that I should be delighted to consider it seriously but felt certain that a psychological study of Wilson could not be compressed into a chapter. To accept would be to abandon my book. Two days later I again called on Freud, and after a long talk we agreed to collaborate.

We started to work on our book at once; but to complete it required about ten years. We read all Wilson's published books and speeches, and all the volumes concerning Wilson published by Ray Stannard Baker, who had been chosen by the President as his biographer and had access to all Wilson's private papers. We then read the *Intimate Papers of Colonel House*, who had been Wilson's closest friend during his years as President; *Woodrow Wilson As I Know Him*, written by his Secretary, Joseph P. Tumulty; and the books on Wilson by William Allen White, James Kearney, Robert Edward Annin, David Lawrence and many others. In addition, I read scores of volumes that dealt with aspects of Wilson's career, like *The Economic Consequences of the Peace,* written by J. Maynard Keynes, and Freud read all that I considered worthy of his attention.

Our discussions of this material compelled us to face two facts: first, our study of Wilson would fill a large book; second, it would not be fair to attempt to write an analysis of Wilson's character unless we could deepen our understanding of his nature by private, unpublished information from his intimates.

I set out to try to collect that information. I was helped by many of my friends among Wilson's associates, some of whom put at our disposal their diaries, letters, records and memoranda, while others talked frankly about him. Thanks to their assistance we felt confident that, although subsequent publication of private papers would amplify and deepen knowledge of Wilson's character, no new facts would come to light which would conflict vitally with the facts upon which we had based our study. Without exception, those who gave us this information did so on the understanding that their names would not be revealed.

From these private documents and conversations I compiled notes which ran to more than fifteen hundred typewritten pages. When I returned to Vienna, Freud read the notes and we discussed thoroughly the facts they contained. We then began to write. Freud wrote the first draft of portions of the manuscript and I wrote the first draft of other portions. Each then criticized, amended or rewrote the other's draft until the whole became an amalgam for which we were both responsible.

To burden our book with fifteen hundred pages of notes seemed outrageous. We decided to eliminate all notes except a few which gave data with regard to Wilson's childhood and youth, and seemed essential for readers unfamiliar with the President's roots. A digest of that data will be found on pages 3-31 of this volume.

Both Freud and I were stubborn, and our beliefs were dissimilar. He was a Jew who had become an agnostic. I have always been a believing Christian. We often disagreed but we never quarreled. On the contrary, the more we worked together, the closer friends we became. In the spring of 1932, however, when our manuscript was ready to be typed in final form, Freud made textual changes and wrote a number of new passages to which I objected. After several arguments we decided to forget the book for three weeks, and to attempt then to agree. When we met, we continued to disagree.

I wished to return to the United States to participate in Franklin D. Roosevelt's campaign for President, and I believed that I would never again find time to work on the manuscript. Freud and I had previously decided that our book should first be published in the United States and that I would control the publication date. Finally, I suggested that, since neither one of us was entirely impervious to reason, it was likely that some day we would agree; meanwhile the book should not be published. Both of us, however, should sign each chapter, so that at least a signed unpublishable manuscript would exist. We did so.

Six years passed. In 1938 the Nazis permitted Freud to leave Vienna. I met him at the railroad station in Paris, where I was then American Ambassador, and suggested that we might discuss our book once more after he was settled in London.

I carried the manuscript to Freud, and was delighted when he agreed to eliminate the additions he had written at the last minute, and we were both happy that we found no difficulty in agreeing on certain changes in the text.

Once more I visited him in London and showed him the final text which we had both accepted. This is the text printed here. We then agreed that it would be courteous to refrain from publishing the book so long as the second Mrs. Woodrow Wilson lived.

I did not see Freud again. He died in 1939. He was a man of ruthless intellectual integrity: A great man.

CONTENTS

INTRODUCTION

BY SIGMUND FREUD

WHEN AN AUTHOR publishes his opinion of a historical personage, he seldom neglects to assure his readers at the outset that he has endeavored to keep himself free from bias and prejudice, that he has worked *sine ira et studio,* as the beautiful classic phrase expresses it. I must, however, commence my contribution to this psychological study of Thomas Woodrow Wilson with the confession that the figure of the American President, as it rose above the horizon of Europeans, was from the beginning unsympathetic to me, and that this aversion increased in the course of years the more I learned about him and the more severely we suffered from the consequences of his intrusion into our destiny.

With increasing acquaintance it was not difficult to find good reasons to support this antipathy. It was reported that Wilson, as President-elect, shook off one of the politicians who called attention to his services during the presidential campaign with the words: "God ordained that I should be the next President of the United States. Neither you nor any other mortal or mortals could have prevented it." The politician was William F. McCombs, Chairman of the Democratic National Committee. I do not know how to avoid the conclusion that a man who is capable of taking the illusions of religion so literally and is so sure of a special personal intimacy with the Almighty is unfitted for relations with ordinary children of men. As everyone knows, the hostile camp during the war also sheltered a chosen darling of Providence: the German Kaiser. It was most regrettable that later on the other side a second appeared. No one gained thereby: respect for God was not increased.

Another obvious peculiarity of the President, to which he himself often called attention, is largely to blame for the fact that we do not know how to begin to grasp his personality but feel it an exotic in our world. Through a long laborious evolution we have learned to set frontiers between our psychic inner world and an outer world of reality. The latter we can understand only as we observe it, study it and collect discoveries about it. In this labor it has not been easy for us to renounce explanations which fulfilled our wishes and confirmed our illusions. But this self-conquest has repaid us. It has led us to an undreamed-of mastery over nature.

Recently we have begun to apply the same procedure to the content of our psychic inner world. Thereby even higher demands have been made upon our self-criticism and our respect for facts. In this field also we expect a like success. The wider and deeper becomes our knowledge of the inner life, the more will our power increase to hold in check and guide our original desires. Wilson, on the contrary, repeatedly declared that mere facts had no significance for him, that he esteemed highly nothing but human motives and opinions. As a result of this attitude it was natural for him in his thinking to ignore the facts of the real outer world, even to deny they existed if they conflicted with his hopes and wishes. He, therefore, lacked motive to reduce his ignorance by learning facts. Nothing mattered except noble intentions. As a result, when he crossed the ocean to bring to war-torn Europe a just and lasting peace, he put himself in the deplorable position of the benefactor who wishes to restore the eyesight of a patient but does not know the construction of the eye and has neglected to learn the necessary methods of operation.

This same habit of thought is probably responsible for the insincerity, unreliability and tendency to deny the truth which appear in Wilson's contacts with other men and are always so shocking in an idealist. The compulsion to speak the truth must indeed be solidified by ethics but it is founded upon respect for fact.

I must also express the belief that there was an intimate connection between Wilson's alienation from the world of reality and his religious convictions. Many bits of his public activity almost produce the impression of the method of Christian Science applied to politics. God is good, illness is evil. Illness contradicts the nature of God. Therefore, since God exists, illness does not exist. There is no illness. Who would expect a healer of this school to take an interest in symptomatology and diagnosis?

Let me now return to the starting point of these observations, to the avowal of my antipathy to Wilson, in order to add a word of justification. We all know that we are not fully responsible for the results of our acts. We act with a certain intention; then our act produces results which we did not intend and could not have foreseen. Thus often we reap more blame and disrepute, and occasionally more praise and honor than we deserve. But when, like Wilson, a man achieves almost the exact opposite of that which he wished to accomplish, when he has shown himself to be the true antithesis of the power which "always desires evil and always creates good," when a pretension to free the world from evil ends only in a new proof of the danger of a fanatic to the commonweal, then it is not to be marveled at that a distrust is aroused in the observer which makes sympathy impossible.

To be sure, when I was led through the influence of Bullitt to a more thorough study of the life of the President, this emotion did not remain unchanged. A measure of sympathy developed; but sympathy of a special sort mixed with pity, such as one feels when reading Cervantes for his hero, the naïve cavalier of La Mancha. And finally, when one compared the strength of the man to the greatness of the task which he had taken upon himself, this pity was so overwhelming that it conquered every other emotion. Thus, in the end, I am able to ask the reader not to reject the work which follows as a product of prejudice. Although it did not originate without the participation of strong emotions, those emotions underwent a thorough subjugation. And I can promise the same for William C. Bullitt, as whose collaborator I appear in this book.

Bullitt, who knew the President personally, who worked for him during the period of his great prominence, and at that time was devoted to him with all the enthusiasm of youth, has prepared the Digest of Data on Wilson's childhood and youth. For the analytic part we are both equally responsible; it has been written by us working together.

A few further explanations seem desirable. The reader may perhaps object that our work is presented to him as a "Psychological Study" although we have employed the psychoanalytic method in examining our subject and have used psychoanalytic hypotheses and terms without restriction. This is not a misrepresentation made in deference to the prejudices of the public. On the contrary our title expresses our conviction that psychoanalysis is nothing but psychology, one of the parts of psychology, and that one does not need to apologize for employing analytic methods in a psychological study which is concerned with the deeper psychic facts.

To publish the results of such a study of deep psychic mechanisms and to expose them to public curiosity so long as the individual concerned lives is certainly inadmissible. That the subject would consent to publication during his lifetime is altogether unlikely. Therapeutic analyses are carried on between physician and patient under the pledge of professional secrecy, all third persons being excluded. When, however, an individual whose life and works are of significance to the present and future has died, he becomes by common consent a proper subject for biography and previous limitations no longer exist. The question of a period of post-mortem immunity from biographical study might then arise, but such a question has rarely been raised. It would not be easy to achieve agreement as to the duration of such a period or to insure its observation. Thomas Woodrow Wilson died in the year 1924.

Finally we must attack the misconception that we have written this book with a secret purpose to prove that Wilson was a pathological character, an abnormal man, in order to undermine in this roundabout way esteem for his achievements. No! That is not our intention. And, even if it were, our book could achieve no such effect. For belief in a stiff frame of normality and a sharp line of demarcation between normal and abnormal in the psychic life has long since been abandoned by our science. An increasingly delicate technique of diagnosis has shown us all sorts of neuroses where we least expected to find them; so that the statement is almost justified that neurotic symptoms and inhibitions have to a certain extent become common to all civilized human beings. We even believe that we understand the exigency which has produced this phenomenon.

Furthermore, we have been compelled to conclude that for the judgment of psychic events the category normal-pathological is as inadequate as the earlier all-inclusive category good-bad. Only in a minority of cases may psychic disturbances be traced back to inflammations or the introduction of toxic substances into the organism; and even in these cases the effect of these factors is not direct. In the majority of cases quantitative factors produce the eruption of pathological results: factors such as exceptionally strong stimuli applied to a certain part of the psychic apparatus, a greater or smaller supply of those internal secretions which are indispensable for the functioning of the nervous system, disturbances in point of time, precocious or retarded development of the psychic life.

We again find this sort of quantitative causation when, with the help of psychoanalysis, we study what now seems to us the elementary material of psychic phenomena. The relative strength of any one of the many instincts which supply the psychic energy, the especial depth of one of those identifications upon which ordinarily the character is constructed, an exceptionally strong reaction-formation against which an impulse must be repressed; such quantitative factors decide the final form of a personality, stamp upon it a certain individuality and direct its activity into a certain channel.

In his description of the dead Brutus, Shakespeare's Marc Antony says:

> the elements
> So mixed in him that nature might stand up
> And say to all the world: "This was a man!"

As a footnote to these words of the poet we are tempted to declare that the elements of the psychic constitution are always the same. What changes in the mixture is the quantitative proportion of the elements and, we must add, their location in different fields of the psychic life and their attachment to different objects. According to certain criteria we then evaluate the personality of the individual as normal or pathological or as exhibiting pathological traits. But these criteria are in no way uniform, reliable or constant. They are difficult to grasp scientifically, for at bottom they are only practical aids, often of conventional origin. "Normal" usually means merely average or close to average. Our judgment of whether or not a character trait or an action is to be considered pathological is often determined by the standard of whether or not it is injurious to the individual or to the community of which he is a member. In spite of the vagueness of these concepts and the uncertainty of the fundamental principles upon which judgment is based, we cannot in practical life do without the distinction between normal and pathological; but we should not be amazed if this distinction does not fit other important antitheses.

Fools, visionaries, sufferers from delusions, neurotics and lunatics have played great roles at all times in the history of mankind and not merely when the accident of birth had bequeathed them sovereignty. Usually they have wreaked havoc; but not always. Such persons have exercised far-reaching influence upon their own and later times, they have given impetus to important cultural movements and have made great discoveries. They have been able to accomplish such achievements on the one hand through the help of the intact portion of their personalities, that is to say in spite of their abnormalities; but on the other hand it is often precisely the pathological traits of their characters, the one-sidedness of their development, the abnormal strengthening of certain desires, the uncritical and unrestrained abandonment to a single aim, which give them the power to drag others after them and to overcome the resistance of the world.

So frequently does great achievement accompany psychic abnormality that one is tempted to believe that they are inseparable from each other. This assumption is, however, contradicted by the fact that in all fields of human endeavor great men are to be found who fulfill the demands of normality.

With these remarks we hope that we have allayed the suspicion that this book is anything more than a psychological study of Thomas Woodrow Wilson. We cannot, however, deny that, in this case as in all cases, a more intimate knowledge of a man may lead to a more exact estimate of his achievements.

DRAMATIS PERSONAE

AXSON, Ellen Louise, Wilson's first wife.

BAKER, Ray Stannard, authorized biographer of Wilson. Director of press bureau for American Commission to Peace Conference.

BALFOUR, Arthur James, British Prime Minister (1902–1906); Minister for Foreign Affairs (1916–1919).

BARUCH, Bernard M., American businessman. Associated with American Commission to Negotiate Peace, Paris (1919).

BERNSTORFF, Johann-Heinrich von, Count, German Ambassador to Washington (1908–1917) who tried to promote better U.S.–German understanding before U.S. entry into World War I.

BONES, James, uncle of Woodrow Wilson.

BONES, Jessie, cousin of Woodrow Wilson.

BRIDGES, Robert, friend and classmate at Princeton.

BROOKE, Francis J., Wilson's first friend.

BROUGHAM, Herbert B., editorial writer for *New York Times*.

BRYAN, William Jennings, Democratic political leader instrumental in swinging nomination to Wilson in 1912. U.S. Secretary of State (1913–1915), resigned because of lack of sympathy for Wilson's policy after sinking of *Lusitania*.

CLEMENCEAU, Georges, French Prime Minister, headed French delegation to Paris Peace Conference.

CLEVELAND, Grover, 22d and 24th President of the U.S.

COBB, Frank, editor-in-chief of the *New York World*.

CREEL, George, American journalist.

DEBS, Eugene V., American Socialist, and oft-times Presidential candidate.

DISRAELI, Benjamin, British statesman.

DODD, William E., historian.

EBERT, Friedrich, first President of the German Reich.

FOCH, Ferdinand, Marshal of France, Commander in Chief of the Allied Armies (1918).

GALT, Edith Bolling, Wilson's second wife.

GERARD, James W., American lawyer. U.S. Ambassador to Germany (1913–1917).

GLADSTONE, William E., British statesman, idol of Wilson.

GLYNN, Martin H., Governor of New York, active in Presidential campaign of 1916.

GRAYSON, Admiral Cary T., Wilson's White House physician.

GREY, Sir Edward, British Foreign Minister.

HALE, William Bayard, Wilson's confidential agent in Mexico (1913).

HANKEY, Sir Maurice, British Army officer and public official, Secretary at Council of Four meetings.

HARDING, Warren G., 29th President of the U.S., opposed to League of Nations.

HARVEY, Colonel George, American journalist, instrumental in Wilson's nomination for Governor of New Jersey. Supported Wilson for President in 1912, opposed re-election (1916). Instrumental in selection of Harding as Republican candidate.

HIBBEN, John Grier, President of Princeton (1912–1932), beloved, then discarded friend of Wilson.

HITCHCOCK, Gilbert M., Wilson's chief Presidential representative in Senate.

HOOVER, Herbert, 31st President of the U.S.

HOUSE, Colonel Edward M., friend and confidant of Wilson. Wilson's personal representative to European nations (1914–1916), member of American Commission to Negotiate Peace (1918–1919), and member of commission to frame Covenant of League of Nations.

HUGHES, Charles Evans, American jurist, defeated by Wilson in election of 1916.

JOHNSON, Hiram, U.S. Senator from California.

JUSSERAND, Jean Jules, French Ambassador to U.S.

KNOX, Philander Chase, U.S. Senator (1917–1921) prominent in opposition to U.S. entry into the League of Nations.

LANSING, Robert, Secretary of State (1915–1920).

LLOYD GEORGE, David, British Prime Minister, directed British policies to victory in war and in settlement of terms of peace.

LODGE, Henry Cabot, Chairman of Senate Foreign Relations Committee who led opposition to Peace Treaty and Covenant of League of Nations.

McADOO, William G., Wilson's son-in-law.

McCORMICK, Vance C., adviser to Wilson on American Commission to Negotiate Peace.

MASARYK, Tomáš, first President of Czechoslovakia.

MAXIMILIAN, Prince of Baden, last Chancellor of the German Empire, who in 1918 initiated negotiations for armistice.

MEZES, Sidney Edward, director of House Inquiry for policy at Peace Conference.

MORGANTHAU, Henry, U.S. Ambassador to Turkey.

ORLANDO, Vittorio, Italian Prime Minister, leader of Italian delegation at Peace Conference.

ORPEN, Sir William, British artist.

PATTON, Francis L., President of Princeton (1888–1902).

POINCARÉ, Raymond, President of the French Republic, noted for conservatism and fight against defeatism.

POLK, Frank Lyon, counselor for State Department (1915–1919).

ROOSEVELT, Theodore, 26th President of the U.S.

SAYRE, Francis B., Wilson's son-in-law.

SHARP, William Graves, U.S. Ambassador to France (1914–1919).

SMUTS, General Jan Christian, Prime Minister of the Union of South Africa, and representative to Peace Conference.

SONNINO, Baron Sidney, Italy's Minister of Foreign Affairs, and Italian representative at Peace Conference.

TAFT, William Howard, 27th President of the U.S.

TUMULTY, Joseph P., private secretary to Wilson when Governor of New Jersey and President.

TYRRELL, William George, British diplomat, Ambassador to France (1928–1934).

VAN DYKE, Henry, Professor of English Literature at Princeton, and U.S. Minister to Netherlands and Luxembourg.

WEST, Andrew F., dean of Graduate School, Princeton (1901–1928).

WHITE, Henry, American diplomat, member of U.S. Peace Commission who favored U.S. entry into League of Nations.

WHITLOCK, Brand, U.S. Minister to Belgium (1913–1922).

WILSON, Anne, sister of Woodrow Wilson.

WILSON, Jessie Woodrow, mother of Wilson.

WILSON, Reverend Joseph Ruggles, father of Wilson.

WILSON, Joseph Ruggles, Jr., brother of Wilson.

WILSON, Marion, sister of Wilson.

WOODROW, Harriet, cousin.

WOODROW, James, uncle.

WOODROW, Reverend Thomas, grandfather.

WOODROW, Thomas, uncle.

Digest of Data
on the
Childhood and Youth
of
THOMAS WOODROW
WILSON

by

William C. Bullitt

IN THE MANSE of the Presbyterian Church of Staunton, Virginia, on December 28, 1856, a son was born to the Reverend Joseph Ruggles Wilson, the Presbyterian Minister. The baby was named Thomas Woodrow in honor of his mother's father, who, like the baby's own father, was a Presbyterian Minister.

All the blood of the infant, Thomas Woodrow Wilson, was lowland Scotch. He had no American-born grandparent. His mother was a Scotch Presbyterian immigrant from North England. His father's parents were Scotch Presbyterian immigrants from Ulster.

His father was a handsome man who talked too much. He was vain: proud of his personal appearance and prouder of his command of words and gestures. His pride in his personal appearance was justified. He was of good height and solidly built. He had clear, deep-set eyes and a broad, finely modeled forehead with a shock of dark hair above it. His cheek bones were high and his well-rounded chin stood out from a fringe of black whiskers that circled his throat below the jaw. His mouth was sensitive and well formed. He had a big, straight nose. Only his ears were ugly. They were large and protuberant. He never lost his mane of hair. In later years it turned white and he began to have the look of a plump old lady; but when his son was a child he was a handsome man.

He had a passion for words, and cherished them for their own sake, for their sounds, caring more for the expression of a thought than for its substance. He sought unusual words in the dictionary and used sumptuous phrases to give splendor to commonplace ideas. At the deathbed of a parishioner he would remark: "He has no speculation in his eyes." He wrote his sermons and delivered them with rhetorical intonations and polished gestures. To preach from the pulpit was not enough. He preached incessantly to his family and to all his friends and acquaintances. He loved to hear himself talk. He had served at Jefferson College, a small Presbyterian institution in Pennsylvania, as Professor Extraordinary of Rhetoric, and that in his heart he remained. He was an exceptionally successful preacher. In his life he had two great passions: words and his son, who was invariably called Tommy.

Jessie Woodrow Wilson, the mother of little Tommy, was a sallow, undervitalized woman of thirty when he was born. She had a long thin face, a long nose, protuberant eyes and a wide, weak mouth. She was silent and solemn. Her childhood had been hard. Her father, the Reverend Thomas Woodrow — the first of his family in five hundred years to leave Scotland — became Minister of a church in Carlisle, England. He had eight children. Jessie was the fifth. The church was so poor that the Reverend Thomas Woodrow had to eke out his income by teaching school. In November 1835 his poverty became so painful that he emigrated to America with his wife and eight children. Jessie was a girl of nine. The voyage on an inferior immigrant boat was a horror to her, and she acquired a dread of the sea that endured all her life. The ship was so beaten that it took two months to sail from Liverpool to New York. The mother of the eight children — also Scotch — never recovered from the voyage and died in New York a month after landing. The Minister then moved his family to Brockville, Canada, in an endeavor to raise a congregation. The hamlet of Brockville was bleak, and he failed. He moved his family to Chillicothe, Ohio. There he became pastor of the First Presbyterian Church. There Jessie Woodrow did housework, took care of the younger children and studied the Bible, until she married Joseph Ruggles Wilson. She produced two daughters — Marion and Anne — before giving birth to the future President of the United States.

Tommy Wilson was a healthy baby. When he was four months old, his mother wrote to her father: "The boy is a fine healthy fellow — he is much larger than either of the others were — and just as fat as he can be. Everyone tells us he is a *beautiful* boy — What is best of all, he is just as *good* as he can be — as little trouble as it is possible for a baby to be." The Reverend Thomas Woodrow, having seen the infant, who was still very plump and extraordinarily quiet, remarked: "That baby is dignified enough to be Moderator of the General Assembly."

Before the baby was a year old the Reverend Joseph Ruggles Wilson was called from Staunton, Virginia, to the pulpit of the First Presbyterian Church of Augusta, Georgia. This was a notable advancement. Augusta was a prosperous town of about twelve thousand inhabitants, including slaves. There the Minister preached until Tommy was fourteen years old. There the character of the child was formed.

The Civil War was approaching. The Minister, born and brought up in Ohio, had moved to the South only eighteen months before Tommy's birth. The fact that the Minister was a Northerner might have made life unpleasant for him and his family; but it did not because he became an ardent convert to the Southern cause.

In the Augusta Manse, Tommy Wilson grew from a fat healthy infant into a sickly little boy. He had inherited neither his father's strong body nor his handsome features; but he had inherited his father's protuberant ears. In physique he resembled his mother. He had pale gray eyes and dull blond hair. He was thin, sallow and weak. His eyes were exceptionally deficient. He had scarcely put off baby skirts before he put on spectacles. Moreover, in his childhood he began to suffer from the indigestion that harassed him all his life. He was coddled by his father, mother and two elder sisters; but his indigestion persisted, giving him days of headache and pain in his stomach. So sickly was he that his parents did not send him to school. He did not begin to learn the alphabet until he was nine, and could not read until he was eleven.

"My earliest recollection," Thomas Woodrow Wilson said fifty years later, "is of standing at my father's gateway in Augusta, Georgia, when I was four years old, and hearing someone pass and say that Mr. Lincoln was elected and there was to be war. Catching the intense tones of his excited voice, I remember running in to ask my father what it meant."

To run to his father was the child's habitual reaction to any uncertainty. Of this dominant trait, Mr. Ray Stannard Baker, his official biographer, who had all the Wilson family papers, wrote: "To be running in to his father was the most natural thing in the boy's life. His father was the greatest figure of his youth — perhaps the greatest of his whole life. 'My incomparable father.' Until after he was forty years old, Woodrow Wilson never made an important decision of any kind without first seeking his father's advice. A great love bound them together — love and admiration and profound respect." On the same subject, Professor Winthrop M. Daniels, who knew the Wilsons intimately at Princeton, wrote: "I have never seen filial affection and regard equal to that of Mr. Wilson for his father. It is hard to say whether genuine admiration for the father's ability or unbounded affection for the man himself was the stronger ingredient in this dominant passion."

"Dominant passion" is a strong expression to use with regard to the affection of a man for a father; but there is a mass of evidence to prove that it describes accurately the feeling of Thomas Woodrow Wilson for his father. His passionate love of his father was the core of his emotional life. "The letters between the two can be called nothing but love letters," wrote Mr. Baker, who had them all. "My precious son," "My beloved father," "Darling boy," they wrote to each other. They invariably kissed emotionally when they met. The son quoted his father endlessly, and told stories about him until those who were frequently with the son became bored by his accounts of his father's trite sayings and insignificant acts. "My incomparable father" was a true expression of the son's feelings. To Tommy Wilson his father was above all other fathers.

Anything his father said or did was of the utmost importance because it issued from his father. He considered his father not only the wisest man in the world but also the handsomest. "If I had my father's face and figure, it wouldn't make any difference what I said," the son adored.

Every circumstance of Tommy Wilson's life conspired to increase the natural admiration of every small child for every father. The Minister was the great man of the Presbyterian upper middle class to which the Wilsons belonged. He was the leader of the elect of God: the interpreter of God on earth. He was everything that the son wished to be and was not. He was strong and handsome, the child was sickly and ugly. The father was undisputed master of the household. His wife had no existence beyond the service of his wishes. The best room of the Manse was his study, book-lined, where he sat smoking incessantly a long clay-bowled pipe. He was the sun of life in the Manse. He had health and vigor. He talked, joked, punned. His wife was silent, solemn, dutiful, negative. Five times a day the father prayed to God while his family listened. Twice a day he read the Bible to his family, and in the evening usually led his family in the singing of hymns. On Sunday he stood in the pulpit and laid down the law of God. Tommy Wilson, according to those who remember the scene, sat with his mother and sisters in the fourth pew and gazed up into the face of his "incomparable father" with rapt intensity, his sharp nose and chin poked forward, his weak eyes straining upward through his spectacles.

So completely did the child take into his heart the teachings of his father that for the remainder of his life he never doubted the exact and literal truth of Presbyterianism. All his life he prayed on his knees morning and evening. Every day he read the Bible. He wore out two or three Bibles in the course of his life. He said grace before every meal. He believed absolutely in the immortality of the soul and the efficacy of prayer. "I do not see how anyone can sustain himself in any enterprise in life without prayer," he once wrote. "It is the only spring at which he can renew his spirit and purify his motive. God is the source of strength to every man and only by prayer can he keep himself close to the Father of his spirit." In crises he felt himself "guided by an intelligent power outside himself." He never doubted. He never allowed himself to entertain doubt for an instant. When his first wife read Kant and questioned, he squelched her promptly. He said to his White House physician, Admiral Cary T. Grayson, "so far as religion is concerned, argument is adjourned." He could not doubt. To have doubted would have been to doubt his own father. At the close of a speech in San Francisco on September 17, 1919, he said, "I believe in Divine Providence. If I did not I would go crazy." That was perhaps true.

The father, who loved the son as passionately as the son loved him, contributed by the intensity of his affection to his son's adoration. He liked to handle the child physically, to embrace him, to chase him through the house and into the garden and catch him in a great hug, crying, "I've caught you now, you young rascal." He loved to pour into his son the thoughts which were in his own head, and thus increased the child's intellectual dependence on him. Since little Tommy was considered too sickly to be sent to school, his father read to him daily and talked to him incessantly, in the house and out of it when they walked together. Pickwick and the prophets, Presbyterianism and phrases, words, synonyms, similes, were driven into the son's head: above all, words; words as live things to be loved. The father did his utmost to beget in the son as great a love of words as he had himself. He never permitted the child to use an incorrect word or to utter a slipshod sentence. After their walks together, the boy and his father would talk over the whole experience, the Minister insisting that every description, every idea be expressed completely in perfect English. "What do you mean by that?" the Minister would ask the boy. Tommy would explain. "Then why don't you say so?" As soon as the boy learned to read, they played by the hour the game of "synonyms," taking turns holding the dictionary. Later the father would choose passages from Lamb or Daniel Webster and compel the boy to try to improve the expressions of the authors. His son was a class of one for the former Professor Extraordinary of Rhetoric. The son loved the teaching. Synonyms became his favorite game. He began to love words as much as his father loved them.

Early the father became convinced that his son would be a great man, and he did not conceal this belief from Tommy or from any-one else. He was unstinting in aid to his son throughout difficult years. In spite of his meager income, which varied from fifteen hundred to four thousand dollars a year, he kept his son in abso-lute economic dependence on him for twenty-nine yaers. And Tommy was content to be so kept.

Often the Reverend Joseph Ruggles Wilson gushed over his son. For example, when he received his son's first book, *Congressional Government*, which had been dedicated to him, he wrote: "My precious son — your book has been received and gloated over. The dedication took me by surprise, and never have I felt such a blow of love. Shall I confess it? — I wept, and sobbed in the stir of the glad pain. God bless you, my noble child, for such a token of your affection."

Yet along with this sort of syrup the father gave the son assets that set him apart from most of his contemporaries and made them feel that he was morally and intellectually superior. Thanks to his early education, Tommy Wilson always tried to be on the side of the angels; he endeavored to think about serious matters; and he attempted to express his thoughts in distinguished phrases. Those were exceptional attributes in the United States after the Civil War, when most men of ability were concentrating on the acquisi-tion of wealth. They gave Tommy Wilson both prestige and an endearing idealism. He was so serious about himself that others took him seriously. To make fun of him was easy; to ignore him was impossible. He was a prig; but a prime prig.

Although the central fact of Tommy Wilson's childhood was his relationship to his father, his sick body attached him to his mother. He needed to be nursed. His mother had little vitality and much housework; but she coddled her son devotedly. She was solemn and apprehensive, full of warnings about the dangers of life, and did her utmost to protect her little boy from rough impacts. His dependence on her was prolonged. "I remember how I clung to her (a laughed-at 'mama's boy') 'till I was a great big fellow," he wrote to his wife in 1888, "but love of the best womanhood came to me and entered my heart through those apron strings. If I had not lived with such a mother, I could not have won and seemed to deserve — in part, perhaps, deserved through transmitted virtues — such a wife."

Although he was a "laughed-at 'mama's boy' " and clung to his mother, he never quoted her, never recounted her acts. He regretted that he had inherited her feeble body, weak eyes and shyness. He wanted to be like his father, not like his mother — a Wilson, not a Woodrow. Yet physically he remained a Woodrow.

His sisters completed the group which surrounded him in his early life. Marion was six years older than he, Anne two years older. The girls helped their mother and father to protect him from the outside world. Of the two he preferred Anne. She loved him dearly. She was a charming little girl with a gay smile. His first wife somewhat resembled her.

His brother, Joseph Ruggles Wilson, Jr., was not born until Tommy was ten years old. He never had much use for that brother. He was old enough when little Joseph was born to take a fatherly attitude toward the boy. When he was at home after a nervous breakdown at the University of Virginia, he even tutored his brother. But Joseph was by no means inclined to take his elder brother seriously. In fact he revolted against the dominance of his father and his elder brother. He became a rolling stone, and slid into newspaper work. When Tommy Wilson was President of the United States, it was suggested to him by some Senators who wished to please him that his brother Joseph should be made Secretary to the Senate. The President refused to allow his little brother to have the position.

Sickly, spectacled, shy, guarded by father, mother and sisters, Tommy Wilson never had a fist fight in his life. His emotions were satisfied in the church and the Manse. The organist of the church "discovered that the Minister's boy, whom she thought shy and reserved, was particularly affected by music, and that when certain solemn selections were played, such as the hymn 'Twas on that dark and doleful day,' sung often at communion services, the little boy would sit crying."

He liked to play with well-brought-up girls rather than boys, especially with his sisters and his cousins. Above all, he liked to play with a little girl cousin who was younger than he and was named after his mother: Jessie Woodrow Bones.

One day when he was eleven, they were playing that she was a squirrel in a tree, and he, with bow and arrow, was an Indian hunter trying to shoot her. An arrow struck her and she tumbled to the ground at his feet. She had fainted but was uninjured. He carried her limp body into the house crying with wild remorse: "I am a murderer. It wasn't an accident. I killed her."

Lincoln was elected before Tommy Wilson was four years old. Lee surrendered when he was eight. During those years the South went through agony. Tommy suffered no agony whatsoever. In later years he said that he remembered only two incidents of the war. One day he was sitting on the gatepost of the Manse. A ragged group of Southern soldiers marched by. He shouted at them in the slang of the day, "Oh Joe — here's your mule!" He also remembered the delicious taste of the soup made from cowpeas by his mother when peace-time food was not to be had.

Why the war left so little trace in his memory is a mystery. He was old enough to remember, and many exciting events occurred in Augusta. His father had become a fervent Southern sympathizer. He served for a time as a chaplain in the Confederate Army. From the pulpit he defended slavery and the right of secession. One Sunday he mounted the pulpit and announced "that a great battle was impending, that the Southern Army was desperately in need of ammunition, and that he would therefore dismiss the congregation at once, with a benediction, that they might repair, men, women and children, to the ammunition factories to help with the cartridge rolling." The Presbyterian Church itself was turned into a hospital. The churchyard became a camp for Northern prisoners. When Sherman's approach was announced, the entire population of Augusta turned out to carry cotton from sheds and warehouses and pile it in the main street in the hope that Sherman might burn only the cotton and not the town.

It is possible but not probable that Tommy Wilson was shielded from all this excitement. He was sensitive, " a bundle of nerves," his mother called him, and his parents protected him from all unpleasantness. Yet it seems scarcely possible that he could have been kept away from the prison-camp churchyard, or from the wounded in the church, which had become a hospital. Perhaps he was. It seems more likely that he saw it all and forgot it. It did not concern him personally, and all the coddling and loving had concentrated most of his interest on his own weak body and the family circle which protected it. The gate post and the cowpea soup, which he remembered, did concern him personally. Then the struggle ended in defeat: an unpleasant thing, a thing to be forgotten. In his later years he was often able to forget unpleasant things.

The Civil War left scars in the souls of almost all Southerners of his generation. It left no scar in him. He could remember without bitterness standing at the age of nine behind the drawn blinds of the Manse and watching Northern soldiers drive the captured President of the Confederate States, Jefferson Davis, and one of the chief Southern leaders, Alexander Stephens, through the streets of Augusta on their way to prison. Yet no passion for the Lost Cause ever burned in him. In his heart he was not a Southerner but a Scotch Presbyterian who by accident was born in Virginia.

The same year that he saw Jefferson Davis, he learned his letters. Two years later, at the age of thirteen, he set foot in school for the first time. A Confederate officer named Derry had opened a small school in Augusta. There Tommy Wilson began to measure himself for the first time against other boys. There he received the only whipping of his life. Professor Derry whipped him and a number of other boys who cut school to follow a circus parade.

He did badly at school, considerably worse than the average boy. "It was not because he was not bright enough, but because he was apparently not interested," said Professor Derry. This judgment seems correct. His father had given him a concentration of interest on one activity: speech. All his life he had this same concentration of interest. He always did badly in studies unless they were connected with speech. To learn enough about a subject to make a speech about it was his objective. If a subject was somehow connected with speech, he did well.

The love of speech and the surroundings of speech showed itself even in his first contact with boy's sports. Some of the boys of the Derry School formed a baseball club. They called it the "Lightfoot." It met in the barn loft behind the Manse, and although Tommy played baseball badly, he was elected president. He drew up a constitution for the club and presided over the meetings seated beneath a large portrait of the Devil torn from a poster advertising deviled ham. Later he told William Bayard Hale, whom he had chosen as his biographer, that "the Lightfoots held meetings characterized by much nicety of parliamentary procedure. Every one of the little chaps knew perfectly well just what the previous question was and that only two amendments to a resolution could be offered which would be voted upon in reverse order." This domination of the play of American small town boys by Robert's Rules of Order is a tribute not only to the thoroughness with which the Professor Extraordinary of Rhetoric had driven respect for parliamentary procedure into his adoring son but also to the eminence of the Minister and his family in a small Presbyterian world. The Minister was the interpreter of God on earth, and his son was his interpreter in the hayloft.

Tommy Wilson's attendance at the Derry School lasted little more than a year. Then his father was appointed to a professorship at the Columbia, South Carolina, Theological Seminary, where his uncle James Woodrow was Professor of Science. The Wilson family moved to Columbia.

Before Tommy left Augusta, however, he had an experience that he remembered all his life. General Robert E. Lee came to Augusta. Tommy stood in the crowd and looked up to Lee's face. He did not forget that noble head. Later when he wrote of Lee, as when he wrote of Washington, he adorned the great Captain of the Confederacy with his own virtues and weaknesses. He always thought that Lee and Washington were like him. He never doubted his kinship with the greatest men. Deep within him was the conviction that his father was the greatest man in the world.

Tommy Wilson was fourteen years old when he left Augusta, yet in later years he did not refer to Augusta as the home of his boyhood. When he thought of his youth, he thought of Columbia. "My own very happy boyhood in Columbia," he wrote. Over Augusta he drew a veil of forgetfulness.

Columbia was a charred ruin when the Wilson family arrived. Five years before, Sherman had burned the little town. Then carpetbaggers from the North had dropped on it and, with the legislature of freed Negro slaves, were making life hideous. If Tommy had not felt the sufferings of the war while it was being fought, he did realize fully in Columbia the horrors that war and a vindictive peace may create. He went to school in a barn. He saw drunken Negroes and thieves from the North sprawled in the Capitol. A schoolmate describes him at that time as "extremely dignified. He was not like other boys. He had a queer way of going off by himself." In fact he went off from the ugly reality of life into dreams, into romance. He had been reading Marryat's and Cooper's tales of the sea. He began to write sea stories.

From the escape of romance, he progressed to the escape of revival meetings by way of his first intense friendship. A deeply religious young man named Francis J. Brooke came to Columbia to study for the Presbyterian ministry. He was a few years older than Tommy Wilson. He held religious meetings in his room and later in the one-story stable which was the chapel of the Theological Seminary. Tommy attended the meetings. He loved Brooke deeply, and the memory of that love endured. When he visited Columbia as President of the United States, he stood before the doorway of the stable and said: "I feel as though I ought to take off my shoes. This is holy ground." And again, "I have never heard greater speaking in my life than I have heard from that rostrum." Under the influence of Brooke, at the age of sixteen and a half, he confessed, "exhibited evidence of a work of grace begun in his heart" and was admitted to membership in the First Presbyterian Church of Columbia, on the fifth of July 1873.

The effect of this religious experience was profound and lasting. From that moment to the end of his life he felt himself in direct communication with God. He felt that God had chosen him for a great work, that he was "guided by an intelligent power outside himself." He had never had religious doubts. From that time on, he was convinced that God would use him and preserve him till his work was done. He never doubted the righteousness of his acts. Whatever he did was right because God directed him.

He had been doing badly at school; at once he began to do better. He tacked a portrait of the British Prime Minister, Gladstone, the "Christian statesman," on the wall behind his desk, and applied himself to the study of shorthand as well as to his school work. When Jessie Woodrow Bones asked whose portrait was on the wall, he replied, "That is Gladstone, the greatest statesman that ever lived. I intend to be a statesman, too."

His father and mother expected him to become a Presbyterian Minister. Gladstone somehow crept between him and the ministry. The step was not a great one. The "Christian statesman" per-

haps seemed to him but a greater preacher who had the House of
Commons for pulpit and the Empire for congregation. And the
handsome "Christian statesman" resembled his handsome father.
To the adolescent Tommy, to be a Christian statesman was perhaps to be a greater preacher than even his father. His concept of
statesmanship always remained the picture of a Minister laying
down the law of God to his flock. Ultimately the White House
became his pulpit and the world his congregation.

In the autumn of the year of his religious experience, he and
Brooke left Columbia to go to Davidson College, then a poverty-
stricken Presbyterian institution lost in the cornfields twenty
miles north of Charlotte, North Carolina. It was the understanding of his family that he was to study for the ministry. His "very
happy boyhood in Columbia" was over. Why it was "very happy"
must remain somewhat of a puzzle to men who are not constituted
as he was. There was no gaiety in the town; he had no love, light
or serious. His emotions were expressed through prayer meetings.
Perhaps the source of his happiness was Brooke. He had found a
man in addition to his father whom he could admire and love intensely.

His career at Davidson was short. He did worse than the average
boy in his studies, debated much, played a little baseball. He was
ill most of the time. In May 1874 his indigestion became so severe
that the next month he left Davidson, never to return. He re-
joined his family in Columbia and followed his father to Wilmington, North Carolina, where in November 1874 the Reverend Joseph Ruggles Wilson was installed as Minister of the First Presbyterian Church.

From June 1874 to September 1875 Tommy Wilson stayed with
his family, studying Greek and taking care of his ailing body. "An
old young man," the intelligent Negro butler of the Wilson family
described him. "Outside Mr. Tommy was his father's boy. But
inside he was his mother all over. She had English ways . . .
Tommy inside was like that, good and all that, but he didn't mix

up with the other boys — like her, a little standoffish with all the boys but John Bellamy. Sometimes Tommy would work with his father so's I could go swimming with him, and the old doctor would say, 'Now Dave, don't you let Mr. Tommy get into fights or anything down there.' But there was no danger. He wasn't the fighting kind; but his little brother, Mr. Josey — say, there was a real boy."

Tommy was in fact still a "laughed-at 'mama's boy.' " He still adored his father. "I have just received one of the finest letters I ever had from Tommy," said his father at about that time. "It is a regular love letter." Even his friend Bellamy, who was sincerely fond of him, found him a bit of a prig. "The only trouble with Wilson," said Bellamy, "is that he was a confirmed and confounded Calvinist."

In spite of the love of his father and mother and the friendship of Bellamy, he was acutely unhappy. He felt that he had been chosen by God to do a great work in the world; but he had to face his sick headaches, his burning stomach, his weak eyes, his nervousness. He seems at one time to have doubted his vocation and to have decided to go to sea. His mother, who still dreaded the sea, dissuaded him.

It was with a desperate, now-or-never spirit that he went to Princeton in the autumn of 1875. He was badly prepared, especially deficient in Greek and mathematics; but he was determined to make himself the leader that his God expected him to be. "We went to college without an objective, but Wilson always had a definite purpose," said one of his classmates. That was true.

In his first year at Princeton, he joined a debating club and looked after his health. His second year at Princeton was one of the decisive years of his life. In 1873 he had experienced a religious awakening, in 1876 he experienced an intellectual awakening. He happened to draw from the library a bound volume of the English *Gentleman's Magazine* for 1874. In the April number he found an article entitled "The Orator." So electrifying was this article to his intellect "that he remembered all his life the exact place at the head of the south stairs in the Chancellor Green Library where he read it." The article described the orators in the House of Commons, praising especially Mr. Gladstone and Mr. Bright, calling the latter "the orator par excellence of the House of Commons," describing him as "precisely the moral and political antithesis of Mr. Disraeli." It lauded Bright's moral earnestness, and concluded: "To an orator this atmosphere of sincerity and honest conviction is a mighty power." Tommy Wilson read the article, and at once felt that he was like Gladstone and Bright. He, too, could debate with moral earnestness. He would lead men by his oratory. He would conquer the world by his moral earnestness and his choice of words and gestures. At once he wrote to his father, announcing that he had found at last that he had a mind.

His father and mother were by no means delighted by his discovery. They counted on his becoming a Presbyterian Minister. His feeling for Gladstone had not impressed them. He was perhaps uncertain whether he wished to be a Minister or a Christian statesman until he read that article. After reading it, he no longer doubted his vocation. He never again considered entering the ministry. His father, to the end of his life, regretted that Tommy had turned aside from the ministry. One day when Tommy had read to him an early essay, "he sprang up and kissed his son — they always kissed when they met — and exclaimed, 'Oh my boy, how I wish you had entered the ministry with all that genius of yours.' " Throughout his life a great part of Thomas Woodrow Wilson's intellectual output consisted of sermons and articles on religious subjects, and he was an Elder of the church; but his vocation was determined: to be an orator, a Christian statesman. He sat in his room at Princeton, a sophomore, and wrote out a number of visiting cards inscribed *Thomas Woodrow Wilson, Senator from Virginia.*

The seriousness with which he took his vocation to be a Christian statesman can scarcely be overestimated. He continued to do badly in those studies which were not connected with speaking or writing, but in those which had to do with words he did well. He threw himself into the work of the debating societies and was elected Speaker of the Whig Society. He devoured the speeches of Burke and Bright and the political essays of Bagehot. He walked in the woods at Princeton and delivered Burke's orations to the trees. He wrote for the *Princetonian,* of which he had become an editor, an article on oratory, saying, "The greatest and truest model for all orators is Demosthenes. One who has not studied deeply and constantly all the great speeches of the great Athenian, is not prepared to speak in public." He stood in front of his mirror and practiced gestures. When he returned to Wilmington for his holidays, he mounted the pulpit of his father's church on week days and delivered to an imaginary congregation the speeches of Demosthenes, Patrick Henry, Daniel Webster, Bright and Gladstone.

He came across the writings of Walter Bagehot on the English Constitution, and found that the English system of government was much more to his liking than the American system. There was more room for the orator in it. In the English system, the orator on the floor of the House of Commons was the central figure of British life, his words were followed by an empire, on his success or failure depended the fate of the government. In the American system, the business of government was carried on in committee rooms, behind closed doors. Senators and Representatives spoke to empty seats. Their speeches were rarely if ever reported in the press. A government might go from scandal to scandal and remain the government, until the time for the next election. The English system of government was perfectly adapted to the career he wished to pursue. The American system of government was ill-adapted. Radio broadcasting did not exist and the orator of the type that Tommy Wilson aspired to be was becoming a joke. Gladstone was no joke. He wielded the greatest power on earth.

Tommy Wilson wished to be the American Gladstone. He thought he could not lead America by the power of words unless the system of government should be altered. Therefore, he set out to persuade the American people to change the Constitution. He wrote an article advocating Cabinet Government in the United States and sent it to the junior editor of the *International Review:* Henry Cabot Lodge. Lodge accepted Wilson's article. He was later to reject a more important article from the same hand.

Tommy's triumphant discovery that he had a mind did more for him than merely release his passion for oratory. It freed him somewhat from his shyness. He had a sweet tenor voice and he began to sing with the Glee Club. There were many serious-minded men like himself rooming in Witherspoon Hall, where he lived. A number of them became his friends and remained his friends all his life: friends in the ordinary sense of the word. He had had an intense attachment to Brooke. At Princeton he had one intense friendship and many friendships on a less emotional level.

Princeton at that time was just beginning to outgrow its Presbyterian beginnings, and was still called the College of New Jersey. The mass of the student body was composed of earnest young men; but there were also young blades from the upper classes of New York, Philadelphia, Baltimore and the South. They drank and had small use for puritans like Tommy Wilson. Tommy acquired for them a distaste and contempt that lasted all his life; but for his classmates who were of his own kind he had a warm affection. Charles Talcott and Robert Bridges became his closet friends.

With Talcott he developed an intimacy that resembled his intimacy with Brooke at Columbia and Davidson, except for the fact that Wilson was the older partner in the friendship. Later he wrote: "I remember forming with Charlie Talcott (a class-mate and a very intimate friend of mine) a solemn covenant that we would school all our powers and passions for the work of establishing the principles we held in common; that we would acquire knowledge that we might have power; and that we might have facility in leading others into our ways of thinking and enlisting them in our purposes. And we didn't do this in merely boyish enthusiasm, though we were blinded by a very boyish assurance with regard to the future and our ability to mould the world as our hands might please. It was not so long ago but that I can still feel the glow and the pulsations of the hopes and purposes of that moment — nay, it was not so long ago but that I still retain some of the faith that then prompted me."

Tommy Wilson became a leader of the serious-minded men of his class. Although he did not play baseball, he was elected President of the Baseball Association. He was respected for his knowledge of political writers. "It was as natural for him as an undergraduate to talk about Burke, Brougham or Bagehot, as for the rest of us to allude to Cooper or Mayne Reid," wrote his friend Bridges. He took great pleasure in the writers who used language with precision and imagination. To him this was not a scholastic pursuit. It was full of the stuff of existence. He would trail a word or a phrase with that eagerness that R.L.S. so exalted. They would pop out in his conversation at the Club table as a part of a jest or a noisy dispute. There was a twinkle in his eye, but he knew and you knew that he had scored."

It became his habit to jest, "When I meet you in the Senate, I'll argue that out with you."

His passion for speech was not satisfied by his debating society, Whig. He organized and wrote the constitution of a new debating club, in which governments rose and fell as in the House of Commons. Whenever he had a chance to speak, he spoke. On one occasion he did not. The chief oratorical event of each year was the Lynde prize debate between teams from Whig and Clio. In his senior year he was considered the best debater of Whig and was expected to win the prize for his team. The subject for debate was "Free Trade Versus a Tariff for Protection." A preliminary debate in Whig was to be held to determine the Whig debaters in the final contest. When lots were drawn, Tommy Wilson found that he must defend the tariff side. He at once announced that he would not debate because he believed in free trade. Without him the Whig team lost the contest. To win for his society and his friends, he would not argue in a mock contest against his convictions. Oratory to him had become a holy vocation.

In June 1879 he was graduated from Princeton and returned to Wilmington, North Carolina, to practice gestures in front of his mirror and to deliver orations from the pulpit of his father's church. Every day he practiced elocution.

"The profession I chose was politics; the profession I entered was law. I entered the one because I thought it would lead to the other. It was once the sure road; and Congress is still full of lawyers." Thus wrote Wilson to Ellen Axson in 1883. He definitely refused to fulfill his father's hope that he should enter the Presbyterian ministry, and in the autumn of 1879 he entered the Law School of the University of Virginia.

The University of Virginia was then, as it has been since its foundation by Thomas Jefferson, a distinguished institution. It was founded by Jefferson in the hope that it would be the most liberal seat of learning in the world. Tommy Wilson disliked Jefferson intensely. The life and principles of Jefferson were not Presbyterian. So great was this dislike that while Wilson was at the university he never once visited Jefferson's home, Monticello, although it stood nearby in all its beauty. He went to Jefferson's university merely because at that time it had as good a law school as there was in the United States, and was not far from his father's Manse. At once he found himself "most terribly bored by the noble study of law." He joined a second-rate fraternity and made speeches in the debating societies. Throughout his residence at the University of Virginia, he was harassed by indigestion. It became so acute in December 1880 that he left the university without a degree. He had established a close friendship with R. Heath Dabney, and two months before his departure had been elected President of the Jefferson Debating Society.

He crept back to the shelter of the Manse in Wilmington, suffering from sick headaches, sour stomach and intense nervousness. He became profoundly discouraged. "How can a man with a weak body ever arrive anywhere?" he asked. "As for my health," he wrote to Dabney, "I know now that to leave the University was the most prudent step I could have taken. My doctor found my digestive organs seriously out of gear and has confirmed me in the belief that, had I remained at the University, and there continued to neglect systematic medical treatment of myself, I might have confirmed myself in dyspepsia and have fixed on myself a very uncomfortable future." He studied law at home, walked with his father and mother, tutored his little brother Joseph in Latin and was acutely unhappy.

The only ray of light in his life was his correspondence with his cousin Harriet Woodrow, daughter of his mother's brother, Thomas Woodrow. Harriet, like his own mother, came from Chillicothe, Ohio. In 1879, she was a student in a Female Seminary which had been established in the old church at Staunton, Virginia, where the Reverend Joseph Ruggles Wilson had preached at the time of Tommy's birth. There Wilson met and fell in love with his cousin Harriet. She was his first love.

Throughout the fifteen months of his illness in Wilmington he wrote to her and she replied. In the summer of 1881, when he was twenty-four years of age, he visited the family of Harriet Woodrow in Chillicothe, Ohio, and proposed marriage to his cousin. Promptly and decisively she refused him. He returned to Wilmington. There, after the loss of hope that he might marry Harriet Woodrow, he dropped his name Thomas and began for the first time to call himself Woodrow Wilson.

After taking care of his stomach for eighteen months, Woodrow Wilson felt himself well enough in the spring of 1882 to start his career as a lawyer. He had not been admitted to the bar. Nevertheless, he formed a partnership for the practice of the law with a friend from the University of Virginia, E. I. Renick, and opened an office in Atlanta, Georgia, then a growing town of thirty-seven thousand inhabitants. In October 1882 he was admitted to the bar. His career as a lawyer is quickly recounted: he never had a client. In the spring of 1883, he abandoned Atlanta and the law.

He was deeply hurt by his failure in Atlanta. To his friend, Dabney, he wrote: "Here the chief end of man is certainly to make money, and money cannot be made except by the most vulgar methods. The studious man is pronounced impractical and is suspected as a visionary. All students of specialities — except such practical specialties as carpentering, for instance — are classed together as mere ornamental furniture in the intellectual world — curious, perhaps, and pretty enough, but of very little use and no mercantile value."

Atlanta forced on him his first and only contact with the world of ordinary life, of ordinary men and women living ordinary lives. He had passed all his life in one cloister or another. He was twenty-six years old, and he had never lived outside the sheltering walls of a Manse, a college or a university. The crudity of Atlanta was too much for him. He could not get along with men who were neither students nor Presbyterians. He fled back to the shelter of the cloister. To his intense relief, his father, who had become worried because "that boy in Atlanta isn't earning a cent," agreed to support him through further years of study at Johns Hopkins University, so that he might become an instructor in some college.

At that moment Wilson was blessed by the greatest stroke of luck that befell him in a life not unmarked by fortunate events. Just before he abandoned the law, he went to Rome, Georgia, to visit his uncle James Bones, father of Jessie Woodrow Bones. At Rome, he met Ellen Louise Axson, daughter of the Minister of the First Presbyterian Church.

She was not only daughter of the Minister but mistress of the Manse as well. Her mother was dead and she was acting as mother to the Minister's three small children. Her domestic situation was that of his own mother when his father had asked her to marry him. Her life had been as completely Presbyterian as Woodrow Wilson's own life. Her grandfather was Minister of the Presbyterian Church of Savannah, Georgia; her father Minister of the Presbyterian Church of Rome. She was small and somewhat resembled his much loved sister Anne. The Axson and Wilson families had long been friends and Woodrow Wilson had, so he said, held Ellen Axson on his lap when he was a boy of six or seven. She had bright cheeks, a charming nature, great kindness and common sense. She painted pictures and hoped to have a career as an artist. She knew poetry and literature. She was serious-minded; but her breadth of interest and lack of prejudice made her able to open new worlds to Woodrow Wilson.

Wilson fell in love with her in April 1883. In September they became engaged. They were not married until two years later. He still had to learn how to earn a living. She went to New York to study art, and he went to Baltimore to study history and economics at Johns Hopkins.

In Ellen Axson, Woodrow Wilson found an emotional security as durable as the love of his mother. "I am the only one who can rest him," she once told a friend. That was true. He could rest on her shoulder with as complete confidence as ever he had had as an infant sleeping on the breast of his mother. He trusted her absolutely. Never in the slightest degree did she betray that trust. She gave him the most sustaining love. "To an extraordinary extent, she protected him, guided him, established the environment in which his intense nature could best function." She gave him wise advice at the most critical moments of his life and mitigated somewhat the violence of his prejudices and hatreds. Always he felt a nervous fear of letting people get close to him, as if he had something to hide. With her he could be frank. He never left her for a day without writing her a love letter recounting all his doings. He became as dependent on her as ever he had been on his mother in the days when he was "a laughed-at 'mama's boy.'" "... you are the only person in the world — except the dear ones at home

— with whom I do *not* have to act a part, to whom I do not have to deal out confidences cautiously; and you are the only person in the world — without *any* exception — to whom I can tell *all* that my heart contains." This he wrote to her while they were engaged. It remained true for the twenty-nine years of their marriage.

She died on August 6, 1914, at the moment when he had to face his greatest tasks. Emotionally he went to pieces. He wanted to be dead. He hoped to be assassinated. He did not die. Instead, a year and four months later, he married again. He could not do without a woman on whose breast he could rest.

In applying for admission to Johns Hopkins University, Woodrow Wilson cited various authorities in history with whose work he was familiar: after Bagehot, he listed Henry Cabot Lodge. Hopkins was at that time the center of a distinguished intellectual life. In and about the university were men who had the best training that Europe could provide, and attacked their problems with intelligence and intellectual integrity. Woodrow Wilson's work fell under the supervision of two professors of high quality, Dr. Herbert B. Adams and Dr. Richard T. Ely. Wilson found them inadequate. Adams he considered "too smooth, too much of a showman to be a thorough scholar." He confided to Dabney that Adams was a "disciple of Machiavelli, as he himself declares," and that "he allowed his pupils to starve on a very meager diet of ill-served lectures." Ely, he wrote, was "a hard worker, a conscientious student and chuckfull of the exact data of his subject (like Schonberg's *Handbuch,* which is his economic bible); but he moves only by outside impulse and is not fitted for the highest duties of the teacher." Nevertheless, he was delighted when Ely invited him to be one of his assistants in the preparation of a history of American economic thought.

Under these masters Woodrow Wilson did the best literary work of his life. Their hard-headed thoroughness checked his love of fleeing from facts to phrases. He produced an article on his favorite subject, "Committee or Cabinet Government," which was ac-

cepted by *The Overland Monthly*. On January 1, 1884, he wrote
to Ellen Axson, "I've opened the new year by a day of diligent
work on my favorite constitutional studies. I've planned a set of
four or five essays on the 'Government of the Union,' in which it is
my purpose to show as well as I can, our constitutional system as it
looks in operation. My desire and ambition are to treat the American Constitution as Mr. Bagehot has treated the English Constitution." He worked hard on this small book under the supervision
of Professor Adams and called it *Congressional Government*. It
was good, and established the foundation of his reputation for intellectual eminence.

Washington was about an hour by train from Baltimore when
he was writing this book, and his object was to show "our constitutional system as it looks in operation." Congress was in session and
highly illuminating political struggles were in progress. The students of Johns Hopkins often went to Washington to see the Federal Government at work. Woodrow Wilson never went. He
produced the impression in his book that he knew the Congress
intimately from personal contact; but not once did he go to look at
the Congress he was describing. This shrinking from actual contact
with men and events persisted throughout his life. He preferred to
gather his ideas from the experiences of other men.

When his *Congressional Government* was accepted by the publishers he was in ecstasy; but within a week he was "down with the
'blues.'" That also became characteristic. No success satisfied him
for more than a moment.

As usual under the pressure of work, although it was congenial
work, he began to break down. He had been at Johns Hopkins
only a month when he wrote to Ellen Axson: "With the utmost
indiscretion, I over-taxed my eyes yesterday and am today suffering
with a dull ache through my head and with throbbing orbs that
refuse all use." Two months later he felt his habitual nervous
breakdown impending, and wrote to her: "I am not often subject
to the dominion of my nerves, and it requires only a very little

prudence to enable me to maintain that mastery over myself and that free spirit of courageous, light-hearted work in which I pride myself." This was whistling to keep up his courage. Two weeks later he collapsed, and fled to the Manse at Wilmington "to be nursed."

On his return to Hopkins he constantly complained of "ominous headaches," that he was in a "low state of health," and he "worried." "I am too intense," he wrote to Ellen Axson. "I am as you have no doubt found out for youself an excessively proud and sensitive creature." He complained that he was "ignorant of women," "shut up in his own heart," that he was full of the "sadness doubtless natural in a person of passionate loves and hatreds, but sadness for all that," that he had a "terrible ambition, a longing to do immortal work." Finally he wrote to her: "It isn't pleasant or convenient to have strong passions . . . I have the uncomfortable feeling that I am carrying a volcano about with me. My salvation is in being loved."

All his life he kept insisting on his "intensity" and his "strong passions." But at the age of twenty-eight he was almost certainly a virgin. All the evidence we have been able to collect indicates that his sexual life was confined to his first wife and his second. When he was in the White House, his political enemies circulated stories about liaisons with Mrs. Peck and others. Those stories were, without exception, untrue — inventions of men who hated him but had no knowledge of his character.

In 1885 he was twenty-eight years old, about to be married, about to begin to earn his living. Physically he was thin, weak and ugly. His ugliness obsessed him. His face was out of proportion, there was too much below the eyeglasses, too little above. In an attempt to improve his appearance he had grown a long, silky mustache and short side-whiskers. They did not conceal his beaked nose, his protuberant ears, his jagged jaw or his loose, meaty upper lip. When he sent a photograph to a friend he remarked that "it is an excellent likeness, not one whit uglier than I was when it was taken." All his life he was acutely sensitive about his appearance and took refuge in jokes about his looks. Again and again he repeated the limerick:

> For beauty I am not a star
> There are others more handsome by far.
> But my face I don't mind it,
> For I am behind it,
> It's the people in front that I jar.

On June 9, 1919, after sitting to Sir William Orpen for his portrait, he looked at the work, which was far from finished. Then he told Sir William that he would not sit again. Sir William was in despair. He asked for at least one more sitting. The President refused. Friends intervened to persuade Wilson to sit again. They discovered that he could not bear the appearance of his ears as Orpen had recorded them. A few diplomatic words on both sides resulted in another sitting and less protuberant ears.

He never forgave Theodore Roosevelt for saying that he looked too much like an apothecary's clerk to be elected President of the United States.

His ugly features were further disfigured by the eyeglasses which straddled his jutting nose, and by a surprisingly bad set of teeth. He never smoked, but decay had mottled his teeth; so that when he smiled, patches of yellow, brown and blue with glints of gold were exhibited. His skin was putty colored with unhealthy blotches. His legs were too short for his body, so that when he sat he looked more distinguished than when he stood.

He held himself erect, however, and made the most of the poor endowment his mother had given him. At the time of his marriage he was in the habit of wearing a coat buttoned up to his chin. He complained in a letter to Ellen Axson, "I am quite used to being taken for a Minister. There seems to be something about the cut of my jib that leads a great many people to conclude that I am a missionary craft of some sort — though I could myself never discover what it is."

He had modeled himself so completely on his father that he, too, had the look of a Presbyterian Minister. He wore the sterilized, disinfected expression which then characterized ministers and Y.M.C.A. secretaries. Yet he could turn on warmth of expression like an electric light. He could suddenly confront a person or a camera with momentary expression of almost lover-like understanding and affection. Then his face would fall back into its habitual astringence. He always addressed audiences with this turned-on, intimate warmth. It increased his power as an orator. In this connection, he wrote to Ellen Axson on December 18, 1884: "I have a sense of power in dealing with men collectively which I do not always feel in dealing with them singly. In the former case the pride of reserve does not stand so much in my way as it does in the latter. One feels no sacrifice of pride necessary in courting the favor of an assembly of men such as he would have to make in seeking to please one man." He was, in fact, ill at ease with men of any distinction.

He was neat and orderly in all his habits. His handwriting was precise, never hurried or slipshod. He rarely touched alcohol in any form and then only in minute quantities for medicinal purposes. He was never drunk. He never smoked, although his father had been a prodigious smoker, and said: "My father did enough of it in his lifetime to answer for both of us." In the later years of his life he rarely touched either tea or coffee, and he followed a rigid diet. He would not play cards. His father considered cards immoral.

The outstanding feature of his physical life was a tendency to nervous breakdown. His pleasures as a young man did not help to combat this tendency. He did not participate in sports or games of any kind. At Johns Hopkins, as at Princeton, he enjoyed singing with the Glee Club and he enjoyed debating. At Johns Hopkins, as at Princeton and the University of Virginia, he drew up a constitution for a new debating society modeled on the British House of Commons. His pleasures were all connected with the use of his mouth.

He read essays and poetry. Walter Bagehot, whom he called "My Master Bagehot," was his favorite essayist. He loathed Byron. His favorite poem was Wordsworth's "Character of the Happy Warrior." He found himself as he liked to think of himself in every line. To his death it remained his favorite poem.

> Who is the happy Warrior? Who is he
> That every man at arms should wish to be?
> It is the generous Spirit, who, when brought
> Among the tasks of real life hath wrought
> Upon the plan that pleased his childish thought;
> Whose high endeavors are an inward light
> That makes the path before him always bright;
> Who, with a natural instinct to discern
> What knowledge can perform, is diligent to learn;
> Abides by this resolve, and stops not there,
> But makes his moral being his prime care . . .

A

Psychological Study

of

THOMAS WOODROW
WILSON

by

Sigmund Freud and

William C. Bullitt

I

ANY BOOKS have been written about Thomas Woodrow Wilson, and many of his friends have attempted to explain him to themselves and to others. The explanations have one quality in common: they end with a note of uncertainty. Wilson remains, even to his biographers and intimates, a character of contradictions, an enigma. On June 10, 1919, in the final month of the Peace Conference, Colonel Edward M. House recorded in his diary: "I think I never knew a man whose general appearance changed so much from hour to hour. It is not the President's face alone that changes. He is one of the most difficult and complex characters I have ever known. He is so contradictory that it is hard to pass judgment upon him." To this conclusion, with greater or less emphasis, all Wilson's intimates and biographers come at last.

Wilson was, indeed, complex; and it will not be easy to discover the clue to the unity underlying the apparent contradictions of his character. Moreover, we should not set out with false hopes. We shall never be able to achieve a full analysis of his character. About many parts of his life and nature we know nothing. The facts we know seem less important than those we do not know. All the facts we should like to know could be discovered only if he were alive and would submit to psychoanalysis. He is dead. No one will ever know those facts. We cannot, therefore, hope to comprehend the decisive events of his psychic life either in all their details or in all their connections. We cannot, consequently, call this work a psychoanalysis of Wilson. It is a psychological study based upon such material as is now available, nothing more.

On the other hand, we do not wish to underestimate the evidence we possess. We know much about many aspects of Wilson's life and character. We must give up hope of full analysis; but we know enough about him to justify the hope that we may be able to trace the main path of his psychic development. To the facts we know about him as an individual we shall add the facts which psychoanalysis has found to be true with regard to all human beings. Wilson was, after all, a human being, subject to the same laws of psychic development as other men; and the universality of those laws has been proved by the psychoanalysis of innumerable individuals.

To say this is not to say that psychoanalysis has revealed the ultimate mysteries of human life. It has, so to speak, opened the door which leads to the inner life of man and has allowed us to recognize the existence of a few objects which lie close to the door, though the objects which lie deeper are still veiled in obscurity. It has let a little light into the darkness, so that we are now able to distinguish the outlines of certain objects in the murk. We can describe certain mechanisms that are used by the ultimate reality which we cannot describe. Our science is still very young, and further research will doubtless prove that the lines with which we now attempt to delineate those objects have not been altogether truly drawn. But our expectation that the details of present conceptions will later have to be modified should not prevent us from using the conceptions we now have. The work of Newton was not rendered useless because Einstein followed; and had it not been for Newton there would probably not have been an Einstein. We shall, therefore, as a matter of course, employ certain theorems which psychoanalysis has developed from the facts it has discovered, for which it now demands belief. It seems necessary to set forth as briefly as possible a few of these conceptions and suppositions before we attack the psychological problem presented by Wilson's character.

We begin with the axiom that in the psychic life of man, from birth, a force is active which we call libido, and define as the energy of the Eros.

The libido must be stored somewhere. We conceive that it "charges" certain areas and parts of our psychic apparatus, as an electric current charges a storage battery or accumulator; that, like a charge of electricity, it is subject to quantitative alterations; that, dwelling without discharge, it shows tension in proportion to the quantity of the charge and seeks outlet; further, that it is continually fed and renewed by physical generators.

The libido first stores itself in love of self: Narcissism. This phase is clearly visible in an infant. His interest are confined to the acts and products of his own body. He finds all his courses of pleasure in himself. To be sure, even an unweaned child has a love-object; the breast of his mother. He can, however, do nothing but to introject this object into himself and treat it as a part of himself.

In contrast to Narcissism we place object-love. Occasionally, a condition similar to the Narcissism of the new-born child is preserved by an adult who then appears to us as a monstrous egoist, incapable of loving anyone or anything except himself; but normally in the course of life a part of the libido is directed toward objects outside the self. Another part continues to adhere to the self. Narcissism is the first dwelling of the libido and remains its most enduring home. In different individuals the proportion between narcissistic and object-love varies greatly; the chief charge of the libido may be stored in the self or in objects; but no man is utterly without love of self.

Our second theorem declares: all human beings are bisexual. Every individual, whether man or woman, is composed of elements of masculinity and femininity. Psychoanalysis has established this fact as firmly as chemistry has established the presence of oxygen, hydrogen, carbon and other elements in all organic bodies.

When the primary phase of pure Narcissism has been lived through and the love-objects have begun to play their role, the libido begins to charge three accumulators: Narcissism, masculinity and femininity. As expressions of femininity we consider all those desires which are characterized by passivity, above all the need to be loved, and in addition, the inclination to submit to others which reaches its apex in Masochism, the desire to be hurt by others. On the other hand, we call masculine all desires which display the character of activity, like the desire to love, and the wish to achieve power over other men, to control the outer world and alter it in accordance with one's desires. Thus we associate masculinity with activity and femininity with passivity.

The primary love-objects the child finds are his mother and father or their substitutes. His earliest relationships to his parents are passive in nature: the child is nursed and caressed by them, guided by their orders and punished by them. The libido of the child first discharges itself through these passive relationships. Then one may observe a reaction on the part of the child. He wishes to give his parents tit for tat, to become active toward them, to caress them, command them and avenge himself upon them. Thereupon, in addition to Narcissism, four outlets stand open for his libido, through passivity to his father and mother and through activity toward them. Out of this situation grows the Oedipus complex.

In order to explain the Oedipus complex we must introduce the third axiom of psychoanalysis, an assumption from the theory of the instincts, which declares that in the psychic life of man two chief instincts are active: the Eros, that is to say love in the widest sense, whose energy we have called libido, and another instinct, which we have named after its final aim, the Death Instinct. The Death Instinct displays itself to us as an impulse to attack and destroy. It is the opponent of the Eros, which strives always to produce larger and larger unities held together by the libido. Both instincts are from the beginning present together in the psychic life and seldom or never appear in pure form but are, as a rule, welded together in varying proportions.

Thus, what appears to us as masculinity and femininity never consists of libido alone but always carries with it a certain additional element of desire to attack and destroy. We assume that this additional element is much greater in the case of masculinity than in the case of femininity; but it is not absent from the latter.

Let us stress once more the fact that every charge of libido brings with it a bit of aggression and return to the Oedipus complex. We shall, however, discuss only the Oedipus complex of the male child.

We have noted that the libido of the child charges five accumulators: Narcissism, passivity to the mother, passivity to the father, activity toward the mother and activity toward the father, and begins to discharge itself by way of these desires. A conflict between these different currents of the libido produces the Oedipus complex of the little boy. At first the child feels no conflict: he finds satisfaction in the discharge of all his desires and is not disturbed by their incompatibility. But gradually it becomes difficult for the little boy to reconcile his activity toward his father and mother with his passivity to them, either because the intensity of his desires has increased or because a need arises to unify or synthesize all these divergent currents of the libido.

It is especially difficult for the little boy to reconcile his activity toward his mother with his passivity to his father. When he wishes to express fully his activity toward his mother he finds his father in the way. He then wishes to sweep his father out of his way as a hindrance to possession of his mother; but on the other hand, the charge of libido stored in passivity to his father makes him desire to submit to his father, even to the point of wishing to become a woman, his own mother, whose position with respect to his father he desires to occupy. From this source arises later the mother identification which becomes a permanent ingredient in the boy's unconscious.

The little boy's wish to thrust aside his father becomes irreconcilable with his wish to be passive to his father. The desires of the child are in conflict. The discharge of the libido from all its accumulators except Narcissism thus becomes hindered and the child is in the conflict which we call the Oedipus complex.

The solution of the Oedipus complex is the most difficult problem that faces a child of man in his psychic development. In the case of a little boy, fear turns the greater part of the libido away from the mother to the father, and his major problem becomes the irreconcilability of his desire to kill his father with his equally ardent desire to submit utterly to his father.

One method of escape from the major dilemma of the Oedipus complex is employed by all males: identification with the father. Equally unable to kill his father or to submit utterly to him, the litte boy finds an escape which approximates removal of his father and nevertheless avoids murder. He identifies himself with his father. Thereby he satisfies both his tender and hostile desires with respect to his father. He not only expresses his love and admiration for his father but also removes his father by incorporating his father in himself as if by an act of cannibalism. Thenceforth he is himself the great admired father.

This early step of father identification makes comprehensible the later ambition to outdo the father and become greater than the father which we so often observe in youth. The father with whom the little boy identifies himself is not the father as he actually is in life and will later be recognized to be by the son, but a father whose powers and virtues have undergone an extraordinary expansion, whose weaknesses and faults have been denied. He is the father as he appears to the little child. Later, measured by the side of this ideal figure, the real father must necessarily seem small; and when a youth wishes to become a greater man than his father, he merely turns back from the actual father as he is in life to the father figure of his childhood.

This almighty, omniscient, all-virtuous father of childhood, as a result of his incorporation in the child, becomes an internal psychic power which in psychoanalysis we call the Ego-Ideal or the Super-Ego. The Super-Ego makes itself known during the remainder of the child's life through its commands and prohibitions. Its negative prohibiting function is well known to us all as conscience. Its positive commanding side is perhaps less easily perceptible, but certainly more important. It finds expression through all the conscious and unconscious aspirations of the individual. Thus out of the unsatisfied desire of the boy to kill his father arises father identification, the Ego-Ideal and the Super-Ego.

The establishment of the Super-Ego does not, to be sure, solve all the difficulties of the Oedipus complex; but it creates an accumulator for a certain portion of the current of libido which was originally aggressive activity toward the father. In exchange, however, it becomes the source of new difficulties with which the Ego thenceforth has to deal. For the Super-Ego throughout the remainder of life admonishes, censures, represses and strives to insulate and turn away from their goals all desires of the libido which do not satisfy its ideals. In many human beings this struggle in the Ego between the libido and the Super-Ego is not severe, either because the libido is feeble and allows itself to be guided easily by the Super-Ego or because the Super-Ego is so weak that it can only look on while the libido goes its own way; or because the ideals of the Super-Ego are not exalted above the limitations of human nature, so that it demands nothing more from the libido than the libido is ready to concede. The latter variety of Super-Ego is an agreeable one for the person who harbors it; but it has the disadvantage that it permits the development of a very ordinary human being. A Super-Ego which does not demand much from the libido does not get much; the man who expects little from himself gets little.

At the opposite extreme stands the Super-Ego whose ideals are so grandiose that it demands from the Ego the impossible. A Super-Ego of this sort produces a few great men, many psychotics and many neurotics. The manner in which such a Super-Ego develops is easy to understand. We have noted that every child has an exaggerated idea of the greatness and power of his father. In many cases this exaggeration is so excessive that the father with whom the little boy identifies himself, whose image becomes his Super-Ego, expands into the Almighty Father Himself: God. Such a Super-Ego continually demands the impossible from the Ego. No matter what the Ego may actually achieve in life, the Super-Ego is never satisfied with the achievement. It admonishes incessantly: You must make the impossible possible! You can accomplish the impossible! You are the Beloved Son of the Father! You are the Father Himself! You are God!

A Super-Ego of this sort is not a rarity. Psychoanalysis can testify that identification of the father with God is a normal if not a common occurrence in the psychic life. When the son identifies himself with his father and his father with God and erects that father as his Super-Ego, he feels that he has God within him, that he himself will become God. Everything that he does must be right because God Himself does it. The quantity of libido which charges this identification with God becomes so great in some human beings that they lose the ability to recognize the existence of facts in the world of reality which contradict it. They end in lunatic asylums. But the man whose Super-Ego is based upon this supposition, who preserves a full respect for facts and reality, may, if he possesses ability, accomplish great things in the world. His Super-Ego demands much and gets much.

To reconcile himself to the world of reality is naturally one of the chief tasks of every human being. This task is not an easy one for a child. Not one of the desires of his libido can find full satisfaction in the real world. Every human being who lives in the world has to achieve such a reconciliation. The person who entirely fails to accomplish this task falls into psychosis, insanity. The person who is able to achieve only a partial and therefore unstable settlement of the conflict becomes a neurotic. Only the man who achieves a complete reconciliation becomes a normal healthy human being. We must add, to be sure, that the reconciliation of the conflict is never so complete that it may not be broken down by the attack of sufficient external misfortunes. We are justified in saying that all men are more or less neurotic. Nevertheless in some men the settlement is based on such firm foundations that they can endure great misfortunes without falling into neurosis, while others need suffer only slight adversity to induce them to construct neurotic symptoms.

Every human Ego is the result of the effort to reconcile all these conflicts: the conflicts between the divergent desires of the libido, and the conflicts of the libido with the demands of the Super-Ego and with the facts of the real world of human life. The type of reconciliation finally established is determined by the relative strength of the inborn masculinity and femininity of the individual and the experiences to which he is subjected as a little child. The final product of all these attempts at reconciliation is the character.

To unify the desires of the libido with each other and the commands of the Super-Ego and the demands of the outer world is, as we have said, no easy task for the Ego: all the instincts must be satisfied somehow; the Super-Ego insists upon its commandments; and adaptation to reality cannot be escaped. To accomplish this task the Ego employs, when direct satisfaction of the libido is impossible, three mechanisms: Repression, Identification and Sublimation.

Repression is the method of denying the existence of the instinctive desire which demands satisfaction, treating it as if it did not exist, relegating it to the unconscious and forgetting it.

Identification seeks to satisfy the instinctive desire by transforming the Ego itself into the desired object, so that the self represents both the desiring subject and the desired object.

Sublimation is the method of giving the instinctive desire a partial satisfaction by substituting for its unattainable object a related object which is not disapproved by the Super-Ego or by the external world: thus the instinctive desire is transferred from its most satisfactory but inadmissible aim or object to one which is perhaps less satisfactory but more easily attainable.

Repression is the least effective of these methods of achieving the desired reconciliation of the conflict because it is impossible in the long run to disregard the instinctive desires. In the end the pressure of the libido becomes too great, the repression collapses and the libido flashes out. Moreover, the intensity of the repressed libido is greatly increased by the repression since it is not only insulated from all discharge but also withdrawn from the moderating influence of the reason which reckons with reality. The repression may achieve the success that the libido finally does not discharge itself by way of its original object, but is compelled to break open a new outlet and cast itself upon a different object.

For example, a boy who completely represses his hostility to his father does not thereby become free from his instinctive desire to kill his father. On the contrary, behind the dam of repression, his aggressive activity against his father increases until its pressure becomes too strong for the insulator. The repression collapses, his hostility to his father bursts forth and flings itself either against the father himself or against some substitute for him, someone who in some manner resembles him and may therefore be used as a father representative.

Hostility to the father is unavoidable for any boy who has the slightest claim to masculinity. And if a man in his childhood has completely repressed this instinctive impulse, he will invariably in later life fall into hostile relations with father representatives. He will display this hostility whether the father representatives deserve it or not. They draw his hostility upon themselves by the mere accident that in some way they remind him of his father. In such cases his hostility springs almost entirely from himself and has almost no external source. If it happens that in addition he has a real cause for hostility, then his emotional reaction becomes excessive and his hostility expands out of all proportion to the external cause. As a rule such a man will find it difficult to maintain friendly relationships with other men of equal position, power and ability, and it will be impossible for him to cooperate with persons who are superior to him in position, power and ability: such men he is compelled to hate.

We cannot leave the theme of repression without calling attention to the technique which the Ego employs to insure individual acts of repression. For this purpose the Ego constructs the reaction-formations, usually by the strengthening of impulses which are the opposites of those which are to be repressed. Thus, for example, out of the repression of passivity to the father may arise an overdevelopment of masculinity, which may show itself in arrogant rejection of every father representative. The psychic life of man is an extremely complicated thing. Reaction-formations against repressed instinctive impulses play as great a role in the construction of the character as the two primary identifications with the father and the mother.

The method of identification which the Ego employs to satisfy the desires of the libido is a very useful and much used mechanism. We have already explained how father identification and the Super-Ego develop from aggressive activity toward the father; countless other identifications are employed every day by all human beings. A child whose kitten has been taken away may indemnify himself for the loss of this love-object by identifying himself with the kitten, crawling about, mewing and eating from the floor like a kitten. A child who is used to being carried on the shoulders of his father, "playing horse," may, if his father is long absent from home, place a doll on his shoulders and carry it as his father has carried him, thus playing that he is his father. A man who has lost a beloved woman may until he has found a new love attempt to replace the lost love-object by himself. We shall come upon an instructive example of such a mechanism in Wilson's life. The man whose passivity to his father can find no direct discharge will often help himself by a double identification. He will identify himself with his father and find a younger man whom he will identify with himself; then he will give the younger man the sort of love which his unsatisfied passivity to his father makes him desire from his father. In many cases a man whose passivity to his father has found no direct outlet discharges it through identification with Jesus Christ. Psychoanalysis has discovered that this identification is present in entirely normal persons.

There is still another path to a final settlement of the father

problem in the Oedipus complex which leads over a double identification. When the boy has become a man and has himself begotten a son, he identifies the son with himself as a child and himself
with his own father. His passivity to his father then finds discharge
through his relationship to his son. He gives his son the love which
in his childhood he longed to receive from his own father. This
solution of the major dilemma of the Oedipus complex is the only
normal one offered by nature; but it requires that one should have
a son. Thus passivity to the father adds itself to all the other motives for wishing to have a son.

We have already mentioned that a mother identification arises
from passivity to the father. Now we must call attention to a
strengthening of this identification which occurs when, at the time
of the dissolution of the Oedipus complex, the boy gives up his
mother as a love-object. He transfers a portion of both his active
and passive desires with regard to his mother to other women who
represent her; but these desires are never fully satisfied by the substitutes and mother identification serves to store this unsatisfied libido. By use of the mechanism we have already described, the
child compensates himself for the loss of his mother by identifying
himself with her. He will then for the remainder of his life give to
other men who represent himself as a child a large or small proportion of the love which he desired as a child from his own mother.

Sublimation, the third method employed by the Ego to reconcile
its conflicts, involves, as we have noted, the replacement of the original objects of the libido by others which are not disapproved by
the Super-Ego or by society. This replacement is achieved by
transference of the libido from one object to another. For example, the boy turns a portion of his libido away from his mother to
his sisters, if he has any, and later to his cousins or friends of his
sisters, and then to women outside the family group with whom he
falls in love, until by this route he finally finds his wife. The more
his wife resembles his mother, the richer will be the flow of his
libido into his marriage; but many instinctive hostile impulses

which tend to disrupt marriage also cling to these mother relationships.

Innumerable sublimations are employed by human beings to discharge libido and to these sublimations we owe all the higher achievements of civilization. Unsatisfied desires of the libido sublimated produce all art and literature. Human society itself is held together by sublimated libido, the passivity of the boy to his father transforming itself into love of his fellow men and a desire to serve mankind. If the bisexuality of human beings seems at times a great misfortune and the source of endless trouble, we should remember that without it human society could not exist at all. If man had been nothing but aggressive activity and woman nothing but passivity, the human race would have ceased to exist long before the dawn of history, since the men would have murdered one another to the last man.

Before we close this brief exposition of some of the fundamental principles of psychoanalysis it seems advisable to describe a few more discoveries.

Every hindrance to the discharge of the libido produces a damming up of psychic energy and an increase of pressure in the accumulator concerned which may extend to other accumulators. The libido always seeks storage and discharge, it cannot be dammed up either permanently or above certain levels. If it cannot find storage and discharge by the use of one accumulator, it stores itself and discharges itself by the use of other accumulators.

The intensity or, to continue our simile, the quantity of the libido varies greatly in different individuals. Some possess a tremendously powerful libido, others a very weak one. The libido of some may be compared to the electrical energy produced by the huge dynamos of a central power station, while the libido of others may resemble the feeble current generated by the magneto of an automobile.

The libido will always abandon an outlet if another is opened which lies closer to the original instinctive impulses, provided the resistance of the Super-Ego and the outer world is not greater in the case of the new outlet. For example, it will always be ready to give up a sublimation if it can find another closer to its original object.

It is perhaps a law and at least a very frequent phenomenon that a human being turns toward a person whom he loves with especial intensity a considerable bit of hate, and toward a person he hates with especial intensity a considerable bit of love. One or the other of these antithetical instinctive impulses is repressed either wholly or in part into the unconscious. We call this the fact or principle of ambivalence.

The birth of a younger brother regularly produces a certain re-action in a little boy: he feels betrayed by his father and mother. The reproach of betrayal and the hatred of his parents may then be transferred by him either wholly or in part to his younger brother. A child who develops normally frees himself from this hatred and the feeling of betrayal by a typical identification: he transforms himself into the father of the child and converts the younger brother into himself. But in less normal development the reproach of betrayal continues to cling to the younger brother, and the elder throughout his life continues to suspect that those of his friends who later represent his younger brother will do things to him in which the betrayal will be repeated.

The feeling of betrayal described above springs from disappoint-ment of both active and passive desires of the libido; but some-thing much more serious may arise from the repression of passivity to the father. It may drive men into the persecutory form of para-noia: persecution mania. As a rule the sufferer from persecution mania believes himself to be persecuted and betrayed by the per-son he most intensely loves. The mania of betrayal and persecu-tion has often no basis in fact but springs solely from the need to escape from the beloved person because the beloved excites but does not satisfy the passivity of the invalid. If the sufferer can be-lieve that the person he loves so ardently betrays him and persecutes him, then he is able to place hate in the place of love and is able to escape from his beloved. It is easy to trace back all cases of unjustified mistrust and persecution mania to repressed passivity to the father.

Frustrations and misfortunes of all sorts tend to drive the libido back to former dwelling places; for example, to drive it back from sublimations to its original objects of desire. This we call regression.

In the course of human life it may happen that the psychic development suddenly halts and comes to an end instead of continuing its evolution. In such a case some overwhelming experience has forced the libido into accumulators to which it clings until death or mental disintegration. This we call fixation.

II

WE HAVE NOW set forth a few of the discoveries of psychoanalysis which we shall treat as axioms in making our psychological study of Thomas Woodrow Wilson. Hitherto we have stated facts which are true of all men born in the world; let us now consider the human being who was born in the Manse at Staunton, Virginia, on December 28, 1856, and passed his childhood in the Manse at Augusta, Georgia.

The reader will doubtless expect us to begin our discussion of Wilson's character with a precise estimate of the power of his libido. We should be glad to make such an estimate if we knew sufficient facts about Wilson. Unfortunately we do not know enough facts about him to justify us in making any estimate whatsoever. The libido becomes manifest only at its outlets. To estimate the strength of the libido one must know all the outlets. One must in addition know how much of the libido remains bound in the inner life. Some of the libido of all men remains so bound. The amount which remains bound in the inner life may be small or great. The libido of an Indian hermit, for example, may be strong, yet find outlet only through contemplation. We have no evidence upon which to base an estimate of the amount of Wilson's libido which remained thus bound, and we do not know anything about many of the outlets of his libido to the outer world.

Thus, to attempt to estimate the magnitude of his libido by a study of its discharge through the few outlets with which we are familiar would be as unreasonable as to attempt to estimate the quantity of electricity generated by the central power station of a city by examining the amount of current employed by a few of the houses and factories in the city. We cannot estimate accurately the magnitude of his libido and we are unwilling to indulge in guesses as to the total strength of his libido.

The reader will doubtless consider us over-cautious and come to his own conclusions with regard to the power of Wilson's libido. He may, perhaps, observe the fact that Wilson almost certainly remained a virgin until he married his first wife at the age of twenty-eight and a half years, and conclude that Wilson's libido was extremely weak. Before jumping to such a conclusion, the reader should remember several facts: first, that the libido may find expression through thousands of outlets aside from direct sexual expression; second, that Wilson was physically weak and presumably had no great somatic pressure to satisfy; third, that the "ideal of purity" was a part of Wilson's Super-Ego and may in some measure have helped to turn the discharge of his libido away from direct sexual expression.

On the other hand, the reader, contemplating Wilson's frequent remarks about his own "intensity," may be tempted to conclude that Wilson's libido was extremely powerful. But this feeling of intensity has in fact little to do with the total strength of the libido. It merely accompanies certain desires of the libido, and may be caused by the withdrawal of these individual desires from control by the Ego or by overcharging of them as a result of an unresolved conflict. A neurotic or psychotic whose total libido is weak may, therefore, display greater intensity than any normal man. A normal man with a very powerful libido neither feels nor exhibits intensity if he has no unresolved conflicts in his Ego. When Wilson wrote, "I am too intense," he indicated, therefore, not that he possessed a powerful libido but rather that he had within him an unresolved conflict between opposed desires; not that his desires were strong but that his Ego had not achieved a satisfactory solution of the Oedipus complex.

If the reader, contemplating Wilson's great love for his father, his great love of speech and his great hatred for many men, should be tempted to draw the conclusion from this evidence that Wilson's libido was especially powerful, he should remember that many men give the appearance of possessing a powerful libido by concentrating its flow into a few channels; but that psychoanalysis of such men often shows that in fact the libido is weak and that, by this concentration, a great part of the psychic life has been left without sufficient flow of the libido to maintain it adequately. We know nothing about the richness of Wilson's inner life; but we do know that the portion of his libido which flowed to the outer world was concentrated into a few channels. His range of interests was extremely narrow. Moreover, within that narrow range of interests he further concentrated the flow of his libido. One of the most striking features of Wilson's character was what he called his "one-track mind." He found it impossible to direct his interest to more than one intellectual object at a time. That is to say, one intellectual object was sufficient to take all the flow of his libido which found outlet through intellectual interests. This may well have been because his libido was so weak that in order to take an adequate interest in any intellectual object he had to concentrate the flow of his libido upon that object. Thus, again, it is wiser to come to no conclusion. And let us not be ashamed to admit our ignorance. To learn to say, "I don't know," is the beginning of intellectual integrity.

However unsatisfactory this incertitude may be to the reader, it must be insisted that the question of the strength of Wilson's libido is not, for the purposes of this study, of primary importance. We are interested primarily in attempting to understand the particular reconciliation of the opposed desires of his libido which was achieved by his Ego: that is to say, his character. We can trace the course of his libido without knowing its exact strength. Let us, therefore, assume merely that his libido was neither extraordinarily powerful nor extraordinarily weak and proceed to the vital question of the outlets through which it discharged itself.

The libido of little "Tommy" Wilson, like the libido of all other human beings, first began to store itself in Narcissism and to find discharge through love of himself. The only son of his father and mother, sickly, nursed, coddled and loved by father, mother and sisters, it would have been remarkable if he had avoided a great concentration of interest on himself. He did, in fact, greatly love himself always. We can find no evidence that he was ever deficient in admiration for himself or in attention to his own aggrandizement.

Moreover, as we shall see later, to be happy he had to have a representative of himself to love. Through this love he achieved an additional outlet for the abundant charge of his libido which dwelt in Narcissism. Unquestionably a large portion of his libido continued throughout life to find outlet through Narcissism — even of the portion which discharged itself through love-objects.

There are two forms of object-choice: direct and narcissistic. In the direct form of object-choice the libido flows directly to some outside person: to the child's mother or father or brother or sister or other person. The object is valued for itself, for its own personality, however little that personality may resemble the personality of the child. This sort of object-choice we call love of the "leaning" type because the child first "leans" or "props" his sexual instincts against his self-preservative instincts and first chooses as his love-object the same persons who satisfy his physical needs. On the other hand, in the narcissistic type of object-choice, the child's libido flows to an outside person who in some way resembles himself. He loves the portion of himself which he sees in the object. He does not love the object for the qualities in which the object differs from himself but only for the qualities in which the object resembles himself. Thus, through an object he loves himself, and his Narcissism finds in this roundabout way an additional outlet.

We shall see later that Wilson made frequent use of the narcissistic type of object-choice. Nevertheless, he was not one of the unfortunates whose libido finds outlet through Narcissism alone.

His Narcissism, preserved from childhood, contained perhaps a greater charge of libido than is usual, but not an abnormally great charge. A considerable portion of his libido found outlet as it does in all normal men by way of active and passive object relations.

It is unnecessary to restate the facts with regard to Wilson's childhood which have been recorded in the Digest of Data. Let us merely recall that one fact stands out with such prominence that it dwarfs all the rest; the fact that Tommy Wilson's father was his great love-object. His father was the great figure of his childhood. In comparison, his mother was a very small figure indeed. It is clear that much more of Wilson's libido found outlet through his relationship to his father than found outlet through his relationship to his mother. We should, therefore, expect that the task of his Ego in reconciling his conflicting desires with regard to his father would be more difficult than the task of his Ego in reconciling his conflicting desires with regard to his mother. That proved to be true. His Ego achieved easily a reconciliation of his conflicting desires with regard to his mother. His relations to women became normal and commonplace; but his Ego was never able to achieve a reconciliation of his conflicting desires with regard to his father.

The reader may perhaps be inclined to remark that Wilson's desires with regard to his father were not in conflict, that never in his life by any thought, word or act did Wilson express hostility to his father, that while an extraordinarily large proportion of Wilson's libido charged his passivity to his father, none whatever charged aggressive activity toward his father. The reply to this is simple: Wilson was a human being and subject to the same laws of development as all other human beings. He was certainly not one of those unfortunate men who is born with no masculinity. And the analysis of thousands of men has proved that the libido charges both aggressive and passive desires with regard to its love-objects. There can be no question whatever that the proportion of Wilson's libido which charged passivity to his father was enormous, and we are therefore obliged to conclude that a considerable portion of his libido must have found storage in aggressive activity toward his father. If we can find in his life no direct expression of hostility toward his father, we must look for evidence of indirect expression of hostility to his father. We know that hostility to his father must have existed and must eventually have found some sort of expression. In point of fact, nearly all the unusual features of Wilson's character were developed from the repressions, identifications and sublimations which his Ego employed in its attempt to reconcile his aggressive activity toward his father with his overwhelming passivity to his father. Wilson's relationship to his father and to father representatives will, therefore, necessarily occupy the greater part of our study of his character.

The Ego of little Tommy Wilson found no great difficulty in reconciling his conflicting desires with regard to his mother. They were not violent desires: the main charges of his libido were stored in his desires with respect to his father. Moreover, he had the good luck to have sisters and little girl cousins to whom his Ego could easily transfer the desires which were originally directed toward his mother.

Little boys who have sisters possess an enormous advantage over little boys who have no sisters. Sisters form a bridge over which the libido may be transferred easily from the mother to women outside the family. The Ego of a little boy who has no sister is compelled to force his libido to cross with one leap the chasm between his mother and the outside world. As we have already pointed out, the little boy who has a sister normally transfers to the sister a portion of the libido which has been attached to his mother, and from the sister transfers it to friends of the sister. Thus, by easy transfers, his libido reaches women outside the family. The Ego of a little boy who has no sister is compelled to transfer his libido directly from the mother to some woman outside the family, which is a much more difficult task, and, to many men, presents an insuperable difficulty. The libido of such men may remain fixed on the mother throughout life. They are incapable of detaching themselves from the mother. If, in one way or another, the mother is lost, the unfortunate son not rarely replaces the lost mother by identification of himself with the mother and gives to other men who represent himself the love that he desired to receive from his own mother.

Tommy Wilson was especially fortunate. The path to women outside his family was made exceptionally broad and smooth by the existence not only of sisters who loved him deeply and took care of him and played with him but also of little girl cousins who loved him. A large part of his libido remained attached to his mother throughout his boyhood and youth but a part also passed to his sisters and cousins. His passivity to his mother seems to have clung to her, indeed, for an exceptionally long time, longer perhaps than his activity. In this connection the letter Wilson wrote to his wife in 1888 is worth another glance: "I remember how I clung to her (a laughed-at 'mama's boy') 'till I was a great big fellow; but love of the best womanhood came to me and entered my heart through those apron strings. If I had not lived with such a mother, I could not have won and seemed to deserve — in part, perhaps, deserved through transmitted virtues — such a wife." In addition to showing how prolonged was the direct flow of Wilson's libido through the outlet of passivity to his mother, this letter indicates somewhat remarkably the amount of his passivity toward his mother which found expression through his first wife.

The fact that so soon after the death of his first wife, with whom he had lived in intimate marriage for twenty-nine years, he married another wife should not cause anyone to doubt his love for Ellen Axson. Experience teaches that men who have been happily married are apt to marry again. The speed with which he remarried nevertheless indicates how indispensable to him, entirely apart from personality, was a mother substitute.

His activity toward his mother, and with it of course some of his passivity, seems to have passed at an early age to his elder sisters, especially to his sister Anne, who was two years older than he and loved him as deeply as he loved her. He liked to play with these sisters and their little girl friends, especially with a little girl cousin who was younger than he and bore his mother's name: Jessie Woodrow Bones.

The extent to which like names produce identifications in the unconscious can scarcely be appreciated by one who has not made special study of the subject. It seems almost certain that little Tommy Wilson identified Jessie Woodrow Bones with his mother, Jessie Woodrow, and transferred to her, from his sister Anne, a considerable portion of the libido which originally had been directed toward his mother. The reader will remember that he was fond of playing "Indians" with this little girl, and that one day when she was up a tree pretending that she was a squirrel, he, the Indian hunter, shot an arrow from his bow into her body. She fell to the ground unconscious but uninjured and Tommy carried her into the house crying out in wild remorse: "I am a murderer. It wasn't an accident. I killed her."

One should not place too much emphasis on such incidents; but we find it impossible to avoid the impression that this episode indicates that by the time Tommy Wilson was eleven years old his Ego had successfully transferred a considerable portion of his activity toward his mother to Jessie Woodrow Bones, and that he was well started along the road to normal relations with women. Had it been otherwise, he would have felt less exaggerated remorse. His libido did not become completely detached from his mother until after his marriage to Ellen Axson seventeen years later; but by the time he was eleven, the detachment had already proceded so far that there was little danger of his being driven back to entire dependence upon his mother. Thus before his adolescence his Ego had so nearly solved the minor dilemma of Oedipus complex that there was every reason to expect that his relations with women would be normal throughout life. They were. For that he had to thank his sisters and his cousin Jessie Woodrow Bones.

Before we consider his adolescence and his later relations with women, let us turn to his childhood relationship to his father. That presents a very different picture.

The facts recorded in the Digest of Data with regard to Wilson's childhood relationship to his father present a remarkable picture of adoration. Many little boys adore their fathers; but not many adore so intensely and completely as did Tommy Wilson. The child's earliest memory was of running to his father to ask for an explanation, and throughout his life he continued to run to his father for guidance. The sickly boy did not go to school. He did not learn to read. All his early education came from the lips of his father and he drank in the words which came from his father's mouth with extraordinary avidity. The father talked much; but never too much for the thirst of his son. Whether the words of the father were uttered at home, in instruction, in prayers, at meals, in evening reading and conversation, or on walks, or from the pulpit, Tommy swallowed them with joy and gazed up to the face of his father with utter adoration. "My incomparable father," was his own description of the Reverend Joseph Ruggles Wilson.

Mr. Ray Stannard Baker was correct when he stated: "His father was the greatest figure of his youth — perhaps the greatest of his whole life. . . . The letters between the two can be called nothing but love letters." And Professor Daniels was correct in calling Wilson's love for his father his "dominant passion."

When we try to find evidence of a direct expression of Tommy Wilson's hostility to his father, we discover that in all the sixty-eight years of his life we can find no hostile thought or act directed in this respect. He continued to ask and to follow his father's advice so long as his father lived; and to the end of his own life, he continued to speak of his father with love and admiration. Only in his choice of a profession did he refuse to submit to the will of his father. His father wished him to become a Minister. He insisted on becoming a statesman. We shall later discuss this decision and, for the moment, ask the reader to suspend judgment upon it, with the hint that even this resolution may prove to have been an expression not of hostility to the father but of admiration for the "incomparable father" of his childhood. What, then, became of Tommy Wilson's aggression towards his father?

As pointed out, the Ego employs three methods of reconciling conflicting desires: repression, identification and sublimation; and that the type of reconciliation finally made by the Ego depends upon the strength of the original inborn masculinity and femininity, and the accidents of childhood. Tommy Wilson in his childhood was subjected to an overpowering father; a strong, handsome father who lectured him incessantly, kissed him, hugged him, preached to him and dominated him as the representative of God on earth. If the masculinity of the boy had been more powerful than his femininity, he would have found the weight of that father intolerable; he would have hated that father, as so many Ministers' sons have hated their fathers. But, in fact, Tommy Wilson's femininity was far stronger than his masculinity, at least at that period of his life. The portion of his libido which charged passivity to his father was far greater than the portion which charged aggressive activity toward his father; and it is obvious that his Ego employed the method of repression to handle the conflict between his powerful passivity and his relatively feeble aggressive activity. His aggressive activity toward his father was repressed. A portion of it found storage, to be sure, in his Super-Ego, but none of it ever found discharge through direct hostility to his father.

We have pointed out that repression is the least effective of all the methods of reconciliation employed by the Ego because the repressed desire continues to seek discharge and is immune from criticism by the reason, since it is cut off from consciousness, and that, in consequence of the insulation of the desire and its withdrawal from the moderating influence of reason, it accumulates a large quantity of libido. We find that the portion of Tommy Wilson's hostility to his father which was repressed was so completely repressed that it never once discharged itself against his father; but it continued to seek discharge and many times during his life broke out against father substitutes, driving him to violent and unreasonable hatreds of men who were to him father representatives, like Dean Andrew F. West of Princeton. At all times, because of this repressed hostility, he found it difficult to maintain friendly relations with men of superior intellect or position, and preferred to surround himself with women or inferiors.

The portion of his aggressive activity toward his father which found outlet through a father identification build up in him a tremendously powerful and exalted Super-Ego. We have noted how normally a little boy substitutes for his desire to kill his father another method of overcoming his father, the method of father identification, and how this produces the Super-Ego. Tommy Wilson identified himself with his father to an extraordinary degree. He thought the thoughts of his father, spoke the words of his father, adopted his father completely as his model, caring for words as his father had cared for them, despising facts as his father despised them, carrying his imitation to the length of delivering speeches from his father's pulpit to an imaginary congregation, dressing himself so that as a young man he was frequently mistaken for a Minister, and marrying like his father a woman born and reared in a Presbyterian Manse.

He never grew beyond this father identification. His qualities and defects remained the qualities and defects of his father. He could not imagine any more perfect man than his father. His father had found his supreme expression in sermons from a pulpit. Tommy Wilson found his supreme expression in sermons from a pulpit which was the White House. His father was not in the habit of devising practical methods to compel the translation of the principles he expounded from the pulpit into reality. Wilson did not devise practical methods to compel the translation of his Fourteen Points into reality. His father sang, so did Tommy. His father read in the evenings to his family, so did Tommy. What his father had done was worth doing. What his father had not done was not worth doing. His father smoked incessantly. Tommy never smoked. "My father did enough of it in his lifetime to answer for both of us," he explained. So that even in this case, in which for once he failed to imitate his father, he did not fail to express most clearly his feeling that he and his father were one: completely identified. He lived again his father's life on a grander scale.

The picture in his unconscious of his "incomparable father," developed from his earliest exaggerations of his father's qualities, which became his Super-Ego, had an immense effect on the course of his life. His career has, indeed, exceptional interest as an illustration of the power of an exalted Super-Ego to drive a man of deficient physique to the attainment of great position and power.

We have described how a large number of little boys, with much less provocation than Tommy Wilson, in the unconscious so exaggerate the powers and virtues of the father that they identify him with the Almighty, All Virtuous Father Himself, God; and by identification install this Almighty Father as the Super-Ego. This unquestionably happened in the case of little Tommy Wilson. It would, indeed, have been remarkable if it had not happened. The little boy looking up to the father in the pulpit whom he considered the most beautiful man on earth and listening to the words of God coming from his mouth could scarcely have avoided identifying his father with the Almighty. The God whom Thomas Woodrow Wilson worshiped to the end of his days was the Reverend Joseph Ruggles Wilson, the "incomparable father" of his childhood. Until he was ten years old, he was the only beloved son of that God. His identification of himself with the Saviour of Mankind, which became so important and obvious a feature of his character in the later years of his life, seems to have commenced as an inevitable conclusion in his unconscious during his first years: if his father was God, he himself was God's Only Beloved Son, Jesus Christ.

We shall see effects of these identifications appearing throughout his life and we do not wish to anticipate later developments; but it seems desirable to record here two invariable results of the possession of a Super-Ego made in the image of the Almighty. As we have already pointed out, such a Super-Ego can never be satisfied. No matter what its unfortunate possessor may achieve, he will always feel that he has not done enough. He will take no joy in work accomplished but will always be dissatisfied with himself and driven by a feeling that he has not accomplished what he expects of himself. He can never accomplish what he expects of himself because his Super-Ego demands that he accomplish the impossible. Throughout Wilson's life this was one of his characteristics. When he had achieved something he took only a momentary joy in the achievement. Almost at once he was harassed by the feeling that he must accomplish more. Invariably this is the outward and visible sign of a too exalted and powerful Super-Ego.

A second result of the establishment of God as the Super-Ego is that the child feels that he has God within him. In his unconscious he himself is God. Whatever he does is right because God does it. Tommy Wilson was able to justify to himself many curious actions of his own because of this unconscious conviction. Whatever he did must be right because God did it. He could on occasion admit that he had been mistaken. He could never admit that he had done wrong. His Super-Ego would not permit that. Rather than admit that he had done wrong he preferred to forget or distort facts, to turn away altogether from the world of reality and to construct imaginary facts to suit the demands of his Super-Ego.

It is not remarkable that the possession of such a Super-Ego as this drives some men to greatness and others to neurosis and psychosis. Its demands are insatiable; but if they are not in large measure satisfied the Super-Ego tortures its unfortunate possessor. Therefore, the possessor of such a Super-Ego first attempts to satisfy it by actual accomplishment, and often accomplishes great things; but, if his accomplishment is not in fact nearly sufficient to satisfy his Super-Ego, it scourges him anew. He cannot accomplish in reality more than he has accomplished. To escape the scourges of his Super-Ego, he therefore invents imaginary accomplishments.

He distorts the world of fact. He may become a psychotic. If his hold on reality is stronger, he merely suffers the scourgings of his Super-Ego and becomes a neurotic. Thus the man who installs God as his Super-Ego walks on a thin ridge up the mountain of greatness balancing precariously between the abyss of neurosis on one side and the abyss of psychosis on the other. He is lucky if before the end of his life he does not fall into one abyss or the other. We shall see how the Super-Ego of little Tommy Wilson drove him up this narrow ridge, how he slipped many times toward neurosis, how finally toward the end of his career he nearly plunged into psychosis.

III

BEFORE WE CONSIDER Wilson as a youth and man we must complete our examination of his desires when he was a child, and we have not yet considered his passivity to his father. We trust that during our discussion of this element in Wilson's nature the reader will remember that his own character, and the character of every other man, is as firmly rooted in bisexuality as was Wilson's character. Nearly all men have learned to contemplate the physical elements in the human body without shame. To call attention to the presence of oxygen and hydrogen in the body of a man no longer causes excitement; but not all men have yet learned to look calmly at the psychic elements of human nature. To mention the bisexual nature of man still seems somewhat scandalous to the ill-educated. Yet bisexuality is a fact of human nature which, in itself, should arouse no more emotion than the fact that fifty-nine percent of the body consists of water. If human beings were not bisexual, they would not be human beings. To be born bisexual is as normal as to be born with two eyes. A male or a female without the element of bisexuality would be as inhuman as a Cyclops. Just as an artist may employ the same paints to produce either a beautiful picture or an ugly picture, so the Ego may combine the original masculinity and femininity of a man to compose either a beautiful character or an ugly character. To judge the final product, whether picture or character, is legitimate. To condemn the elements is absurd. Masculinity may be employed to produce the heroism of Leonidas or the act of a murderer. There is everything to praise and blame in the results the Ego produces with the original masculinity and femininity, but there is nothing praiseworthy or blameworthy in the mere existence of these elements. They exist. That is all. When Margaret Fuller, "high priestess of New England transcendentalism," declared, "I accept the universe," Carlyle remarked, "By God, she'd better." Like the universe, the bisexuality of mankind has to be accepted.

The outlets employed by Wilson's Ego for his passivity to his father were all outlets approved by his Super-Ego. His chief outlet was through direct submission to the will of his father. He did what his father wanted him to do and did not do what his father did not want him to do. He accepted his father's thoughts without question and his father's leadership with adoration. He submitted every problem of his life to his father. In Mr. Ray Stannard Baker's words: "Until after he was forty years old, Woodrow Wilson never made an important decision of any kind without first seeking his father's advice." He depended on his father financially until he was twenty-nine years old. His father wished him to be a good moral Presbyterian. He became one. His father wished him to become a specialist in words and a speaker. He became one.

Throughout Wilson's life much of his libido found outlet by way of speech-making. His excessive interest in making speeches would be surprising if it were not obvious that he found in the performance outlet not only for passivity to his father but also through identification, for activity toward his father. When he spoke, he was doing what his father wished him to do; but he was also by identification becoming his father. The Reverend Joseph Ruggles Wilson was, after all, essentially a speaker. Thus speech-making gave expression to Thomas Woodrow Wilson's two strongest desires.

A portion of Wilson's passivity to his father found outlet through direct submission to his father; but the submission which, in his unconscious, he desired to make was far more profound and specific than the submission he was able to make in life. He therefore sought more ways in which to submit. He found an outlet, fully approved by his Super-Ego, through submission to the God who represented his father. All his life he enjoyed daily acts of submission to that God: morning prayers, evening prayers, grace before each meal and Bible reading each day. Moreover, so great was his need to submit to his God that never in his life could he allow himself to entertain religious doubt. To have doubted would have been to cut off an outlet which he needed for his passivity. "God is the source of strength to every man and only by prayer can he keep himself close to the Father of his spirit," he said. Twice, at least, he remarked: "I believe in Divine Providence. If I did not I would go crazy." Inasmuch as he made this remark about himself one need not feel that it is indecent to agree with him. So considerable a portion of his passivity to his father found outlet through his daily submissions to the God who represented his father that he might have found it impossible to discover another adequate and acceptable outlet. If he had not been able to make his daily submissions to God, he might indeed have taken refuge in paranoia and developed a "persecution mania"; he might have become not the occupant of the White House but the inmate of an asylum.

Another outlet for Wilson's passivity to his father was through a mother identification. We do not know enough about Wilson to make any estimate of the relative importance of his mother identification. He know only that he had a mother identification. In spite of his conscious wish to be like his father, Wilson resembled his mother not only in physique but in character. He had not only her thin weak body but also her severity, shyness and aloofness. He often felt like his mother, and he knew it. His remark to Dudley Field Malone is striking: "When I feel badly, sour and gloomy and everything seems wrong, then I know that my mother's character is uppermost in me. But when life seems gay and fine and splendid, then I know that the part of my father which is in me is in the ascendance." He usually felt "badly, sour and gloomy."

Were Wilson alive and would he submit to psychoanalysis, we would doubtless find that mother identification played a momentous part in his life. As it is, we must content ourselves with noting that we shall find evidence of mother identification when we consider the later stages of his life. Available evidence permits us to say merely that he, like all other men, had a mother identification and through it a portion of his passivity to his father found outlet.

Another vital tie with regard to which we have almost no evidence is his relationship to his brother Joseph. When Joseph Ruggles Wilson, Jr., was born, Thomas Woodrow Wilson was ten years old. Therefore, in spite of the fact that his development was retarded, it seems certain that he had passed the most important stages of his psychic development before the birth of this little brother. Nearly all children by the end of their sixth year have achieved some sort of a reconciliation of the conflicts of the Oedipus complex and have entered a period of sexual latency which usually lasts until adolescence. In consequence, most boys who are ten years old at the time of the birth of a younger brother find it comparatively easy to accept the intruder. Normally, the elder brother in his unconscious becomes father to the younger brother and also identifies himself with the younger brother, so that in the relationship he plays father to himself: to the elder brother, the younger brother represents himself as a small child. Through the passivity of his little brother (himself as a small child) to himself (representing his father) he obtains an outlet for his own passivity to his own father.

There is invariably present also an element of hostility. The younger brother is a rival for the love of the father and mother; and the birth of the younger brother, as we have already pointed out, gives rise to a feeling of "betrayal." Usually neither the hostility to the younger brother nor the sense of betrayal is pronounced in the case of a normal boy who has passed into the period of latency before the birth of his younger brother. If the elder brother has reached the age of ten before the birth of the younger brother, he ordinarily finds it easy to adopt a fatherly attitude toward the infant in the manner we have described and either preserves this attitude throughout life or follows the pattern of this relationship in his friendships with smaller and younger men who represent his brother.

We have no evidence as to Tommy Wilson's emotions at the time of the birth of his brother Joe, and we know little about their future relations. We know that Thomas Woodrow Wilson at one time taught his little brother as his father had taught him, that he helped his brother in various ways, that he wrote, "I love my brother passionately," that he refused, when President, to appoint his brother to a postmastership or to allow his brother to be made Secretary to the Senate. Our information is so scanty that we should be glad to pass over this relationship without attempting to discuss it; but we must mention the probability that Joe Wilson played a far larger part in the emotional life of Thomas Woodrow Wilson than either realized.

In later life Thomas Woodrow Wilson always needed to have at least one affectionate relationship with a younger and physically smaller man, preferably blond. In these friendships Wilson clearly played the part of his own father and his friend represented himself as a boy. The pattern for these relationships probably was established by the emotions aroused in the ten-year-old Tommy Wilson by the birth of the infant Joe. We have noted that normally the elder brother identifies himself with the younger brother and plays father to himself and in addition that a sense of hostility, distrust and betrayal may accompany the affectionate emotions. Wilson's intense friendships were characterized by just such manifestations. He loved John Grier Hibben and Colonel House intensely so long as they preserved the obedient little brother attitude toward him. He finally concluded that each had betrayed him and cast each into the outer darkness as a Judas. We have seen that this paranoid sense of betrayal springs always from passivity to the father, and that it is often connected with the birth of a younger brother. We must, therefore, mention the probability that the birth of Joe Wilson inaugurated two important characteristics of his brother Thomas Woodrow Wilson. First, Joe's birth may have marked the beginning of his inclination to establish friendships in which he played father to a younger and smaller man who represented himself. Second, it may have established his inclination to protect himself from his passivity by a paranoid mechanism. Briefly, his little brother Joe may have been the original much-loved betrayer who was followed many years later in his unconscious by Hibben and House. The original emotion involved was, of course, Tommy Wilson's passivity to his own father; but it seems to have reached his friends by way of his brother Joe. It is noteworthy that the most unjustified distrust of Wilson's life — his distrust of his White House Secretary, the faithful Joseph P. Tumulty — was directed toward a younger, smaller blond male named Joe. Joe Tumulty, to Wilson's unconscious, may well have represented Joe Wilson. The actions of a human being are often determined by far more absurd identifications than this.

When one considers Wilson's later relations with his brother Joe, Hibben, House, Tumulty and others, one is driven to conclude that the birth of the infant Joe Wilson must have aroused far stronger emotions in the ten-year-old Tommy Wilson than are usual in a child of that age confronted by an infant brother. His over-violent reaction was no doubt produced by the magnitude of his passivity to his father which made it inevitable that he should regard with excessive hostility a brother who ousted him from his unique position as the only begotten son of his father. It seems clear that at the age of ten Wilson's passivity to his father was still his dominant desire and that a portion of this current of libido, accompanied by much hostility and a paranoid sense of betrayal, charged his relationship to his brother Joe.

Another outlet for Wilson's passivity to his father was his identification of himself with Jesus Christ. This identification probably was established in his early childhood as a correlative to his identification of his father with God; but it seems not to have accumulated a large charge of libido until his adolescence. We shall, therefore, for the moment postpone discussion of it.

We have now glanced at the distribution of Wilson's libido in his childhood. We have observed that his love of self was ample; that his father, not his mother, was his chief emotional object; that his relations with women promised to be normal and commonplace; that a part of his activity toward his father had been repressed and a part had produced an exalted Super-Ego; and that his passivity to his father was his dominant emotion and required many outlets, among which were submission to his father and to God and identification with his mother and with his brother Joe. Before we consider Wilson's youth, adolescence and adult life let us for a moment look at the child as a whole.

Thomas Woodrow Wilson was a rather pathetic little boy, a child to whom one cannot refuse sympathy. He was weak, sickly and nervous, retarded in his development, his eyesight was defective and he suffered constantly from indigestion and headaches. That he should have been nervous is not extraordinary. Nervousness is the visible sign of an inner conflict which the Ego has been unable to solve. And, aside from all minor conflicts which may have harassed him, there was plenty of cause for nervousness in the conflict between his Super-Ego which commanded that he should be all masculinity, God Himself, and his passivity to his father which demanded that he should submit to his father in all ways even to the point of becoming all femininity. Thus his early relationship to his father doomed him to expect of himself all his life more than his body or mind could give. The nervousness and discontent which marked his life were early established. For this reason he compels our pity.

Yet it must also be recognized that he was in many ways favored by fate. His sisters and cousins had led him to an easy transfer of his libido from his mother to women outside the immediate family so that he was on his way to a normal sexual life. Moreover, his nature was admirably fitted to the civilization and class into which he was born.

The Lollard tradition of the British non-conformist middle class transferred to America, in which he was brought up, produced an atmosphere in which it was difficult for a man whose masculinity exceeded his femininity to flourish, except economically; but one well suited to women and to men whose femininity exceeded their masculinity. The "Thou shalt not!" of Lollardry is intolerable to a masculine man but congenial to women.

A more masculine boy than Tommy Wilson would have felt hostility to the *mores* of the family and community in which the Minister's son was reared; but he felt no impulse to revolt. His masculinity was feeble. His Ego-Ideal was not hostile to the ideals of his family or his community. The problems of his life arose not from conflicts with his environment but from conflicts within his own nature. He would have had to face those conflicts if he had been brought up in the comparative freedom of European civilization. The screen of rationalizations which allowed him to live all his life without facing his passivity to his father would have fallen early on the continent of Europe. He was fortunate to have been born in a nation which was protected from reality during the nineteenth century by inherited devotion to the ideals of Wyclif, Calvin and Wesley.

IV

Tommy Wilson's first contact with life outside the sheltering circle of father, mother, sisters and cousins came at the age of thirteen, when he went to school. At Professor Derry's little day school he did badly in his studies. The explanation of his teacher is worth noting: "It was not because he was not bright enough, but because he was apparently not interested." Here one seems to see foreshadowed his "one track mind." Some light is thrown on this phenomenon by another event of the same year. We see no lack of interest when we turn to the scene in the Minister's hayloft and behold Tommy Wilson laying down the laws of orderly speech to the Lightfoots.

If, indeed, as Wilson later said, "the Lightfoots held meetings characterized by much nicety of parliamentary procedure," one may be sure that the "nicety of parliamentary procedure" was imposed upon the small boys by the Minister's son in the chair, and that he was able to impose this "nicety" because of his own love of speech. In this action he was both obeying his father and identifying himself with his father. He was finding outlet for his passivity to his father and, by identification, for activity toward his father. The flow of his libido was therefore abundant, his interest was great. But apparently his libido was insufficient in volume to supply both his interest in speech and other intellectual interests, and it naturally flowed first to the outlet which offered sublimation for his conflicting desires with regard to his father. Throughout his life he took intense interest only in subjects which could somehow be connected with speech. Just as, when a boy, he was unable to find sufficient libido to nourish a healthy interest in the subjects of the school curriculum, later, in order to take an adequate interest in subjects unconnected with speech, he had to consider such subjects one at a time, excluding other subjects from his thought though they might demand immediate attention. Thus developed his "one track mind."

He took no interest in mathematics, science, art or music — except in singing himself, a form of speaking. His method of thinking about a subject seems to have been to imagine himself making a speech about it. His literary work was speech-making on paper, and its defects were for the most part defects produced by using the technique of oratory in literary composition. He seems to have thought about political or economic problems only when he was preparing to make a speech about them either on paper or from the rostrum. His memory was undoubtedly of the vaso-motor type. The use of his vocal chords was to him inseparable from thinking.

Adolescence, with its manifold physical alterations, came upon Wilson along with important changes in his environment. When he was fourteen years old, his father gave up his pastorate in Augusta and became a professor in a Theological Seminary at Columbia, South Carolina. His family followed him to Columbia. Thus, when adolescence overtook Tommy Wilson, his life no longer was confined to the community which surrounded the Manse and the church in Augusta. He found himself in the burned capital of South Carolina, in which violent political struggles provided drama. And his father, though still a clergyman, was no longer a Minister but a professor.

The reader will remember that a pious young man named Francis J. Brooke came to Columbia to study for the Presbyterian ministry. He was a few years older than Tommy Wilson. He held religious meetings in his room and in the one-story stable which was the chapel of the Theological Seminary. Tommy attended the meetings and began to love Brooke deeply. Under the influence of Brooke he underwent a religious "conversion." At the age of sixteen and a half he confessed, "exhibited evidence of a work of grace begun in his heart" and was admitted to membership in the First Presbyterian Church of Columbia. Thenceforth he felt himself to be in direct communication with God. He felt that God had chosen him for a great work and would use and preserve him till his work was done. He had been doing badly at school, at once he began to do better. He put a portrait of Gladstone on the wall behind his desk, and when the little cousin he had shot out of the tree asked whose portrait was on the wall, he replied: "That is Gladstone, the greatest statesman that ever lived. I intend to be a statesman, too."

This sequence of events provides the nexus between the childhood and manhood of Thomas Woodrow Wilson. To find such a nexus is, indeed, no great discovery. Wilson was adolescent, and adolesence is the period which connects childhood and manhood. It is also somewhat platitudinous to note that the profound physical changes of adolescence are invariably accompanied by psychic changes no less profound. Every man knows this from his own experience. With the onset of adolescence the need of the libido to find outlet is greatly sharpened. Not only is the demand of the libido for direct expression re-enforced by actual somatic pressure; but alterations in the internal secretions also produce a growth in the masculinity of the boy. The quantity of libido accumulated in activity toward his mother and father is thereby increased. His desire to possess his mother, in the form of a mother representative, is intensified; and his hostility to his father revives, no matter how completely it may have been repressed. This intensification of active desires results occasionally in juvenile delinquency; but happily in most cases its results are comic rather than tragic. The boy's increased activity toward his mother makes him fall desperately in love with an older woman or a girl; and his increased activity toward his father produces a desire to disobey and to escape from the authority of his father, and a tendency to replace his father as a love-object by a father representative.

Adolescence, in the normal manner, produced striking changes in the character of Thomas Woodrow Wilson. But, characteristically, these manifestations appear in connection with desires directed toward his father and not with desires directed toward his mother. There is no evidence that he fell in love with any girl or older woman. He had his mother, sisters and cousins, and they continued to satisfy the small portion of his libido which was directed toward women. As always, he needed to have a mother representative in his life; but apparently he had no great somatic pressure to satisfy and even during his adolescence, as throughout the rest of his life, his relations with women remained polite and dull.

On the other hand, his increased masculinity disturbed considerably his relations to his father. Indeed, adolescence seems to have produced a somewhat exceptional increase in Wilson's masculinity; and he offers an example of the importance of time in considering psychic phenomena. As a child his passivity to his father had been overwhelmingly strong. His Ego had therefore repressed completely his aggressive activity toward his father. But adolescence brought such great re-enforcement to his masculinity that throughout the rest of his life his masculinity was able to battle his femininity on something like equal terms, and as he grew older the preponderance of his masculinity seems to have been established. The repressions, reaction-formations, identifications and sublimations which he had established in early childhood were not thereby altered; but, through physical changes, the proportion of his libido which charged masculinity — that is to say, active desires — became greater than the portion which charged femininity — that is to say, passive desires. It became increasingly necessary for him as he grew older to find expression for his aggressive activity toward his father. In the consideration of psychic phenomena the element of time and physical change must never be forgotten.

When Wilson's increased masculinity first came into conflict with his passivity to his father, his Ego sought the usual escapes. First, it transferred a portion of the libido which was directed toward his father to a father representative. Brooke was unquestionably a substitute for his father. The virtuous young man, who conducted religious meetings which Tommy Wilson attended, represented the "incomparable father" whose religious meetings Tommy had attended from infancy. He fell in love with Brooke.

This transfer to Brooke of a path of the libido which was flowing toward his father did not solve the conflict between his passivity to his father and his newly invigorated activity toward his father but merely diminished the intensity of the conflict. He already possessed, however, an unused outlet through which these conflicting desires could find simultaneous expression: his identification of himself with Christ.

The reader may perhaps be inclined to ask at this point why Wilson's identification of himself with Christ did not receive a large charge of libido at the moment in his childhood when, presumably, he established it as a correlative to his identification of his father with God. That might have happened; but it seems not to have happened. An identification may receive an immense charge of libido at the moment of its establishment, as in the case of a *coup de foudre*, love at first sight. On the other hand, an identification may be established and may carry only a slight charge of libido until a moment of necessity arises. Wilson's aggressive activity toward his father was so feeble during his childhood that it seems to have been almost completely consumed by the maintenance of his Super-Ego. It was not until adolescence had increased his masculinity that he needed greatly to employ a method of reconciling his activity toward his father with his passivity.

There are many bits of evidence which indicate that Wilson's identification of himself with Christ first became the accumulator of a great charge of libido at the time of his "conversion." To discuss here the phenomenon of conversion would carry us too far afield. Let us merely note that the "rebirth unto righteousness" which marks "conversion" may occur by the convert identifying himself with some member of some holy family. He then feels reborn because in his unconscious he has become that deity.

Wilson at the time of his "conversion" began to believe that he was in direct communication with God, to feel that God had chosen him for a great work and would preserve him till that work was done. Wilson, as President of the United States, stood before the door of the stable in which Brooke had led him through his religious experience and made a curiously overcharged remark: "I feel as though I ought to take off my shoes. This is holy ground." This remark, taken in conjunction with his beliefs and behavior at the time of his conversion, makes it difficult to avoid the conclusion that his identification with Christ first began to carry an important charge of libido at that moment in his adolescence. In his unconscious Wilson probably felt that the stable was holy ground because it was the scene of his rebirth as Christ. The setting was appropriate for such an event. Christ also was born in a stable. His conflicting desires demanded such an event. The identification made in his early childhood was ready for use. Brooke did the rest. Throughout the remainder of his life he employed this identification. As he grew older, more and more of his libido found lodgment in it and outlet through it, until toward the end of his life it became absolutely necessary for him to be able to identify himself with the Son of God. Such facts as had to be suppressed or distorted by his conscious mind in order to preserve this outlet for his libido were distorted or suppressed. At all costs he preserved it, even at the cost of declaring the Treaty of Versailles to be ninety-nine percent insurance against war and of inventing betrayals by his friends.

Parenthetically, we may here point out that the step between identification with Christ and the paranoid defense against passivity is made easy by the existence of a convenient bridge. Christ had a betrayer, and the betrayer was a disciple, a friend. In later years Wilson, having fully identified himself in his unconscious with Christ, found it easy to cross this bridge. On the other side of reality, he found among his friends many a Judas.

Wilson's identification of his father and himself with the major figures of the Trinity played so great a part in his life that, before discussing his adolescence, it seems desirable to attempt to recapitulate his unconscious relations with the deity: He seems to have identified his father with God at a very early age and to have established this Father-God as his Super-Ego and thus condemned himself to expect of himself the impossible. He probably identified himself with the Only Begotten Son of God shortly after identifying his father with God, but it seems likely that he did not begin to employ this identification with Christ as a major outlet for his libido until his adolescence, when his increased activity needed to be reconciled with his passivity to his father. He seems to have taken in his unconscious the final step of full identification of himself with God only after his defeat at Princeton by West. Then, when his father was dead, and he was defeated by a father representative, he assumed his father's throne, became God in his unconscious and began to act with a sense of his own inevitable righteousness.

Let us now return to the "converted " adolescent who had identified himself with Christ. And let us first note that although this identification provides a most happy reconciliation for the conflicting desires of passivity to the father and activity toward the father it is based on a misconception. The individual who identifies himself with Christ is not Christ. In the world of men, submission does not often lead to triumph. Yet the neurotic who has lodged a considerable portion of his libido in identification with Christ is apt, when faced by battle and harassed by fear, to take refuge in the comforting illusion that he too by submitting will achieve ultimate victory. He fears to fight. Therefore, through his identification with Christ he convinces himself that he does not need to fight, that by submitting he will achieve his aims. And, if he has not a firm grip on reality, he is apt to convince himself after he has submitted that he has in fact won a victory, although in reality he has suffered complete defeat. Thus, however desirable identification with Christ may be as a means to reconcile an inner conflict, it is disadvantageous in so far as it produces an inclination to submit when facing battle, and a tendency to turn away from the facts of reality. We shall later see that Wilson's identification of himself with Christ was not without influence upon his actions in the crucial days of his life. In Paris at the Peace Conference he feared the consequences of fighting. He submitted, then declared that he had won a victory and announced that the Treaty of Versailles was indeed the peace of "absolute justice" which he had set out to establish. His identification of himself with Christ was the mental mechanism which enabled him to reach that somewhat fantastic conclusion.

Wilson's love for Brooke and his identification of himself with Christ were followed not only by happiness but also by notable changes in his character. He began to do better in his studies, and he announced that he intended to become a statesman, not a Minister. This announcement, which at first sight appears most puzzling, was the expression of a personal wish and was not approved by his family. When he went to Davidson College six months later, his father and mother hoped that he would become a Minister. He himself appears to have been undecided whether to adopt the career which his father had mapped out for him or to attempt to follow in the footsteps of Gladstone. He did not make his irrevocable decision to become a statesman until three and a half years later when he was at Princeton. This decision, which determined not only the course of his life but also in some measure the course of all human life, is so important that it seems worth while to attempt to analyze it in detail. It must be considered as a whole, from the first tentative announcement when he was sixteen and a half years old to the definite decision when he was twenty. We must, thereore, ask the reader to suspend judgment upon it until we have glanced at the events of the intervening three and a half years.

In the autumn of 1873, three months before his seventeenth birthday, Wilson left his father and mother and went with Brooke to Davidson College. Ill health drove him back to his father and mother in the spring of 1874, and he remained at home being nursed for fifteen unhappy months.

This "breakdown" at Davidson was the first of many similar collapses. Nervousness, dyspepsia and headaches characterized his life from childhood to death. His "breakdowns" were merely periods of greater nervousness, more severe indigestion and more continuous headache than his periods of "health." For example, the period from October 1887 to June 1888 when he was acutely unhappy at Bryn Mawr is difficult to classify. At least fourteen times in his life his nervousness, dyspepsia and headaches became so severe as to interfere seriously with his work, to say nothing of his happiness.

1. June 1874 to October 1875
2. December 1880 to June 1882
3. November 1883 to March 1884
4. October 1887 to June 1888
5. November 1895 to August 1896
6. June 1899 to August 1899
7. The summer of 1903
8. January 1905 to March 1905
9. May 1906 to October 1906
10. January 1907 to February 1907
11. September 1907 to September 1908
12. February 1910 to March 1910
13. August 1914 to February 1915
14. April 1919

To discuss these "breakdowns" is not easy. It is, of course, possible, though improbable, that they were organic affections, caused by bodily weakness in which psychic factors had no share or only a small share. In the later part of Wilson's life severe, undoubtedly physical, diseases accompanied them. From the beginning, therefore, they might possibly have been of purely physical origin. We regret deeply the lack of material which might lead to a conclusive answer to this question.

We know, however, that Wilson was physically weak and also that his neurasthenic symptom complex invaribly reappeared as a reaction to difficult situations. We are struck by the fact that he spent three of the ten years between the spring of 1874 and the spring of 1884 being nursed in his father's Manse. He was in the full vigor of his young manhood — seventeen at the beginning of that period, twenty-seven at the end — but he clung to the habits of his childhood and remained a virgin full of dyspepsia, nervousness, headaches and ideals. In default of specific evidence with regard to his physical ailments at that time, we can only conclude that his "nervousness" and "intensity" were caused by the conflict between his femininity and his exalted Super-Ego which demanded that he should be all masculinity. If we are asked why from time to time his symptoms increased to the point of "breakdown," we can answer only by the generalization that his symptoms increased in severity whenever the events of his life produced a sharpening of the fundamental conflict.

V

In September 1875, after fifteen months of illness, Wilson went to Princeton desperately determined to overcome his weakness and to make himself the leader his Super-Ego demanded. To an extraordinary degree he succeeded. His career from 1876 at Princeton to the day when he was received in Paris as the Saviour of Mankind offers a remarkable example of the power of a strong Super-Ego to drive to success a man of weak body and neurotic constitution. During his second year at Princeton, he entered upon the course which was to lead him to the Presidency of the United States and the leadership of the world. His first year had been passed in attempting to remedy the deficiencies in his intellectual preparation for college and in nursing his stomach. In the autumn of 1876 he read one day an article in an English magazine on "The Orator" in which Mr. Gladstone and Mr. Bright were described and praised for possessing just such qualities as Thomas Woodrow Wilson was convinced that he possessed. He wrote to his father that he had discovered that he had a mind and decided definitely and unalterably to become a statesman, not a Minister.

The reader has perhaps observed that the same person appears in Wilson's original statement of his intention to become a statesman at the age of sixteen and in his final decision at the age of twenty: Gladstone. We must, therefore, suspect that Queen Victoria's Prime Minister may offer the key to the riddle of Wilson's refusal to follow in the footsteps of his father. Let us first consider the state of mind of Tommy Wilson when he pinned the picture of Gladstone on the wall above his desk and announced his intention to become a statesman. He was adolescent. His masculinity had increased. His reawakened aggressive activity toward his father demanded outlet. His passivity to his father was still so powerful that even his re-enforced aggression could not find outlet through direct hostility to his father. The reader will recall that every little boy in his early childhood when confronted by the dilemmas of the Oedipus complex normally escapes from his wish to kill his father by a "cannibalistic" method of destroying his father: he absorbs his father into himself by identification and establishes this idealized father of early childhood as his Super-Ego.

It seems clear that at the age of sixteen Wilson turned to the same method of expressing his aggressive activity toward his father. He attempted to identify himself with the "incomparable father" of his early childhood. But that "incomparable father" was no longer present before him in life. Every adolescent boy, because of his reawakened aggression toward his father, looks at his father with an eye wiped clean of illusions. However much he may strive to maintain his adoration of his father, he is compelled to realize that his father is not the handsomest, strongest, wisest, most virtuous, most powerful man in the world. There are some defects. The old man is even a trifle comic and a little pitiful. The boy may repress this knowledge. Wilson did repress it. He continued to talk of his father as if his father were God-like, to quote him, to admire him. Yet, like every other adolescent, he must have known at the bottom of his mind that his father was in fact not perfect. He needed intensely to refind the "incomparable father" of his early childhood and to identify himself with that father, and thus by a cannibalistic identification to give expression to his aggression toward his actual father. He refound the "incomparable father" of his early childhood in Mr. Gladstone.

Mr. Gladstone may have been installed as the object of Tommy Wilson's newly awakened aggression by some other mechanism; but whether or not this was the mechanism by which the substitution was achieved, there is no doubt whatever that Gladstone did begin to represent the "incomparable father" of Tommy Wilson's childhood. Adolescent Tommy then destroyed Mr. Gladstone by the cannibalistic method of identification and announced: "That is Gladstone, the greatest statesman that ever lived. I intend to be a statesman, too." Thus through Gladstone he found expression for his newly awakened aggression toward the father who stood before him in life, and he was able to continue uninterruptedly to love the imperfect actual father of adolescence. His identification of himself with Gladstone received not only a great charge of libido from his aggressive activity but also secondary charges from his tender activity and his passivity to his father. So long as he lived, it continued to accumulate much of the libido derived from his aggressive activity toward his father.

The Reverend Joseph Ruggles Wilson, however, had no intention of allowing his son to become anything but a replica of himself. Tommy was sent to Davidson College to be prepared for the ministry. The boy's passivity to his father was still so strong that he did not revolt or refuse. He went to Davidson. But thenceforth in his unconscious the figure of the "incomparable father" of his childhood bore the face of Gladstone, not the face of the Minister of the Gospel. To feel that he himself was the "incomparable father" of his childhood Tommy Wilson had to become a statesman.

It was necessary for him to identify himself with the father of his childhood not only to obtain an outlet for his aggressive activity toward his actual father but also to escape from his mother identification. If his father identification did not dominate him, his mother identification did: then, as he said, he felt "badly, sour and gloomy." To his increased masculinity that was intolerable.

Nevertheless for three years of ill health and unhappiness Wilson could not bring himself to make his little declaration of independence, which involved resistance to his actual father although to his unconscious it meant merely a turning aside from the father of actuality to the perfect father of childhood. Then he read the article on "The Orator" in which, along with Bright, Gladstone was praised for qualities which he considered his own. He felt himself a man like Gladstone. He dared to make his declaration. Once and for all he renounced imitation of the father of actuality for imitation of the father of his childhood who wore the face of Gladstone. Thenceforth to feel that he was on the way to becoming a statesman was absolutely necessary to his happiness. Only thus could he find discharge for the aggressive activity toward his father accumulated by his identification with Gladstone. Only thus could he avoid domination by his mother identification. In order to feel that he was a man, he had to become a statesman.

VI

THOMAS WOODROW WILSON at the age of twenty-one was a formed character. All the chief outlets for his libido had been established and, except for an intensified identification of himself with God after his defeat by West, he did not greatly change in the remaining forty-seven years of his life. Our study of his character must, therefore, proceed from a slightly altered standpoint. We have hitherto been concerned with determining what accumulators and outlets for his libido were established in his childhood, youth and adolescence. We shall henceforth be concerned with observing his attempts to find happiness through the established outlets. We shall exchange the microscope with which we have been examining isolated portions of his libido for a field glass with which we shall observe him as a human being in action attempting to satisfy his desires.

The problem of finding happiness in life, which preoccupies all men, is in large measure a problem of psychic economics. The individual possesses a certain amount of libido which stores itself in various accumulators and seeks discharge through multiform outlets. If the outlets are approved by the Super-Ego and are nicely adjusted to the quantity of libido demanding discharge, neither restraining the current which is present nor releasing so much libido that the accumulator is drained dry, the individual is happy. Conversely, if the outlets are disapproved by the Super-Ego or are insufficiently large or are too large the individual is unhappy. Modern psychology can add nothing to the classic formula for happiness, "moderation in all things," except the footnote that moderation in the demands of the Super-Ego is as essential as moderation in all other things.

Yet even a man who is ready to live by this antique rule cannot expect to find happiness easily or to possess long the happiness he finds. To find outlets for the fundamental, often opposed desires is extremely difficult; and if satisfactory outlets are found the changing circumstances of life do not allow them to remain unaltered. Death, illness, loss of affection or status are inseparable from human life and all involve the loss of outlets for the libido, so that the wisest and most moderate man cannot count on holding his happiness. Less wise men, among whom Thomas Woodrow Wilson must be numbered, are unable to attain more than momentary flashes of happiness. Wilson's immoderate Super-Ego, which demanded from him the impossible, was alone enough to condemn him to lifelong discontent, and the excessive quantity of libido which charged his passivity to his father demanded outlets difficult to find and to retain.

The young man at Princeton was not greatly troubled by need to find outlet for the somewhat feeble current of his libido which was directed toward his mother. He was not harassed as are most young men by an imperative need to possess a woman. His love for his mother, sisters and cousins sufficed him. His actions at Princeton, like his actions throughout most of his life, were determined by his need to find outlet for his conflicting desires with regard to his father. We have seen that he had found an outlet for both his activity and passivity to his father through identification of himself with Gladstone, and during his college course all other interests were subordinated to this desire to make himself a Christian statesman. He did badly as usual in studies which were unconnected with speaking and writing; but in those which had to do with words he did well. He studied Burke, Bright and Bagehot, practiced gestures in front of a mirror, delivered orations to trees in the woods, wrote out visiting cards inscribed *Thomas Woodrow Wilson, Senator from Virginia,* organized a debating club in which governments rose and fell as in the House of Commons and wrote an article advocating the establishment of the English form of Cabinet Government in the United States.

At that time, Wilson respected highly a man whom later he hated: Henry Cabot Lodge, junior editor of the *International Review*. He submitted his article to Lodge, who accepted it. Later, when Wilson wanted to enter Johns Hopkins University, he listed Lodge among the distinguished authors in the field of history that he had read. Thus Lodge entered Wilson's life as a person in authority: a father representative.

The increase in Wilson's self-confidence during his sophomore year enabled him to step forward as a leader among his fellows at Princeton and to form a number of normal, unpassionate friendships. He also entered into a relationship with Charles Talcott which differed from his attachment to Brooke in the particular that Wilson was older than his friend. Talcott, to Wilson's unconscious, probably was the successor of little Joe Wilson and the forerunner of Hibben and House. In all these relationships Wilson clearly represented his own father and his friend represented himself, so that through them, by the double identification we have discussed, Wilson found outlet for his passivity to his own father.

At Christmas 1879, when Wilson was nearly twenty-three years old, he fell in love with a woman for the first time. We have seen that in his childhood he had transferred some of the libido which was directed toward his mother to his sisters and cousins. And characteristically he fell in love with a cousin: Hattie Woodrow. She was the daughter of his mother's brother, Thomas Woodrow, and she was certainly a mother representative to him. Like his mother she came from Chillicothe, Ohio. Her father, like his mother's father, was named Thomas Woodrow. Wilson began to write "somewhat ardent" letters to her. His increased masculinity for the moment led him no closer to the body of a woman.

The major portion of his libido was still directed toward his father. To become Gladstone was still his great desire. Graduated from Princeton in June 1879, he went in the autumn to the University of Virginia to study law, not because he wished to be a lawyer but because he considered law the "sure road" to statesmanship.

At the University of Virginia the law bored him but debating as usual fascinated him, and as usual he began to try to reorganize the debating club of which he was a member. To draw up a constitution for a debating club gave him intense satisfaction throughout his life. As a boy of twelve he laid down the rules of orderly speech for the Lightfoots. He made or remade constitutions at Davidson and at Princeton. He announced his intention to do so at the University of Virginia. He did so at Johns Hopkins and at Wesleyan. He examined the constitution of New Jersey for the purpose of remaking it. He prepared a constitution for the League of Nations. From the Lightfoots to the League of Nations is a clear line. We have seen that in laying down the laws of orderly assembly for the Lightfoots Wilson was both obeying his father and imitating his father, he was finding outlet both for his passivity to his father and, through identification, for activity toward his father. He found satisfaction for the same desires in preparing the Covenant of the League of Nations. Wilson's share in founding the League of Nations has been exaggerated; but in so far as he was its "father," the League of Nations was the grandchild of the Reverend Joseph Ruggles Wilson, the Professor Extraordinary of Rhetoric, whose interest in words and the rules of speech so bored his acquaintances, and so impressed his son.

At the University of Virginia Wilson was elected President of the Jefferson Society, in spite of his dislike of Jefferson. This hostility to Jefferson, and a similar hostility to Disraeli, at first sight seems somewhat extraordinary in a young man who aspired to become a statesman. Jefferson was one of the most distinguished of American statesmen and Disraeli was not the least distinguished of British. The explanation of Wilson's hostility is, however, not far to seek. He saw himself as a "Christian statesman": Gladstone.

Neither Jefferson nor Disraeli was a Christian statesman. Jefferson was a Deist, Disraeli a Jew. Disraeli, indeed, was the personal opponent of his master, Gladstone. They were appropriate devils for the Father-God with whom he had identified himself. When Wilson later became a statesman and a deity in his own unconscious, he was always somewhat inclined to clothe his opponents in the habiliments of Satan.

In December 1880, when he was twenty-four, Wilson's habitual indigestion and headaches became so severe that he had to leave the University of Virginia without a degree, and return to his father's Manse to be nursed. There is no evidence that he had ceased to be a virgin. He was still writing letters to his cousin Hattie. He was acutely unhappy. Six months later he visited the family of Hattie Woodrow in Chillicothe, Ohio, where his father had married his mother thirty-two years before, and proposed marriage to his cousin. She refused him. He returned to his father's Manse and for the first time began to call himself Woodrow Wilson, dropping Thomas.

In later years Wilson gave various explanations of this action; but no one of his explanations is convincing. And when a man gives various unconvincing explanations of an act one must suspect that the real reason for the act lies in his unconscious. The unconscious reason for Wilson's dropping his name Thomas is, in fact, clear. The reader will recall that the Ego normally replaces a lost love-object by identification of the self with the lost object. The little boy who loses a kitten may crawl about mewing. The little boy who has to give up his mother as a love-object at the time of the dissolution of the Oedipus complex identifies himself with his mother. Wilson employed this familiar mechanism. He went to Chillicothe to win a Woodrow cousin who represented his mother. Her father, like his mother's father, was Thomas Woodrow. In his unconscious he was unquestionably his own father going to Chillicothe to marry his mother. He was rejected. He was acutely unhappy. He had lost a mother representative whose name, like his mother's name, was Woodrow. Like the child who mews, he replaced the lost mother representative by himself. He dropped Thomas — the name of the father of the girl who had rejected him — and became unadulterated Woodrow. Thus he identified himself with his mother and satisfied his need for a mother representative by becoming himself his mother.

To his increased masculinity this identification of himself with his mother was intolerable, and it is not surprising that the year and a half which followed were the most unhappy of his life. Not only was his activity toward his mother without outlet but also his activity toward his father. His dyspepsia and headaches barred him from the path he hoped would lead him to a career as a statesman until the spring of 1882. Then after eighteen months at home he went to Atlanta to begin the legal labors which he felt confident would lead him to statesmanship. But in Atlanta he did not find even one client. He began to despair. The road to statesmanship seemed closed to him. In the spring of 1883 at the age of twenty-six, he sat in his office in Atlanta an utterly unhappy man. The flow of his libido through the channels of activity toward both his father and mother was blocked.

At this critical moment in his development, the stroke of good fortune without which it is almost impossible for any man to achieve distinction befell him. He went to visit the beloved little cousin he had shot out of the tree. The cousin was married; but there he met Ellen Axson, and she became to him the mother representative he needed in his life. That he should have fallen in love with her at once is not remarkable. She was cast in the same mold as his mother, sisters and cousins. Like his mother and sisters she was daughter of a Minister of the Presbyterian Church. Like his mother she was not only daughter of the Minister but mistress of the Manse as well. Her mother was dead and she was acting as mother to the Minister's three small children. Her position in life was almost precisely the position of his own mother when his father had married her. In asking Ellen Axson to marry him, Wilson was again identifying himself with his father. There are a thousand indications in their later relations that Ellen Axson was not only a mother representative to Wilson but a close, full and complete mother representative.

To fall in love with a mother representative is to give hostages to fortune. Such a relationship takes so completely the flow of the libido directed toward women that it becomes either a source of the greatest happiness and strength to a man or a source of the greatest unhappiness and weakness. If Ellen Axson had not loved Woodrow Wilson, or if having once loved him she had ceased to love him, he would have received a shattering blow from which, given his neurotic constitution and his habitual neurasthenic symptoms, he might never have recovered. But the contrary happened. She not only loved him deeply but continued to love him so long as she lived. From the day in the autumn 1883 when she promised to marry him to the summer day in 1914 when she died, Woodrow Wilson possessed the greatest source of strength which may exist in the life of any man: the undivided love of a complete mother representative. It is difficult to exaggerate the help she gave him. His relations to men continued to be unsettled throughout his life, producing conflicts which exhausted him. His relations to women were settled. He could always creep back to the sheltering arms of a perfect mother representative for rest. "I am the only one who can rest him," she said. That was true. He called her "the center of quiet" for his life. Without that center of quiet Woodrow Wilson would early have succumbed to the conflicts in his nature. His career was as much the product of Ellen Axson's love as of his own Super-Ego. She was for him a magnificent wife.

VII

THUS FROM THE AUTUMN of 1883 onward Woodrow Wilson possessed an outlet for his activity toward his mother and his passivity to her. At the same time, however, he abandoned the outlet his Ego had chosen for his activity toward his father. The way to statesmanship through the practice of law in Atlanta seemed closed. He went to Johns Hopkins to learn to earn his living as an instructor at some college. In order to undertake this new career he had to convince himself that somehow through professorship he would eventually reach statesmanship. He persuaded himself that by becoming an authority on political questions, he might influence political thought and enter political life by this side door. But to reach politics by way of the classroom was at that time unheard of in America, and he had to recognize that there was not much chance that he would ever become a Gladstone. So firmly had identification with Gladstone been established as the major outlet for his activity toward his father that anything less than a direct march to statesmanship left unsatisfied this portion of his libido, and much of his apparently unreasonable discontent and ill health during the years of his teaching and writing may be attributed to the loss of this outlet for his aggressive activity toward his father.

His letter of February 24, 1885, to Ellen Axson contains a remarkable bit of self-revelation: "Yes . . . there is, and has long been, in my mind a 'lurking sense of disappointment and *loss*, as if I had missed from my life something upon which both my gifts and inclinations gave me claim'; I do feel a very real regret that I have been shut out from my heart's *first* — primary — ambition and purpose, which was, to take an active if possible a leading part of public life, and strike out for myself, if I had the ability, a *statesman's* career. That is my heart's — or, rather, my *mind's* — deepest secret." Wilson's framing of the word primary in this sentence makes one feel that, when he wrote primary, his unconscious was thinking: Prime Minister: Gladstone.

As a student at Johns Hopkins, he wrote *Congressional Government*. He produced the impression in this book that he knew Congress intimately from personal contact. But he never once went to look at the Congress he was describing, although Washington was about an hour by train from Baltimore, where he was writing. This shrinking from contact with men and facts persisted throughout his life.

When *Congressional Government* was accepted by the publishers he was in ecstasy. But within a week he described himself as "down with the 'blues.'" Throughout his life his satisfaction in accomplishment invariably was overcome almost at once by a feeling that he had not done enough. His Super-Ego was insatiable. When the book was published he dedicated it not to his fiancée but to his father; and he asked his father to decide whether or not he should return to Johns Hopkins for a second year and take a degree, thus inviting his father to decide whether his marriage should be accelerated or postponed. He was twenty-eight years of age at the time and fond of writing letters describing himself as having "strong passions" and feelings as if he were "carrying a volcano" about with him; but this double subordination of his fiancée to his father shows clearly how weak was the flow of his libido directed toward women when compared to the flow of his libido directed toward his father.

Since his chosen outlet for aggressive activity toward his father was blocked, it is not surprising that he was highly critical of his Johns Hopkins professors. They were in fact distinguished scholars and it was due to their restraining hands that *Congressional Government* was the best literary work of his life. But anyone in authority over Woodrow Wilson remained to him always a father representative and thus offered an outlet for his repressed hostility to his actual father. We shall see this repressed aggression breaking out many times during the course of his life against men who deserved gratitude from him.

In June 1885 Woodrow Wilson married Ellen Axson. Until her death in August 1914, he had not the slightest sexual interest in any other woman. To be sure he wrote hundreds of long sympathy-seeking letters to Mrs. Hulbert and other ladies. These letters seem attempts to re-create his relationship to his older sisters rather than his relationship to his mother. It was on Ellen Axson's breast, not on the breast of one of his correspondents, that he found rest.

Woodrow Wilson took his newly married bride to a college for girls, at Bryn Mawr, Pennsylvania, and commenced his work as an instructor in history. Almost at once he became acutely unhappy. In spite of his young love, at a time when most men find themselves on the heights of happiness, he found himself in an abyss of misery. His nervous wretchedness at Byrn Mawr was so acute and extraordinary that it cannot have sprung solely from his Super-Ego. We must expect to find other accumulators of his libido without satisfactory outlet. Let us glance at his complaints.

His chief lament was that he did not want to teach girls; he wanted to teach boys. Here we find ourselves once again contemplating the relations of little Tommy Wilson to his father. Neither his activity nor his passivity to his father was finding satisfactory outlet. To teach boys offered an outlet for both desires. In lecturing to boys he could identify himself with the boy as well. Thus he could play son to himself and father to himself and re-establish the infantile relationship which had made him so happy. But unless the student to whom he lectured was a male, the identification became not only impossible but worse than impossible; he became his father lecturing to a girl who represented himself; he felt himself again a woman and that had become intolerable to him. Before he had been at Bryn Mawr six months he was searching for avenues of escape.

To teach at Princeton became his hope. He went to New York to speak at a Princeton alumni banquet hoping to impress his auditors sufficiently to obtain an instructorship at the college. The audience laughed at him, jeered, walked out. The wound to his Narcissism must have been immense, and it is not remarkable that thereafter he had little love for anything connected with New York.

He recoiled to his cherished identification with Gladstone. He went to Washington and tried to get a position in the Department of State. He failed. Again his activity toward his father was blocked.

His wife was pregnant. He wanted a son, as he wanted men pupils, through whom to find outlet for both his activity and passivity to his own father. His wife gave birth to a girl. Once again the stream of libido running toward his father was dammed. He grew more and more nervous. His wife again became pregnant. Again a child was born and again the child was a girl. His nervousness increased. He wrote to his friend Robert Bridges: "I almost fear I shall break down in health here if I stay another year." Again he tried the outlet of statesmanship, attempting to secure an appointment as Assistant Secretary of State. He failed. He approached breakdown, described himself as "hungry for a class of *men*," and called that winter, 1887–1888, "a terrible winter."

The reader contemplating all this nervous unhappiness in the life of a young married man who had a charming home and the esteem of Bryn Mawr may perhaps be tempted to conclude that his relations with his wife did not give him satisfaction. That is certainly not true. As always Ellen Axson was taking care admirably of the minor portion of his libido which was directed toward women. And he found pleasure in his daughters. But the main stream of his libido had been turned back again and again from outlets it had striven to open. His relations to men were so much more important to him than his relations to women that no amount of domestic felicity could make him happy.

His reaction to the death of his mother at the end of the "terrible winter" throws some light on this disproportion in his nature. To a friend he wrote: "My mother was a mother to me in the fullest, sweetest sense of the word, and her loss has left me with a sad, oppressive sense of having somehow suddenly *lost my youth*. I feel old and responsibility ridden . . . And yet the worst of it is not my own bereavement, but my father's, whose daughters are both married, and who, with my college-boy brother, is left practically without a home. My own happy little home seems to reprove me on his account in my morbid moments . . . " He invited his father to come and live with him.

This letter is no cry of pain for a lost love-object. His words about his mother are polite and conventional. Ellen Axson had taken her place. But his passivity to his father was stirred deeply by the thought that his father needed a wife. In his unconscious he had always wished to take the place of his mother with his father. Promptly in his unconscious he took it. He was filled with a feeling not that he had lost his mother but that he had lost his youth. The death of his mother removed the one obstacle to becoming in his unconscious the wife of his father. He felt "old and responsibility-ridden," felt that he must make a home for his father. One is tempted to say that in his unconscious he felt himself an old woman: his mother. It is not surprising that he invited his father to come to live with him or that, in so far as possible, he played he part of devoted wife to his father till the Reverend Joseph Ruggles Wilson died. Thus his passivity to his father found an outlet.

On March 9, 1890, he wrote to his wife, ". . . a distinct *feeling of maturity* — or rather of maturing — has come over me. The *boyish* feeling that I have so long had and cherished is giving place consciously to another feeling . . ." and added that he was "at last, perhaps, becoming a self-confident (mayhap a self-assertive) man." Consciously he thought that he was becoming at last a grown man, but it seems likely that in his unconscious he had become a grown woman. Thus even the death of his mother was made to serve his unsatisfied desire to be loved as a wife by his father. He did not in his unconscious become a grown man until after the death of his father.

"Hungry for a class of men" through whom he could loose his activity and passivity to his father, he leaped at a chance to leave Bryn Mawr for Wesleyan. There he had his class of men, and his health and spirits improved at once. The seven years which followed were in fact the happiest and healthiest of his life. He had no "breakdown" during the entire period and his habitual symptoms did not greatly harass him. All the major accumulators of his libido were provided with comparatively satisfactory outlets. His Narcissism was satisfied by the success of his lectures and the general esteem which greeted him everywhere. His wife cared perfectly for his activity and passivity to his mother. His passivity to his father was finding outlet not only through playing wife to his father when his father visited him, but also through identification with the youths to whom he lectured. His activity toward his father was to be sure not altogether satisfied; but a sufficient portion of it escaped through identification with his father when he lectured to diminish his need for the outlet of statesmanship. Even his Super-Ego must have been more or less appeased by the strides he was making in the academic world. His lectures, in which he played father to himself, pouring over his male auditors a loving warmth and rolling out magnificent generalities in the manner of the pulpit preacher, were most successful. Yet only the outlet of statesmanship could fully satisfy his aggressive activity toward his father and he was delighted when, after two years at Wesleyan, he obtained a position at Princeton which offered a field of labor closer to the current of national life.

Even during this period of comparative happiness, whenever Woodrow Wilson was separated from his father he wrote longing love letters to the old Presbyterian Minister. His letter of December 16, 1888, for example, is a notable outpouring on the part of a man of thirty-two:

106 High St., Middletown, Ct.
16 December 1888.

My precious father,

My thoughts are full of you and dear "Dode" all the time. Tennessee seems *so* far away for a chap as hungry as I am for a sight of the two men whom I love. As the Christmas recess approaches I realize as I have so often before, the *pain* there is in a season of holiday and rejoicing away from you. As you know, one of the chief things about which I feel most warranted in rejoicing is that I am your son.

I realize that benefit of being your son more and more as my talents and experience grow: I recognize the strength growing in me as of the nature of your strength: I become more and more conscious of the hereditary wealth I possess, the capital of principle, of literary force and skill, of capacity for first-hand thought; and I feel daily more and more bent toward creating in my own children that combined respect and tender devotion for their father that you gave your children for you. Oh, how happy I should be, if I could make them think of me as I think of you! You have given me a love that grows, that is stronger in me now that I am a man than it was when I was a boy, and which will be stronger in me when I am an old man than it is now — a love, in brief, that is rooted and grounded in reason, and not in filial instinct merely — a love resting upon abiding foundations of *service,* recognizing you as in a certain very real sense the author of all I have to be grateful for. I bless God for my noble, strong, and saintly mother and for my incomparable father. Ask "Dode" if he does not subscribe? And tell him that I love my brother passionately . . . Ellie joins me in unbounded love to you both.

Your devoted son,
Woodrow.

No less remarkable as an exhibit of mother identification is the following passage from his letter of March 20, 1890:

. . . I find that everybody regards my election to P. as a sort of crowning success; congratulations pour in from all sides; evidently I am "writ down" in the category of "successful men." I suppose I ought to feel an immense accession of personal satisfaction, of pride; but somehow I can't manage it. I feel grateful and full of courage at the prospect of having an opportunity to do just the studying and writing I want to do under the most favorable circumstances; but so far as personal gratification is concerned, I would infinitely rather know that I was going to have a chance to be cured of the heart-sickness from which I suffer because of my separation from you and "Dode." My *mind* can't give me gratification: I know it too well, — and know it a poor thing; I have to rely on my *heart* as the sole source of contentment and happiness; and that craves, oh *so* fiercely, the companionship of those I love. It seems to me that the older I get the more I need you; for the older I get the more I appreciate the debt I owe you, and the more I long to increase it. It seems to me that my separation from you, instead of becoming a thing of wont, becomes more and more unendurable. Are you *quite* well, now? Please, sir, let me know as early as possible your plans for the summer — how soon they include us. I suppose dear "Dode" will come North too this summer. I keep his picture on my desk all the time, and all the time long to see him. — Dear Ellie is much better though her foot is still far from being well. She pretends to love you and "Dode" as much as I do: but that is impossible.

Your devoted son
Woodrow.

VIII

THE EXTRAORDINARY preoccupation with literary "style" which marked Wilson's first happy years at Princeton seems to have arisen from the unsatisfied portions of both his activity and passivity to his father. In the words of his brother-in-law: ". . . he was so preoccupied with literary 'style,' that it approached obsession." His father also had been preoccupied to an exceptional degree by "style," and Wilson's "obsession" probably drew its chief charge of libido from his need for an additional identification with the Professor Extraordinary of Rhetoric. But since the Reverend Joseph Ruggles Wilson had done his best to compel his son to become preoccupied with literary "style," this preoccupation also gave outlet to Wilson's passivity to his father. Thus, like speech-making, literary "style" offered outlet to Wilson's most powerful desires.

The features of his "style" leave no doubt as to its parentage. It was the "style" of a boy immensely impressed by the phrases of a pedantic preacher. Archaic affectations, symbolism, alliteration, flight from fact to generalization, the piling of adjective on adjective, the use of superlatives and words with vague connotations like "counsel" and "process" characterized it. He was himself aware that his style was marked by pedantry, but he found himself helpless to alter it. This is not surprising, since it was not essentially a vehicle to convey thought but a means to give expression to his unconscious desires with regard to his father.

The unconscious is apt to push identifications to somewhat ridiculous extremes, and it is not without interest to note that

Woodrow Wilson went too far in his pomposity for even the Professor Extraordinary of Rhetoric. After reading his son's biography of George Washington, in which more than a hundred senences began with 'Tis, 'Twas, or 'Twould, the Reverend Joseph Ruggles Wilson was driven to remark, "Woodrow, I'm glad you let George do his own dying in your book."

When Woodrow Wilson wrote or spoke he was in his unconscious his father preparing or delivering a sermon, and he attempted to make his alliterations sing as sweetly and his generalities flash as brightly as the preacher's had sung and flashed in the mind of the child who sat in the fourth pew and adored his "incomparable" father. That his generalizations might have little to do with fact did not trouble him. They existed for themselves, as outlets for identification with his father. Facts are the enemies of generalizations, and the dislike of facts which he so often expressed was doubtless due in part to their ability to make a generalizations difficult. They interfered with the easy flow of his libido through this father identification. They also threatened his belief in and submission to his Father-God. Thus facts stood in the way of the discharge of his libido from its two greatest accumulators, activity and passivity to his father. It is not remarkable that he developed the habit of forgetting them when he found it inconvenient to remember them. The quality of his work was not thereby improved. He ignored the unpleasant fact of the existence of the secret treaties of the Allies. His fight for a "just and lasting peace" was thereby foredoomed to failure. He forgot the location of the Brenner Pass and thus delivered two hundred and fifty thousand German-Austrians to Italy. Toward the end of his life be became able to forget any fact which conflicted with the flow of his libido through outlets for activity and passivity to his father, and a considerable portion of the human race had to suffer for the overwhelming love which the Reverend Joseph Ruggles Wilson had inspired in his son.

At Princeton he found an additional outlet for his passivity to his father by forming an intense friendship with Professor John Grier Hibben. As usual he re-created through a narcissistic object-choice his own infantile relationship to his father. Hibben was the smaller, younger man who reappears so often in his life as an essential love-object. If possible, he saw Hibben every day and "he made no plans, came to no conclusions, without talking with 'Jack' Hibben." He loved Hibben deeply and, as Hibben was devoted to him, he found great joy in this friendship.

Professor Andrew F. West had been for seven years a prominent member of the Princeton faculty when Wilson went there to teach. West was the son of a Presbyterian Minister, and like Wilson's father was of Scotch blood from Ulster. When Wilson reached Princeton, West was the leader of a number of professors who were attempting to force President Francis L. Patton to raise the standards of scholarship in the undergraduate department and to establish a Graduate College. At first Wilson seems to have had a cordial respect for West, as he had at first a cordial respect for Henry Cabot Lodge. But West, an older, larger man of superior position, unquestionably entered Wilson's unconscious as a father representative, and there stood ready to be used as an outlet for Wilson's repressed hostility to his actual father.

Wilson's respect for West soon turned to dislike, and it is amusing to observe that the first critical note on West recorded by Wilson is a comment on West's Presbyterian bigotry, which was but another variety of the narrowness that distinguished both the Reverend Joseph Ruggles Wilson and his son, Tommy. In 1897 Wilson wrote in his diary: "*Morning,* interview with West, in which he showed the most stubborn prejudice about introducing a Unitarian into the Faculty."

When the Reverend Joseph Ruggles Wilson came to live in his son's home at Princeton, Woodrow Wilson was able to play the part of a tender wife to his father, and his passivity to his father must have found a sweet outlet; but his repressed hostility to his father must often have come close to bursting through its repression. It did not burst through and express itself against his father, nor did it, for the time, burst through against West as father representative. In order to achieve the presidency of Princeton, which had become Wilson's susbstitute for the apparently unattainable presidency of the United States, it was necessary for him to remain on cordial terms with West. His repressed hostility to his father remained repressed and produced a surprising "breakdown." In the autumn of 1895, while Wilson was writing his *George Washington,* his habitual symptoms suddenly became severe. He lay on his back with violent indigestion and great nervousness. He struggled through the winter nursing his aching head and sick stomach, complaining, "I am so tired of a merely talking profession. I want to *do* something." In the spring of 1896 he broke down completely. Neuritis, which deprived him of the use of his right hand, was added to his usual symptoms.

At the time of this "breakdown" Wilson apparently had every reason to be happy. He had a devoted wife and three charming little girls. His beloved father was often with him. He had a friend who was very dear to him. He was building a home in a pleasant town. His hunger for a class of men had been satisfied. He was exceedingly successful. His lectures not only at Princeton but also at Johns Hopkins were received with enthusiasm. His comparative happiness and health of the previous seven years suddenly turned to discontent and illness. Why? We shall probably be not far from the truth if we answer that the presence of his father in his home had excited his repressed aggressive activity against his father, and that this portion of his libido was without adequate outlet.

His recurrent complaint is significant. When Wilson complained that he wanted to *"do* something," he meant that he wanted to enter public life as an executive. We have seen, however, that in his unconscious, to become a statesman meant to identify himself with the "incomparable father" of his childhood who wore the face of Gladstone and thus by a "cannibalistic" identification to destroy the old man. We may, therefore, suspect that in his unconscious the "something" he wished to *"do"* was to annihilate the Reverend Joseph Ruggles Wilson. But his repression of this desire was so powerfully supported by his passivity to his father that he could not think a thought or perform an act of hostility toward his actual father, and he could not at that time become a statesman. Moreover, he was too intent on improving his position at Princeton to be able to loose this desire by acts of open hostility against West or any other father representative. His Narcissism and his Super-Ego always kept him from any action which might jeopardize his career. He, therefore, escaped from his conflict by flight into his habitual neurasthenic symptoms and after seven months of misery ran away to Scotland alone.

IX

IN THIS PSYCHOLOGICAL study of Wilson we have devoted little attention to the conscious portion of his mind, and we have no apology to offer for our concentration on his deeper mental mechanisms. The more important portion of the mind, like the more important portion of an iceberg, lies below the surface. The unconscious of a neurotic employs the conscious portion of the mind as a tool to achieve its wishes. The convictions of a neurotic are excuses invented by reason to justify desires of the libido. The principles of a neurotic are costumes employed to embellish and conceal the nakedness of the unconscious desires.

The civilization in which a child is educated nevertheless influences his character. It determines at least the style of the clothing in which his desires must be dressed in order to appear respectable. The child breathes in from the atmosphere of his home and his community ideas as to the gentleman-as-he-should-be, and these ideas become a part of his Ego-Ideal and determine the form of his convictions. This gentleman-as-he-should-be is not a stable character. His aspect changes continually in time and space. The God of one age becomes the devil of the next. The Christian devil wears the horns of Pan and his cloven hoof.

Although styles in civilization are unstable, like styles in women's clothing, the child does not know this and accepts the principles of his family and community as if they were immutable laws of nature and forms his idea of the gentleman-as-he-should-be in accordance with them. Thereby the style of the convictions in which he later dresses his desires is determined.

Thomas Woodrow Wilson, as a child, inhaled the ideas and ideals of the middle class Bible-reading Britishers who had spread an Old Testament view of life over America. Inevitably Wilson clothed the desires of his libido in the approved habiliments of the British non-conformist middle class.

In all his recorded words there is no sign that he understoood French, German or Italian civilization, to say nothing of the classic Greek. His convictions were British middle class convictions. To him the finest flowers of the human spirit were the products of Lollardry and Presbyterianism. His hostility to other views of life was profound. One American at least could have been understood and esteemed by the ancient Greeks: the free living, free-thinking, many-sided Thomas Jefferson, author of the Declaration of Independence, founder of the University of Virginia, architect, philosopher, President of the United States. Woodrow Wilson excluded Jefferson entirely from a *Calendar of Great Americans* which he drew up in 1894, on the ground that "Jefferson was not a thorough American because of the strain of French philosophy in his thought." He felt that a "thorough American" must have the ideas and ideals of the British middle class.

This somewhat excessive admiration for the British middle class sprang, of course, from his reverence for his own progenitors. They were all members of that class. His mother and the parents of his father were immigrants from the British Isles. By every unconscious identification he must have felt himself to be a middle class Britisher, and his abundant Narcissism made him admire these whose marriages had resulted in the procreation of himself. An early established admiration of this sort is often later corrected by an increased acquaintance with the world; but Woodrow Wilson was cut off from direct contact with European life by his ignorance of European languages. All his heroes were British: Burke, Bright, Bagehot, Gladstone. He found France, Italy and Germany so distasteful when he ventured onto the continent for the first time in 1903, that he fled home after a few unhappy weeks. He did not return to the continent until 1919, when he arrived to rear-range Europe. His conscious mind remained all his life the mind of a North British Presbyterian Minister.

Four times after "breakdowns" he attempted to overcome his habitual symptoms by visits to the British Isles. His experience in Ireland was confined to a few days of contempt; but Scotland he lov(d, the English universities moved him to ecstasy and the English Lake District became the home of his heart. He decided that he would spend his old age not in America but at Rydal in the English Lake District, which he described in terms that recall the feeling of a little boy for his mother: "You know how broad and gracious the slopes of dear Wansfell are, — like some great nour-ishing breast, it always seemed to me . . . Ulpha Fell . . . has infinitely wide and rich expanses of green slope, sweeping up from the wooded spaces of the valley, about the stream in curves of ex-quisite beauty."

In 1896 he remained in Scotland and England until his symp-toms had subsided, then returned to Princeton with a new deter-mination to advance to executive life which impressed those who were closest to him. His brother-in-law Stockton Axson wrote: "He had always been a purposeful man, but now he was a man of fixed and resolute purpose . . . He grew more and more impa-tient of merely theoretical discussions; he must handle facts in all their difficult reality."

To break down, to rest until he had subdued his symptoms, then to return to work with a ruthless determination to assert his mascu-linity became a formula for his life. Thenceforth each of his breakdowns was followed by an exhibition of increased aggression. The cause of this phenomenon is clear. His unsatisfied hostility to his father drove him to escape by his habitual symptoms. His ag-gressive activity was still unsatisfied. He returned to work deter-mined to satisfy it through the long-established outlet of identifica-tion with Gladstone.

An opportunity to advance toward executive leadership came

quickly. He was asked to deliver an address on the occasion of the Princeton Sesqui-Centennial Celebration on October 21, 1896. He chose as his subject, "Princeton in the Nation's Service," remarking in the course of his speech: "There is laid upon us the compulsion of the national life . . . There is nothing that gives such pitch to public service as religion . . . I have had sight of the perfect place of learning in my thought . . . every eye within it bright in the clear day and quick to look toward heaven for the confirmation of its hope. Who shall show us the way to this place?"

He asked the final question of this address with the obvious hope that his auditors would answer, silently at least, Woodrow Wilson. Many of his hearers were thoroughly dissatisfied with the Reverend Francis L. Patton, President of the university. No one in the audience was more dissatisfied than was Woodrow Wilson. He despised Patton; but he was careful to conceal his contempt from Patton himself and from Patton's friends. He wanted to become President of Princeton. Therefore he kept a foot in the camp of Patton, and a foot in the camp of West, concealing his antagonism to both men and angling deftly for the support of both.

The address was received with enthusiasm, but it did not lead to any immediate alteration of Wilson's position in the world and he settled down to six years of chronic discontent, headaches and indigestion. His father was living in his house and the increase in his aggression in this period may almost certainly be attributed to this exciting presence. His increased aggressive activity, having no adequate outlet, drove him to his habitual symptoms, and his discontent was doubtless sharpened by the unsatisfied demands of his Super-Ego. To achieve executive leadership either through political life or through Princeton seemed impossible. He began to see dark forces blocking his way. He spoke of "sinister influences at present dominant in the administration of the college." He suggested that he might leave Princeton. Eight rich men who esteemed him, among them Mr. Moses Taylor Pyne, made a contract with him, agreeing to pay him extra thousands a year in return for his promise not to leave Princeton for a period of five years beginning with the college year 1898–1899.

In the spring of 1899 he broke down once more, and again sought rest in the British Isles. He subdued his symptoms and returned to Princeton and his habitual discontent. By 1900 he so despaired of his future both at Princeton and in politics that he considered seriously the idea of devoting the rest of his life to literary work and, ignoring his contract, asked the Princeton trustees to give him a year of leave to prepare material for a monumental tome on *The Philosophy of Politics,* the writing of which would have involved the abandonment of his academic work. His feeling for West had by this time turned into hostility, and when West was elected Dean of the Graduate School in 1901, Wilson began to employ him as a father representative upon whom the flood of his hostility to his actual father could be loosed.

West had placed himself in frank opposition to President Patton. Wilson was perhaps more bitter in his hostility to Patton than any other member of the Princeton faculty; but Patton did not know it and when Professor Magie and Dean West had made Patton's position impossible, it was the despised Patton himself who nominated Wilson to succeed him as President of Princeton. The election of West would have split the university world into hostile groups. West knew that Wilson was, in fact, hostile to the Patton system, and was unaware of Wilson's personal hostility to him. He, therefore, abandoned his own aspirations and did not oppose Wilson's election. On June 9, 1902, at the age of forty-five, Wilson was elected President of Princeton. He was in ecstasy. "I feel like a new prime minister getting ready to address his constituents," he wrote to his wife. He was Gladstone at last! At last the flow of his libido through the conduit of activity toward his father could find outlet by way of the identification he had established twenty-five years before.

Often during the years of his Princeton presidency Wilson repeated the thought contained in his statement that he felt "like a new prime minister." He remarked, for instance, to the members of an association of Princeton clubs, "I always feel, upon an occasion like this, that I am a responsible minister reporting to his constituents." And he was in the habit of calling education "minor statesmanship." When he was elected President of Princeton he became, in his unconscious, Gladstone.

The opening of this long-desired outlet for his aggressive activity toward his father, plus the satisfaction his election to the presidency of Princeton gave to his Super-Ego and to his Narcissism, relieved his discontent at once. He wrote to his wife: "I find . . . that my election to the presidency has done a very helpful thing for me. It has settled the future for me and given me a sense of *position* and of definite, tangible tasks which takes the *flutter* and restlessness from my spirits." the word "flutter" is so feminine in its connotations that one should hesitate to employ it to describe a man; but since Wilson used it to describe himself and underlined it, we may note that it was admirably descriptive. He spent most of his life in a flutter.

X

THREE MONTHS after Wilson's inauguration as President of Princeton his father died. His entire life had been dominated by his relationship to his father. The loss of his father, therefore, necessitated a considerable rearrangement of the outlets for his libido.

In the customary manner, he replaced his lost father by himself and thenceforth in his unconscious he was more than ever the Reverend Joseph Ruggles Wilson. Thus he found a new outlet for his aggressive activity to his father to add to the freshly opened outlet of identification with Gladstone. For the remainder of his life his primary activity toward his father seems to have possessed adequate outlets; but his father's death deprived him of the chief outlets for his passivity. He could no longer find outlet for this hypertrophied charge of libido by submitting to his father, or by playing wife to his father. These were its major outlets. He did not find outlet for it by submission to a father representative. But after his father's death his addiction to speech-making, which was already excessive, grew to fantastic proportions; his desire for a friend to love became an imperative need; and his interest in all forms of religious activity increased. It is obvious that the loss of the major outlets for his passivity to his father had put severe pressure on its minor outlets and increased the evacuation of libido through speech-making, passionate friendship, submission to God and identification with Christ.

Moreover, after the loss of his father, he began to display increased inclination imperiously to rearrange the world and to hate with unreasonable intensity distinguished men who disagreed with him. The charge of libido lodged in his passivity to his father was evidently too great for the outlets which remained in existence to carry its full flow. After his father's death Wilson had to repress a large portion of it. As we pointed out, the Ego invariably employs a reaction-formation to assist in the repression of a strong desire. The amount of Wilson's passivity to his father which had to be repressed after his father's death was great and it required a large reaction-formation to assist in its repression. That reaction-formation found outlet through his attempts to rearrange the world and through hostile actions against father representatives.

The original source of all these character traits was, of course, little Tommy Wilson's passivity to his "incomparable father." The Reverend Joseph Ruggles Wilson, who incidentally is not to be recommended as a model for fathers, had made his son love him so deeply and submissively that the flood of passivity he had aroused could be satisfied by no other man or activity. To find outlet for it was not easy for a man whose Super-Ego demanded that he should be all masculinity: God Himself. The Professor Extraordinary of Rhetoric, dead, continued to overwhelm his son.

Wilson, installed as President of Princeton, began at once to dominate the life of the university. He dismissed various professors, increased the severity of examinations, sharpened discipline, resisted an agitation for the abolition of compulsory daily attendance at chapel and reorganized the entire course of study. In those activities he had the support of a great majority of the faculty, graduates and students. His most valued collaborator was Professor John Grier Hibben, the smaller, younger man, whom, in the words of Mrs. Wilson, he had "taken to his bosom." After the death of his father his love for Hibben became even more intense than it had been before. It is clear that by identifying Hibben with himself as a child he was contriving to receive from himself the love he wanted and could no longer get from his father.

In spite of the free flow of his activity through his executive actions and the satisfaction his friendship with Hibben gave him, his habitual symptoms began to reappear, and at the close of the college year in the summer of 1903 he sought rest in Europe. His comprehensive dislike of France, Germany and Italy prevented him from obtaining rest on the continent, and he returned to America still somewhat harassed by nervousness, indigestion and headaches. These symptoms continued to trouble him throughout the following year, and in January 1905 he broke down completely. In addition to his habitual symptoms a hernia was bothering him. In February 1905 an operation was performed on his hernia and he spent five weeks in Florida resting.

He returned from Florida determined to push through immediately a project for the reformation of Princeton by the hiring of fifty preceptors. The spirit he displayed on this occasion was very much like the spirit he had displayed after his 1896 breakdown, when he returned from England determined to break through to executive life. He threw an immense flood of energy into his campaign for the preceptorial system, pushing the project with such vigor that, in spite of its cost, he was able to obtain the formal assent of the Board of Trustees in June 1905 and to establish the system in the autumn of the same year. That he should have been able to find such energy in his frail body indicates the dimension of the portion of his libido which had begun to flow into his reaction-formation against his passivity to his father. His campaign for the preceptorial system afforded it outlet. From the first, the preceptorial system was a success and its establishment was a personal triumph for Wilson. He became acutely unhappy.

Wilson's state of mind during the winter of 1906–1907 was admirably described by his chosen biographer, Mr. Ray Stannard Baker: "The new preceptorial system was working with unexpected smoothness and success. Merwick had been opened as a graduate college, money was coming in for new buildings, But he was suddenly impatient with it all. The university was not after all doing all that it should: it was not 'sufficiently inspired,' nor moving fast enough, nor useful enough. To outward view, progress had been astonishing, the success extraordinary, but it did not satisfy the insatiable spirit of the new president. Whenever Wilson began to doubt, began to question whether or not he was doing all that he could or should in the pursuit of the vision which, if it inspired him, also scourged him, he worked harder than ever. He began now to make public addresses outside of college and alumni audiences, and to deal directly, and, it is hardly too much to say, passionately, with the problems of the day . . . As in all the previous crises of his life, it also seemed to have a religious side. We find him speaking again and again that winter and spring on religious subjects or to religious gatherings. Many of his other addresses breathe a religious aspiration." Among these addresses was one in which Wilson asked and answered the question: "What would Christ have done in our day, in our place with our opportunities?"

On February 3, 1906, Colonel George Harvey, a Democrat, at a dinner in New York proposed that Wilson should be nominated as Democratic candidate for President of the United States. Wilson pretended not to take this proposal seriously; but in view of his intense desire to become a statesman it is obvious that Harvey's words must have moved him deeply. Real statesmanship offered a far better outlet for his identification with Gladstone than the "minor statesmanship" of his educational activities. Moreover no "minor statesmanship" could satisfy his Super-Ego. It demanded major statesmanship *in excelsis:* the presidency of the United States, the presidency of the World and the presidency of Heaven. The true impression that Harvey's words made on Wilson may perhaps be judged by the fact that they moved him to transform his intense dislike of Jefferson into admiration. Jefferson was the deity of the Democrats, and the Democratic nomination for President of the United States could not be obtained without lip service to the author of the Declaration of Independence. Shortly after Harvey's speech, Wilson contrived to discover admirable qualities in the statesman in whom previously he had seen only faults. He found the going somewhat difficult, however, and "made no fewer than four versions" of an address on Jefferson which he delivered on April 16, 1906, to an audience of Democrats.

Throughout that winter of speech-making Wilson had been intensely nervous and had suffered not only from his habitual headaches and indigestion but also from pains in his left shoulder and leg and right hand which were attributed to "neuritis." His symptoms gradually grew more severe. He was on the verge of a typical "breakdown" when, one morning in May 1906, he awoke to find that his left eye was blind. The sequence of events from his triumphant establishment of the preceptorial system in October to his collapse in May presents an unmistakable picture of a neurotic succumbing to a conflict in his unconscious. Let us attempt to determine the exact nature of this conflict.

The fact that his triumph of the autumn was followed not by the satisfaction and content which a normal man would have felt but by intense discontent is the first symptom we must consider. Accomplishment followed by unhappiness was no new thing in Wilson's life. Even in the months after his marriage and his first professional successes at Bryn Mawr, when almost any other man would have been joyful, he was acutely unhappy. And the reader may recall that a week after the acceptance of *Congressional Government* had moved him to ecstasy he was "down with the 'blues,' " and that we attributed his unhappiness then to the excessive demands of his Super-Ego, which required of him such God-like achievements that no actual accomplishment could satisfy it.

We have noted that his determination immediately to establish the preceptorial system at Princeton sprang for his reaction-formation against his passivity to his father; that the energy he threw into this task was enormous and that the magnitude of his energy indicated the quantity of libido which had begun to charge this reaction-formation. The task was accomplished. His repressed passivity to his father again demanded outlet. His reaction-formation again was stimulated to feverish productivity. He had no new immediate task upon which to loose a flood of masculine activity. The establishment of the preceptorial system thus neither satisfied the insatiable demands of his Super-Ego nor, when the struggle was ended, did it longer afford outlet for his reaction-formation against his passivity to his father. His passivity demanded outlet, the reaction-formation against it demanded outlet, his Super-Ego demanded that he should become God. His Ego became a battlefield: on one side stood his repressed passivity to his father demanding that he should be all femininity; on the other side stood his activity toward his father, his reaction-formation against his passivity, and his Super-Ego, demanding that he should be all action and masculinity. Thus we find that the conflict which produced his unhappiness, illness and feverish speech-making in the winter of 1905–1906 was the same old conflict which his Ego had never been able to solve: the conflict between his activity and passivity to his father. He was still caught on the horns of the major dilemma of the Oedipus complex. And his unhappiness was increased by the inordinate demands of his Super-Ego.

At no time in his life was his interest in making speeches so excessive as during these months of 1905 and 1906. We have seen that Wilson found in speech-making an outlet for both his activity and passivity to his father: when he spoke he both obeyed his father and identified himself with his father. Thus by speech-making he was able to drain libido from both the desires whose conflict in his Ego was becoming unendurable. The mere delivery of an address drained energy from both antagonists. The subjects he chose for his speeches gave additional outlet first to one stream of libido then to the other. He made many addresses on political subjects which offered additional outlet to his reaction-formation against passivity. On the other hand he made many religious addresses like the speech in which he told his audience what Christ would "have done in our day, in our place with our opportunities." In that address he spoke for Christ; in his unconscious he was Christ: the flow of his passivity through his identification with

Christ swept unimpeded into the ears of his auditors. The conflict in his Ego had in fact become so unendurable that he was compelled either to speak or to take refuge in one of his habitual "breakdowns." Therefore he spoke constantly, passionately, feverishly. In the words of his biographer, Mr. Baker: "He seemed possessed! He devoted to a single address a passion of intensity that would have served half a dozen ordinary speeches." He was possessed by one of the chief devils that tortures man: a conflict between activity and passivity to the father.

His speech-making saved him from one of his ordinary "breakdowns" but drove him into a more serious illness. The hemorrhage of one of the blood vessels of his left eye which ended his feverish activity was found to have been caused by arteriosclerosis. The overwork necessitated by his frantic speech-making must have contributed considerably to his high blood pressure. Thus, although it would be untrue to say that his hemorrhage was caused by the conflict in his Ego, we must note that his neurosis, through the overwork it produced, was a contributing cause. At the same time we should not forget that the physical condition of his arteries undoubtedly intensified the psychic symptoms he displayed before his hemorrhage. Moreover, a subtler question, to which we can give no answer, is raised by this hemorrhage. We have learned that psychic conditions may cause most intense physical effects. For example, to die of a "broken heart" is not a mere poet's fantasy. It is possible for a man to die from rupture of the heart produced by purely psychic causes. A hundred years hence, when the effect of the mind on the body will be, we may hope, better understood than it is today, some scientist doubtless will be able to determine whether or not there was a more direct connection between Wilson's psychic conflict and his hemorrhage than the connection through overwork. In our present ignorance we can only offer a question.

Wilson, his left eye blind, had Hibben, "the friend he had taken to his bosom," appointed acting President of Princeton and went to Rydal, in England, to rest. There he met Fred Yates, the portrait painter. In the absence of Hibben, Wilson's reaction was immediate. "The two men seem to have fallen in love on the spot," wrote Mr. Ray Stannard Baker. So great a quantity of Wilson's passivity to his father had begun to flow through the outlet of passionate friendship that he had to have a substitute for Hibben to love. His symptoms rapidly diminished in intensity and he began to recover the sight of his eye. At the end of the summer he felt well enough to go back to Princeton.

Wilson returned to Princeton in the autumn of 1906 with a determination to assert his executive leadership that recalls the determination with which he returned after his breakdowns in 1896 and 1905. It rose indeed from the same unconscious sources — his activity and his reaction-formation against his passivity to his father had vastly increased. Just as in 1905 he returned determined to establish the preceptorial system, so in 1906 he returned determined to reorganize the entire life of the university by dividing the student body into "Quads" modeled on the colleges of Oxford and Cambridge.

Theoretically there was much to be said in favor of this proposal and much to be said against it. Practically it necessitated abandonment of the familiar American division of the student body into four classes with distinctive privileges and "class spirit," abolition of the clubs which had become a cherished feature of Princeton life, and because of its expense, indefinite postponement of the construction of a Graduate College in accordance with the plans which West had prepared and Wilson had approved. It was, therefore, certain to arouse formidable opposition. But, to Wilson, the fact that the proposal involved not a mere reform like his preceptorial system but a revolution in the life of the university doubtless made it doubly dear. His reaction-formation against his passivity to his father had been so intensified during the previous year that it demanded outlet through an action in which Wilson might show himself as an excessively strong man able to override all opposition, even reasonable opposition.

Before he had time to propose the establishment of the "Quad" system, he had to deal with another matter which also directly involved his reaction-formation against his passivity to his father. Dean West was invited to become President of the Massachusetts Institute of Technology. Wilson by that time thoroughly disliked West. Nevertheless he wrote personally a resolution which was adopted by the Board of Trustees in which he urged West to remain at Princeton saying that his loss would be "quite irreparable," and assuring West "that he cannot be spared and that the Board trusts, should he remain, its hopes and his may be the sooner realized because of this additional proof of his devotion." West, taking the final sentence of this resolution as a pledge that the next objective in the campaign for the development of Princeton would be the collection of funds for the construction of the Graduate College, refused the presidency of the Massachusetts Institute of Technology.

Nine weeks after Wilson had written this resolution, he proposed his "Quad" system, which he knew would be so expensive that its adoption would postpone indefinitely the construction of the projected Graduate College, since funds for both projects would have to come from the same friends of Princeton. Why Wilson, believing that he was about to make the execution of West's plans impossible, nevertheless urged West to remain at Princeton, presents a problem which at first sight appears somewhat puzzling. The answer becomes obvious when one recalls that Wilson at that moment was fully in the grip of a neurosis and that his reaction-formation against his passivity to his father was demanding expression so imperatively that he could not allow to slip out of his grasp any outlet for it. West offered a magnificent outlet. He was a conspicuous father representative and could be used to receive the charge of Wilson's unconscious hatred of his father. In his unconscious, to defeat West meant to conquer his father. The bonds which hatred establishes are no less binding than the bonds of love. Aggressive activity toward the father is as fundamental as any other desire. Hatred like love must find outlet. Wilson was bound to West by unbreakable bonds of hatred; bonds which in fact became so strong that they bound him until death loosed him from all bonds. He could not let West get away from him. He needed West to hate, defeat and humble. He was absolutely sure that he could defeat West. Therefore, he concealed his hatred of West, persuaded him to remain at Princeton, then launched the thunderbolt of his "Quad" proposal.

A few days later West met Wilson and expressed vigorously his opinion of Wilson's action in sidetracking the Graduate College. Wilson took deep offense and an open quarrel was barely avoided. From then on, the relations of the two men were strictly official. Thenceforth, Wilson hated West with an intense neurotic hatred. To push through his "Quad" system by any means available, and to prevent West from establishing the Graduate College of his dreams, became the major aim of Wilson's life. Whatever the cost to Princeton, he had to defeat the big dark man who in his unconscious represented his father. His actions during the remainder of his term as President of Princeton were dictated by this compulsion which drew strength both from his aggressive activity towards his father and from his reaction-formation against his passivity. The compulsion was enormously powerful and it drove Wilson to many strange words and actions. Indeed the manner in which the unconscious employs the conscious portion of the mind as a tool to carry out the wishes of the libido, using reason to find excuses to justify actions desired by the unconscious, has rarely been illustrated more vividly than by the arguments Wilson used during the years from 1906 to 1910. Facts ceased to exist for him if they conflicted with his unconscious desires.

XI

WILSON WAS at the height of his popularity at Princeton when he made his "Quad" proposal; and the mere circumstance that it was his proposal was sufficient to obtain for it considerable support in the university. Yet West was not alone in his opposition. The Board of Trustees did not, therefore, immediately adopt Wilson's proposal but appointed a committee of which Wilson was chairman to consider it; Wilson realized that he would have to fight; but he felt absolutely confident of his ability to win. His symptoms, however, began to return and he went to Bermuda to rest. On two Sundays there he rested by preaching from the pulpits of local churches, thus as usual draining libido from his conflicting activity and passivity by his old outlet of oratory. He returned to Princeton "infinitely refreshed." On June 10, 1907, he presented the report of his committee recommending that he should "be authorized to take such steps as may seem wisest for maturing this general plan." He had originally written "maturing and executing" and had struck out the latter words because a Trustee insisted that the Board should be given the "privilege of further consideration."

At once civil war broke out in Princeton, and Wilson was horrified to find that Hibben, "the friend he had taken to his bosom," opposed him. We have seen how great a flow of his passivity to his father was finding outlet through this friendship by which he had re-created his childhood relationship to his father, and we shall not therefore be surprised to find that Hibben's opposition made him acutely nervous and unhappy. Little Tommy Wilson had never dared to oppose his own "incomparable father," and when any friend opposed him, even in a matter of opinion, the friend ceased to represent Tommy Wilson.

Wilson did his best to persuade Hibben to remain Tommy Wilson; but Hibben possessed that unendurable thing, a will of his own. In spite of Wilson's arguments he continued to oppose the "Quad" project. On September 26, 1907, at a faculty meeting Hibben rose and seconded van Dyke's motion opposing the adoption of Wilson's proposal. Wilson, who was presiding, turned pale. "Do I understand that Professor Hibben seconds the motion?" Wilson asked in steady tones but as one who could scarcely believe what he heard and saw. "I do, Mr. President," replied Hibben. These words shattered Wilson's relationship to Hibben. No longer did he represent little Tommy Wilson. No longer could Wilson by identifying himself with Hibben receive from himself the love he longed to receive from his own father. And to protect himself from the dammed flood of his passivity, Wilson at once converted Hibben into a betrayer: a man to be hated.

The conversion of Hibben into a Judas was doubtless made easy for Wilson by his unconscious identification of himself with Christ. We have seen that the flow of Wilson's passivity to his father through the outlet of identification with Christ had been greatly increased by the death of the Reverend Joseph Ruggles Wilson. In the portion of Wilson's unconscious in which he was Christ his younger friends were certainly his disciples. John Grier Hibben was doubtless John, the Beloved Disciple. But when he joined the enemies of Wilson at the crucial moment in his master's career it was easy for Wilson to convert him into Judas Iscariot. Thus, by employing the mechanism used by paranoiacs, Wilson, who was not a psychotic, protected himself from his unsatisfied passivity.

Hibben did everything possible to preserve the friendship, and Wilson for a time continued to speak to Hibben. Then he stopped speaking altogether. When Hibben was elected President of Princeton, Wilson sent no word of congratulation, and he refused to attend Hibben's inauguration. Hibben later attempted to bring about a reconciliation. Wilson refused. When he was President of the United States, Wilson went to Princeton to vote. Hibben went to the polling booth to pay his respects. Wilson looked at him, turned on his heel and walked away.

The transformation of Hibben from an object of love into an object of hatred because of a difference of opinion illustrates vividly the neurotic nature of Wilson's intense friendships. He had never escaped from his childhood feelings with regard to his father. He was compelled to love passionately men whom he had identified with little Tommy Wilson, and to hate them passionately when in one way or another they ceased to be submissive to him and thus ceased to represent himself looking up to his "incomparable father." He could never permit any friend to meet him on terms of mental and moral equality. Hibben was but the first of several passionately loved friends whom he discarded when they ventured to disagree with him.

Wilson was so stricken by the loss of Hibben that he vowed that he would never have another intimate friend. But he could not do without a man to love. In 1910 he became very fond of a blond young man named Dudley Field Malone, whom he called his "fidus Achates." In 1911 he fell in love with Edward M. House. These friendships and others went the way of his friendship with Hibben. Malone, in 1917, favored woman suffrage, which Wilson opposed. He never again spoke to Malone. All the factors which made and unmade these and other friendships are to be seen in his love and hatred of Hibben. His passionate friendships were all, at bottom, re-creations of his childhood relationship to his father.

On October 18, 1907, the Princeton Trustees met to decide whether to adopt the "Quad" project or to reject it. Wilson, acutely nervous because of the loss of Hibben, surprised them by the disconcerting claim that "the essential idea and purpose of the plan" had already been adopted by them through their approval of his resolution ordering the "maturing" of it. This assertion of

Wilson's seems to mark the beginning of the mental degeneration which led him to sign the Treaty of Versailles and then to call it an "incomparable consummation of the hopes of mankind," "the first treaty ever made by great powers that was not made in their own favor," "a ninety-nine percent insurance against war." He had apparently managed to forget that he had been compelled to strike out of his resolution the words "and executing" because one of the Trustees had insisted that they should be given the "privilege of further consideration."

To point out the source of this distortion of fact seems necessary, not because the incident was in itself important, but because distortion of fact thereafter became a pronounced trait of Wilson's character. Thousands of distorted, ignored or forgotten facts mark the remainder of his life. To discuss them all would require a large volume and we do not wish to encumber this psychological study with detailed examination of his many mental errors. It seems necessary, however, to discuss one typical distortion. The reader may then perhaps discover for himself the sources of later distortions.

We have seen that from childhood onward Wilson was inclined to live in a world of phrases, not facts. It was, therefore, easy for him to distort, ignore, forget or invent facts if the truth conflicted with his desires. The distortion of fact involved in his claim that the Princeton Trustees had already adopted "the essential idea and purpose" of his "Quad" proposal was produced by most violent desires. A large portion of his passivity to his father had been finding outlet through his love for Hibben. He had lost that outlet. Even before the loss of Hibben the reaction-formation necessary to repress his passivity was enormous. The increase in his repressed passivity produced by the loss of Hibben required a further expansion of his reaction-formation to repress it. It is not remarkable that this reaction-formation became expanded beyond normal limits or that a fact which stood in the way of the immense charge of libido in this accumulator should have been swept away. If the

Trustees had indeed adopted the "essential idea and purpose" of the "Quad" system, the plan was already a part of Princeton's official program, the outlets for Wilson's reaction-formation were already established. He wanted them to be established, therefore he declared that they were established. He distorted a fact. He argued before the Trustees that the "Quad" system could be rejected only by a resolution rescinding the alleged adoption of the previous June. His intellect at that moment was the tool of his unconscious desires and nothing else. The Trustees, however, had not forgotten that the words " and executing" had been stricken from Wilson's resolution. They knew well that they had never adopted the "Quad" system. They refused to be stampeded. They voted, and every vote but one was cast against Wilson's proposal.

Wilson was aghast. The turmoil in his mind may be imagined. He had kept West at Princeton to conquer. Defeat cost him the outlets for his reaction-formation against his passivity to his father. Furthermore, to his Super-Ego defeat was intolerable. Moreover, he had lost Hibben and thus the chief outlet for his passivity to his father. The conflict in his Ego between these floods of unsatisfied libido at once became unbearable.

The conscious portion of his mind faced problems almost as difficult to solve as the problems of his unconscious. He did not know what to do. He had talked so vehemently against the conditions of life at Princeton that to remain President of the university while those conditions remained unaltered seemed inconsistent with self-respect. He knew that he could no longer hope to establish his "Quad" system and that his popularity had vanished because of his attacks on the college.

He wrote a letter of resignation; but he did not send it. He had no other job to which to go and he had to earn his living. He was desperate. He hated the practice of the law; but he talked seriously of returning to legal practice in Virginia. He intensely needed his father to tell him what to do, and he seems for a moment to have turned to the Reverend Melanchthon W. Jacobus for advice as he would have turned to his father if the Reverend Joseph Ruggles Wilson had been alive. "I trust that a kind Providence will presently send me some sign of guidance which I shall have sight enough to perceive and to interpret," he wrote on October 23, 1908, to Dr. Jacobus. But he never reached terms of frank intimacy with Jacobus and on November 6 wrote again to Jacobus: "I have never for a moment thought of giving the fight up," forgetting his unsent letter of resignation.

In the fortnight of hectic uncertainty which separated his letters to Jacobus he discovered solutions for both his conscious and unconscious problems. The solution which his Ego contrived for his unconscious conflict was important. He never grew past the pattern in which his character then became fixed and it seems worth while to examine this fixation in detail.

We have seen that submission to God and unconscious identification with Christ were the only two large conduits for his passivity to his father through which his libido was still able to run freely. After the loss of Hibben an increase in the flow of libido through those conduits was inevitable for purely economic reasons: that charge of libido had no place else to go. The outlet of his identification with Christ was further enlarged by his turning Hibben into Judas Iscariot. For the remainder of his life his unconscious identification with Christ carried a large portion of his libido.

The great alteration in his character made at this time by his Ego was, however, on the side of his reaction-formation against his passivity to his father. He had never employed one obvious conduit for the forces of masculinity. In his unconscious, he had identified his father with God, but he had not identified himself with God. Under the pressure of his defeat he became in his unconscious God the Father as well as God the Son. The extraordinary confidence in his own righteousness, the ability ruthlessly to push on to power, which began to mark his life leave no doubt as to what had happened in his unconscious. He could not become superior to West in life. He had to become superior to him. Therefore, he became superior to West in his unconscious. He became God. Thereafter, one portion of his unconscious never failed to tell him: "You are God. You are superior to all men. Whatever you do is right because you do it." For the remainder of his life a large portion of his activity toward his father and his reaction-formation against his passivity found outlet through this identification with God. The reader may perhaps find it difficult to believe that a man may simultaneously identify himself with both God the Father and God the Son. To the unconscious, such paradoxes present no difficulty.

Thenceforth, there was a somewhat unusual amount of deity in the character of Woodrow Wilson. His Super-Ego demanded that he should accomplish God-like achievements, his passivity to his father found outlet through submission to God and through identification with Christ, his activity and his reaction-formation against his passivity through identification with God. It is not remarkable that he began to be superior to such a human limitation as respect for fact. His head was in the heavens, and his feet were clambering up the thin ridge to greatness which lies between neurosis and psychosis.

The decision he reached with regard to his mundane difficulties bears the stigmata of his inner deities. Five years before, to a lady who had pleaded that she would die if her son were expelled from Princeton, he had replied grandiloquently but apparently sincerely: "If I had to choose between your life or my life or anybody's life and the good of this college, I should choose the good of the college." But to the Woodrow Wilson who, in his unconscious, was God, Princeton became not an end in itself but a means to an end. He decided to remain at Princeton, to retain his livelihood, to prevent West from establishing the Graduate College of his dreams and to carry on his fight for the "Quad" system in such a way that whether he should win, which was highly improbable, or lose, which was almost inevitable, he would in any case make Woodrow Wilson Democratic candidate for President of the

United States. He would overcome his defeat in the field of "minor statesmanship" by victory in the field of major statesmanship. He would do whatever was necessary at Princeton and say whatever was necessary about Princeton to make himself President. The sign of guidance for which he had prayed had come to him from Colonel George Harvey.

Colonel Harvey had been quietly gathering conservative Democratic support for Wilson ever since he had personally nominated Wilson on February 3, 1906, and Wilson had done or said nothing to alienate conservative Democrats. All his political utterances had been conservative. But a wave of protest against the control of the United States by New York plutocrats was sweeping the country. Wilson's political problem was to obtain the support of the radical Democrats, whose strength was growing, without losing the conservative support which Harvey had obtained for him. The "Quad" controversy gave him an opportunity to kill several birds with one stone.

He started on a speaking tour in November, ostensibly for the purpose of making an appeal to the "Princeton Constituency," for support of his "Quad" proposal. He did, to be sure, attack his opponents at Princeton vigorously; but his speeches were interlarded with utterances designed to promote his political prospects. He presented the question of establishing imitation English colleges at Princeton as if it were a struggle between democratic poor Americans whom he represented and plutocratic snobs, thus endearing himself to the radicals. Yet at the same time he was careful to pour oil into the ears of New York Conservatives by specific political utterances like his statement of November 19, 1907: "I charge the present financial panic to the aggressive attitude of legislation toward the railroads." Thus by his speeches he not only found outlet for his hatred of West by making him and his allies appear the advocates of plutocratic snobbery but also dramatized himself as the champion of the democratic poor while pleasing the plutocrats. The adroitness which he displayed in promoting his career at this time and later was remarkable. We cannot say that it was surprising. His abundant Narcissism had always made him acutely sensitive to anything which might affect his career. Even before he became God in his unconscious, he showed ability in advancing the fortunes of Woodrow Wilson. The welfare of Princeton, which he depicted as a home of plutocratic snobbery, was not promoted.

In January 1908 Wilson again broke down. His wife ascribed this breakdown to the "loss of the friend he took to his bosom." She was probably right. He had found no adequate substitute for Hibben; and it was doubtless his unsatisfied passivity to his father which drove him to breakdown. He went to Bermuda, tortured by nervousness, neuritis, sick headache and sour stomach. Late in February he returned to America and again dashed about making speeches. His ill health continued; and in June 1908 he again collapsed.

The neurotic who sailed for Scotland on June 20, 1908, to nurse his nerves, sick stomach, aching head and twinging legs and arms crossed the Atlantic ten years later hailed as new Saviour of the World. Throughout human history so many neurotics have risen suddenly to power that Wilson's achievement is far from unique but is extraordinary. Life often demands the qualities which a neurotic possesses in greater measure than normal men. Thus from the point of view of "success in life," psychic disturbance may actually be an advantage. Moreover, Wilson's neurotic character was well suited to the demands of his time. First America, then the world, needed a prophet who could speak as if he were God's mouthpiece on earth. And we should not forget that Wilson had the qualities of his defects: if his passivity to his father was excessive, his activity, developed by his reaction-formation against it, had become even stronger and enabled him to act with harsh masculinity; if his unconscious conviction that he was God raised him above reality, it also produced a powerful self-confidence; if his Narcissism made him unattractive as a human being, it caused a concentration on himself which made him able to preserve his slight supply of physical strength and use all that he had for his own advancement; if his enormous interest in speech-making was somewhat ridiculous, it created an ability to sway crowds by his spoken word; if his Super-Ego tortured him by demanding impossible achievements, it drove him to considerable accomplishments. Yet a neurosis is an unstable foundation upon which to build a life. Although history is studded with the names of neurotics, monomaniacs and psychotics who have risen suddenly to power, they have usually dropped as suddenly to disgrace. Wilson was no exception to this rule. The qualities of his defects raised him to power; but the defects of his qualities made him, in the end, not one of the world's greatest men but a great fiasco.

XII

IN THE REMAINDER of this study of Wilson we shall merely call attention to some of the more obvious consequences of his qualities and defects, the sources of which we believe we now understand. We shall not point out any new identifications, sublimations or repressions because our examination of the rest of his life reveals none. There were, of course, new friends, new enemies, new activities and a new wife. But these were, so to speak, merely new taps attached to old pipes, new bottles for old wine. Wilson was fifty-one years old; an ugly, unhealthy, "intense" Presbyterian, who had little interest in women and none in food, wine, music, art or sport, but enormous interest in speaking, in himself, in his career and in God. The man that Wilson was in 1908, he remained.

Wilson, seeking mental and physical health, bicycled through southern Scotland to the English Lake Country. At Rydal, with Wansfell "like some great nourishing breast" before him and Yates, his best substitute for Hibben, beside him, he soon became "conscious of growing every day more normal both in nerve and muscle, and consequently in mind also." By the middle of August he felt well enough to visit Andrew Carnegie at Skibo Castle in Scotland. He hoped to obtain from Carnegie the millions necessary to establish the "Quad" system at Princeton, and thus to place West and the Trustees in the position of having to adopt the "Quad" system or reject a great gift. But he got no funds from Carnegie and he disliked his reception at the castle. He felt that he was not treated with sufficient respect.

Grover Cleveland, twenty-second President of the United States, the most distinguished of the Trustees of Princeton, died while Wilson was on his way to Scotland. Wilson had admired Cleveland almost to the point of adulation until Cleveland supported West. On hearing of Cleveland's death Wilson wrote: "I do not think that my knowledge of how he failed and disappointed us during the past few years . . . will long obscure my admiration for his great qualities and his singularly fine career." The memory of Cleveland's opposition did, however, "obscure his admiration" for the rest of his life. In the address which Wilson delivered on his return to the university in the autumn he did not refer to Cleveland's death, and, contrary to Princeton custom, he ordered no memorial service for Cleveland. His hatred for West was large enough to embrace all the allies of his favorite enemy.

Cleveland's death deprived West of his strongest supporter on the Board of Trustees, and in February 1909 Wilson dared a direct blow at his cherished father representative. He persuaded the Trustees to transfer control of the Graduate School from the Dean to a faculty committee in the naming of which the Dean was to have no voice although he was to be chairman of the committee. West protested that this action was unjust to him. Wilson replied: "I wish to say to the Dean, somewhat grimly, that he must be digested in the processes of the University." West then referred to the pledges made to him in 1906. Wilson answered: "We must not lay too great stress on commitments." God the Father was in action.

West countered by the precise maneuver which Wilson had attempted. The donation which Wilson had failed to get from Carnegie for his project, West obtained from William Cooper Procter for his project. On May 10, 1909, West handed Wilson a letter from Procter offering half a million dollars for the construction of a Graduate College, on condition that the project should be carried out on the lines of West's pamphlet, that an additional half million should be raised, and that Procter should approve the site for the College. Almost at once an additional half million was pledged by friends of Princeton, so that Wilson faced the dilemma of having to submit to complete defeat by West or having to oppose the acceptance of a million dollars for the construction of the very Graduate College which he had himself endorsed in his preface to West's pamphlet.

The university's need of an adequate Graduate College had been so long and generally recognized that the offer for a million dollars for the construction of the College was hailed with delight by Princeton men everywhere. It was obvious that such a college would enhance the position of Princeton in the world of education and it seemed impossible that anyone should question the value of the gift to the university. Wilson, in the grip of his compulsion, did question. He could not allow West to defeat him whatever the cost to Princeton. He opposed acceptance of Procter's gift. And once again his unconscious began to employ his reason to find excuses for the action it desired.

Procter wished the College to be built either at Merwick, where the graduate students were actually housed, or on the golf links about a half mile from the undergraduate buildings. Wilson's reason, in obedience to his reaction-formation against his passivity to his father, took a firm moral stand on the ground that a Graduate College built on the campus would be a great success and an influence for democracy while a Graduate College built a half mile to the east would be a disastrous failure and an influence for snobbish plutocracy. He used an immense number of words to explain how this slight geographical difference could produce so enormous a moral change. The numbers of those who opposed acceptance of Procter's gift were not greatly increased by this argument, and Wilson's reason found another high moral ground. He argued that to accept gifts with conditions attached was to bow the knee of pure learning before the golden calf of wealth. Since he had joyfully accepted for the Graduate College the Swann legacy, which was far more restricted than the Procter bequest, this argument did not ring true and convinced few. He then shifted to a legal quibble asserting that to accept the golf links site would mean the loss of the Swann bequest, which specified that the Graduate College should be built on the grounds of the university, because the golf links had not belonged to the university when Mrs. Swann made her bequest. On October 21, 1909, the Board of Trustees voted to accept Procter's gift if this legal point could be satisfactorily cleared up. A committee of nine prominent lawyers to whom it was referred decided the point against Wilson, and he appeared to be beaten.

A compulsion is, however, precisely what its name implies. It compels action. Wilson had to go on trying to defeat West. He had made no headway with his high moral arguments and his legal quibble. On Christmas Day 1909 he tried a threat. He wrote to Mr. Moses Taylor Pyne and threatened to resign unless the action of the Trustees of October 21 should be reversed. The real source of his opposition to Procter's gift, which he had attempted to conceal by his high moral arguments, appeared at last in this letter: "A Graduate College which lay in every sense at the heart of things was West's first idea, and the modification of his views and purposes has played no small part in depriving him of the confidence of his academic colleagues. He has now lost their confidence completely, and nothing administered by him in accordance with his present ideas can succeed. Indeed nothing administered by him can now succeed." Wilson was most reluctant to reveal the real source of his opposition. A week after his letter to Mr. Pyne he wrote to another Trustee: "To put the matter explicitly upon the ground of our disapproval of West and what he stands for, would, it seems to me, be to make it appear a personal matter, which the friends of the University would certainly misinterpret greatly to our discredit . . . We now know, indeed, that Mr. Procter's gift is made to put West in the saddle, but we cannot make that a matter of public discussion." He realized that if it should become generally known that he preferred to have Princeton lose a million dollar Graduate College rather than suppress his hatred of West, his position in the 'Princeton Constituency" would become untenable.

The Trustees were somewhat terrified by his threat of resignation. They had already had a foretaste of the criticisms he might launch against themselves and Princeton, and they feared that if he should be allowed to resign as a martyr he would not hesitate to give Princeton a highly undesirable reputation.

It must be noted also that the acceptance of his resignation would have enhanced his political prospects. Colonel Harvey was confident that he could persuade Boss Smith of New Jersey to dictate the nomination of Wilson for Governor the following September. If Wilson had been able to pose as a martyr to plutocratic snobbery, his chance to obtain the support of the radical Democrats for the presidential nomination would have been increased. Defeat in the field of "minor statesmanship" would have helped him in the field of major statesmanship. He was aware of this when he threatened to resign. His personal position was much more secure than at the time of the defeat of his "Quad" proposal in 1908. Not only were his political prospects excellent but also he had been offered the presidency of the University of Minnesota. He was in no danger of having to return to the practice of law in Virginia. Otherwise his careful Narcissism would probably not have permitted his threat to resign.

The Trustees, fearing Wilson's possible speeches, wishing to keep him at Princeton and desiring most intensely to accept the million dollars for the Graduate College, tried to arrange various compromises. Before the meeting of the Trustees on January 13, 1910, the Graduate School Committee met. Wilson informed the committee that he had proposed a compromise to Procter; that Procter's gift should be used to build on the golf links while the Swann bequest should be used to build a second Graduate College on the campus. He expressed his regret that Procter had refused this extraordinary proposal. Thereupon, Mr. Pyne produced a letter from Procter saying that rather than let the whole matter fall through he was ready to accept Wilson's proposal for two Graduate Colleges. Wilson was dumbfounded. After some moments of confusion he said that, as Mr. Procter had once declined his offer, the matter could not be reopened, thus revealing the insincerity of his maneuvers; "then with a marked change of manner, he explained that there had been a lack of frankness in the discussion. 'The matter of site is not essential. Under proper auspices my faculty can make this school a success anywhere in Mercer County. The whole trouble is that Dean West's ideas and ideals are not the ideas and ideals of Princeton.' " In view of his habit of clothing his desires in the raiment of ideals he could scarcely have said more clearly: "The whole trouble is that I hate West."

Some of the Trustees, perceiving this, were then sufficiently cruel to strip the cloak of ideals off Wilson's hatred. His attention was called to his repeated public indorsements of Dean West's plan, including the "ideas and ideals" involved, and especially to the signed preface to the "prospectus." Wilson answered that when he wrote the preface he had not seen the book. Again his memory was convenient. Again he distorted a fact. His preface, indeed, consisted largely of a paragraph taken from his report to the Trustees of October 21, 1902. West's pamphlet was not then completed. But Wilson altered the paragraph in preparing it as a preface after he had read the West pamphlet.

Wilson's opponents among the Trustees, feeling that as soon as the alumni knew what he had said on January 13, 1910, his prestige would be non-existent, and fearing possible public attacks on Princeton and themselves if they compelled his resignation, allowed him to appoint a committee to report on the whole matter to the Board. Wilson appointed three of his supporters and two of his opponents. They prepared majority and minority reports and the stage was set for Wilson's final defeat at the scheduled meeting of the Trustees on February 10, 1910. But a week before the meeting of the Trustees, the "Princeton Constituency" was amazed and enraged to read in the *New York Times* an editorial attack on the university, the content of which indicated that it had been inspired either by Wilson or by someone in his entourage. Wilson's friends denied indignantly that he had had anything to do with it. The fact was that Professor Robert Root, one of Wilson's followers, had suggested the editorial to Mr. Herbert B. Brougham, one of the *Times* editorial writers, that Mr. Brougham had sent it to Wilson for approval before publication and that Wilson had "confirmed the facts." Mr. Brougham altered it slightly after Wilson's suggestions had been received and its publication was approved by Wilson, when by a word he could have prevented it. Mr. Brougham became one of his trusted confidants. Mr. Procter read the editorial, believed that Wilson had inspired it and, thoroughly disgusted with Wilson, withdrew his offer entirely on February 6, 1910, four days before the Trustees were to meet to accept it.

Wilson was overjoyed. Princeton had lost a million dollar Graduate College; but he had defeated West. He persuaded himself that he had won a great moral victory and he seems to have had no qualms caused by the realization that since he was President of the university his duty was to promote the welfare of Princeton, not to find outlet for his hatred of West. Indeed his reason, obeying the libido which charged his reaction-formation against his passivity to his father, was able to convince him that by depriving Princeton of a million dollar Graduate School he had promoted the welfare of the university. Exhausted but elated he sailed, on February 14, 1910, for Bermuda. There he had a foretaste of the dreams which were to disturb his nights until death closed his eyes securely. From Bermuda he wrote to his wife: "I did not realize until I got here how hard hit my nerves have been by the happenings of the past month. Almost at once the *days* began to afford me relief, but the nights distressed me. The trouble latent in my mind came out in my dreams. Not till last night did the distress — the struggle all night with college foes, the sessions of hostile trustees, the confused war of argument and insinuation — cease."

Wilson returned from Bermuda early in March to find that the

Princeton alumni already knew that his personal hatred of West was the cause of the loss of the Graduate College, and that a wave of hostility to him was sweeping the "Princeton Constituency." He had defeated West, but the methods he had employed had shaken his hold on the presidency of Princeton. Through Colonel Harvey, he was already negotiating with the Democratic Boss of Essex County with regard to his nomination for Governor of New Jersey in September, but his nomination was not certain. He decided to go on a speaking tour for the double purpose of justifying his rejection of the Graduate College and increasing his political reputation as the enemy of plutocratic snobbery. The further Harvey progressed in his negotiations with Boss Smith, the less Wilson's speeches dealt with education and the more with politics. After his speech of April 7, to the Princeton Alumni of New York, had been received with hostile silence instead of the applause to which he was accustomed, he remarked: "Well, I don't have to stick at this work. There are large political opportunities opening before me."

On April 14, 1910, at a meeting of the Board of Trustees, Wilson had to face the fact that his victory over West had been more apparent than real. A motion which he sponsored to refer the organization and administration of the Graduate School to a committee of the faculty was defeated, and a plan to persuade Procter to renew his gift was strongly supported. Wilson left this meeting in bitter rage. He saw that his rejection of the Graduate College was recoiling on himself. He had felt that West was definitely defeated. It was now evident that West was stronger than ever because of the anger the loss of the Graduate College had aroused among the alumni. It seemed probable that if Procter should renew his offer it would be accepted in spite of his opposition: West would defeat him.

The turmoil in Wilson's mind caused by the renewed prospect of defeat by West exhibited itself in the address which he made to the Princeton Club of Pittsburgh two days later. It was a violent attempt to obtain radical political support, and it seems to have sprung from the realization that he would have to solace himself for a defeat in the field of "minor statesmanship" by a victory in the field of major statesmanship. For many years he had wanted to leave education for politics. To exchange the presidency of Princeton for the governorship of New Jersey and a chance to become President of the United States would have given him great joy if it had not been for his unsatisfied hatred of West. He still could not allow West to defeat him. His compulsion was as active as ever. No triumph, however dear to him, could fully solace him for defeat by West.

On May 18, 1910, Isaac C. Wyman died and by his will left approximately two million dollars to the Princeton Graduate College, appointing Dean West as one of his two Trustees. Wilson felt destroyed. He wanted to oppose the acceptance of this bequest as he had opposed the acceptance of Procter's gift; but he soon realized that he could not possibly persuade the Trustees to support him. Procter renewed his offer. Wilson became acutely miserable. Victory in the field of statesmanship lay before him; but West had defeated him. He submitted.

He did not at once resign the presidency of Princeton. He was not quite sure that he would be nominated for Governor of New Jersey. Boss Smith personally disliked Wilson, whom he described as a "Presbyterian priest." The Boss had made no definite promise and feared that Wilson, once Governor, would turn on him and attempt to destroy him. He demanded an explicit assurance from Wilson that he would not do this. Wilson gave the assurance, writing on June 23, 1910, to an agent of Smith: "I would be perfectly willing to assure Mr. Smith that I would not, if elected Governor, set about 'fighting and breaking down the existing Democratic organization and replacing it with one of my own.' " Smith accepted this assurance as "entirely satisfactory" and, relying on it, agreed to dictate the nomination of Wilson for Governor of New Jersey the following autumn.

Wilson, struggling against the unhappiness caused by West's victory, put on the best face he could muster for the Commencement exercises; but when the valedictorian of the graduating class delivered his address, the President of the university could control himself no longer. He stood with streams of tears coursing down his face.

In the autumn Wilson left Princeton to enter the political career for which he had longed since the day in his adolescence when he had pinned the picture of Gladstone on the wall above his desk. But the memory of Princeton and West would not leave him. Again and again West appeared in his conversation and his dreams. He could not stop talking about West or dreaming about West. In the White House during the World War, he dreamed that he was fighting West at Princeton. When he was dying in his house in Washington, he had the same dreams. At the end of his life the name of West still stirred him to rage. His aggressive activity toward his father and his reaction-formation against his passivity to his father found in the course of his life many new outlets, but a portion of those streams of libido continued to be fixed upon West. In spite of all his struggles the big dark man had defeated him. In his heart always remained a cankering sore. He called it West. It was the Reverend Joseph Ruggles Wilson.

XIII

Boss Smith, relying on Wilson's promise not to attempt to destroy his power, dictated the nomination of Wilson for Governor of New Jersey to an unwilling convention. On September 15, 1910, Wilson received the votes of the delegates Smith controlled and no others. Seven weeks later Wilson, elected Governor of New Jersey, began to battle Smith. Seven months after his promise not to destroy the Smith organization, he had completely demolished it. Wilson realized that his political stature and his chance to obtain the Democratic nomination for President of the United States would be increased if he should become known to the nation as a Boss-destroyer. Since he believed that he was the representative of God on earth, it was not difficult for him to believe that to promote his own career was a higher moral duty than to keep his word. Later he often argued with his intimates that lying was justified in cases involving the honor of a woman or the welfare of the nation. Since he believed that the welfare of the nation required direction of the nation by Woodrow Wilson, he applied the same principle in cases involving his own career.

When he began to fight Smith, Wilson for the first time became intimate with Joseph P. Tumulty, the able young Catholic lawyer who later served as his Secretary in the White House. Tumulty, considering Wilson the cat's-paw of Smith, had opposed Wilson's nomination; but when Wilson began to battle the boss, Tumulty became devoted to him with a passionate loyalty that endured. In Wilson's affection for Tumulty there was always a curious element of distrust. He was fond of Tumulty and valued him highly for his political acumen; but, in spite of the fact that Tumulty was a smaller, younger, blond male who looked up to him with a respect not unlike Tommy Wilson's adoration of his "incomparable father," he never placed Tumulty in the niche in his heart from which he had thrown out Hibben; and his periods of great intimacy with Tumulty were always followed by periods of aloofness. He would not have taken Tumulty to the White House with him if it had not been for the influence of Mrs. Wilson, who loved Tumulty as much as he loved her.

To determine the exact source of the mingled affection and distrust which Wilson felt for Tumulty seems at first sight somewhat difficult. A number of factors might have been involved. Tumulty was in the habit of speaking frankly to Wilson, and his insufficient subservience might have aroused Wilson's dislike. Tumulty was a Catholic and Wilson possessed the habitual Presbyterian distrust of Catholics. Yet when one examines their relationship from the first day to the last, certain facts appear which point to a different conclusion. Wilson, coming from the room in which his wife, who represented his mother, had just died, ignored his own family and wept on Tumulty's shoulder, sobbing, "Oh, Joe! You know better than anyone what it means to me!" He invited Tumulty to live with him at the White House.

After his second marriage and re-election, Wilson became so displeased with his Secretary that he asked Tumulty to resign; but he was so moved by Tumulty's tears that he withdrew his request. He refused to take Tumulty to the Peace Conference; but he was so sensitive with regard to Tumulty's feelings that he would not take another Secretary. At last, with unnecessary cruelty, he made the devoted Tumulty appear a liar and false friend, and never spoke to him again. All these facts point to a far deeper emotional root for Wilson's mingled affection and distrust than Tumulty's lack of servility and Wilson's religious prejudice. If one recalls the fact that like names almost invariably produce identifications in the unconscious when there is even slight resemblance between the bearers of the names, the conclusion becomes almost inescapable that Wilson's mixed feelings about Tumulty sprang, as we have already noted, from the accident that Tumulty's name, like the name of Wilson's little brother, was Joe. It seems likely that in Wilson's unconscious Joe Tumulty represented the little brother whose birth had aroused in him the mingled feelings of affection, dislike and a sense of betrayal, and that Tumulty, identified with Joe Wilson, became the recipient of those emotions.

Wilson, having destroyed Boss Smith and inaugurated a program of progressive legislation, started on a speaking tour to promote his chances for the presidency by showing the Boss-destroyer to the radical West. The further West he went, the more radical grew his speeches until he began to advocate a series of measures which he had denounced only a short time before. He explained his inconsistency by saying that experience had forced him to new beliefs. He knew that the wave of radicalism which was sweeping the country was moving so fast that he could not hope to obtain the Democratic nomination for President of the United States unless he kept up with it, or at least close behind it.

Meanwhile his campaign in the East was progressing favorably. Harvey was busy as usual. William F. McCombs, a young lawyer who had studied under Wilson at Princeton, opened campaign headquarters for him in New York. McCombs worshipped Wilson, saying that Wilson had an almost hypnotic effect on him. Wilson did not like McCombs. Once after talking with McCombs he described himself as feeling "as if a vampire had been sucking his blood." But he was glad to use McCombs or anyone else who would help to make him President of the United States. Among the men he hoped to use for this purpose was Colonel Edward M. House, who, politically, had Texas in his pocket. He asked House for an appointment, and for the first time they met on November 24, 1911, in New York.

Wilson again was "hungry" for a man to love. The loss of "the friend he had taken to his bosom" had left a running sore in his emotional life. On February 12, 1911, he wrote of Hibben: "Why will that wound not heal over in my stubborn heart? Why is it that I was blind and stupid enough to love the people who proved false to me, and cannot love, can only gratefully admire and cleave to, those who are my real friends . . . Perhaps it is better to love men in the mass than to love them individually." When Hibben was elected President of Princeton, Wilson wrote bitterly: "The worst has happened at the university. Hibben has been elected President!" But, needing a house in which to live, he chose not a house in Trenton, the state capital, but a cottage next to Hibben's house in Princeton! He did not speak to Hibben, and he wrote on April 1, 1911, "We were lucky to find such a place, and I shall find content here, I am sure, even if it is next door to the Hibbens." On its invisible tablets, his unconscious doubtless wrote, *"because* it is next door to the Hibbens." It is obvious that he was still bound to Hibben by powerful ambivalent desires. A considerable portion of his libido was still flowing toward Hibben and finding no outlet. He needed intensely a substitute for "the friend he had taken to his bosom."

Wilson, on November 24, 1911, went to the Hotel Gotham in New York City to use House, and remained to love him. To House he transferred almost immediately the libido which had once found outlet through Hibben. House recorded in his diary: "A few weeks after we met and after we had exchanged confidences which men usually do not exchange except after years of friendship, I asked him if he realized that we had only known one another for so short a time. He replied 'My dear friend, we have known one another always.' " The following year Wilson said: "Mr. House is my second personality. He is my independent self. His thoughts and mine are one. If I were in his place I would do just as he suggested . . . If anyone thinks he is reflecting my opinion by whatever action he takes, they are welcome to the conclusion." Wilson later was frequently unable to remember whether a thought had had its origin in his own brain or in the brain of

House, and often repeated to House, as original, ideas which House himself had suggested. All the thousands of facts we have been able to gather with regard to the friendship of Wilson and House point to the conclusion that House, like the beloved Hibben, in Woodrow Wilson's unconscious represented little Tommy Wilson. Once again by a narcissistic object-choice Wilson had re-established his infantile relationship to his "incomparable father." By identifying himself with House on the one hand and with his father on the other, he was able to receive from himself the love he wanted and could no longer get from the dead Professor Extraordinary of Rhetoric. Once again his passivity to his father was about to find outlet through a passionate friendship.

House was ideally equipped to play the role of little Tommy Wilson. He was a smaller, younger man than Wilson and like Tommy Wilson he had blond hair. He, too, had suffered from illness in his childhood and had to worry about his health. Like Tommy Wilson he had a passion for politics. Yet he could not possibly be considered a rival to Woodrow Wilson because he did not want office. He wanted only to be the quiet friend of the man in power. Thus, through House, Wilson was able to re-create in a singularly perfect form his relationship to his father.

From the point of view of House also the relationship was perfect. He wanted to control a President of the United States. He was fond of Wilson but he could see around, over, under and through the Governor of New Jersey. After looking for the first time through Wilson's eyeglasses at his pale gray eyes, House told a friend that the time would surely come when Wilson would turn on him and throw him on the scrap heap. This did not disturb House. He was happy to use his power so long as it might last. He soon learned that Wilson did not like open opposition but that he could make a suggestion to Wilson, drop the matter if Wilson disapproved, and remake the suggestion a few weeks later in a slightly different form and be reasonably sure that Wilson would answer him in the words of his first suggestion. Thus he was able to influence Wilson without arguments that might have endangered their relationship. He knew that for him to take office under Wilson would be fatal to their relationship, and he refused Wilson's repeated offers of Cabinet posts. He would have had to oppose Wilson openly in Cabinet meetings, and he said rightly: "Had I gone into the Cabinet, I could not have lasted eight weeks." The extraordinary power of House over Wilson was thus maintained by his tact, but the root of it was in the fact that to Wilson he was a part of himself; he was little Tommy Wilson. "Mr. House is my second personality. He is my independent self. His thoughts and mine are one."

Wilson's delight in his friendship with Colonel House was so great that House became at once his most trusted political adviser, and when the Colonel told him that without the support of William Jennings Bryan he could not be nominated, and that Bryan believed him to be a "tool of Wall Street" because of Harvey's enthusiasm for his nomination, Wilson at once bluntly dismissed Harvey.

His dismissal of the man who had first advocated his nomination, and had labored for it through six unprofitable years, produced a general outcry that Wilson would let neither friendship, gratitude nor loyalty stand in the way of his career. Wilson's publicity agents spread the story that his break with Harvey had occurred because he had refused to accept financial aid from one of Harvey's Wall Street friends. Harvey was then publicly damned as a false friend for deserting Wilson because of this honorable refusal, and Wilson was acclaimed as the champion of the "common people" against the "interests." There was no word of truth in the story sent out by Wilson's publicity men, but this fact did not bother Wilson any more than the fact that in the case of Harvey he had added insult to injury. He had become so intent on his career, so narcissistic and so sure of his mission that neither fact nor gratitude could be allowed to stand in his way. He needed the support of Bryan. Therefore, Harvey had to go. He finally captured Bryan by delivering a fervent public tribute to the old Democratic leader, whom he despised. Bryan "put an arm around Wilson and gave him the Bryan benediction." The support of Bryan, the labors of House and McCombs, the money of Cleveland Dodge, Baruch and Morgenthau, and his speeches, were the chief factors which obtained for him the Democratic nomination for President on July 2, 1912.

On November 5, 1912, Woodrow Wilson was elected President of the United States. The two Republican candidates, Theodore Roosevelt and William Howard Taft, had a combined vote of 1,312,000 more than Wilson, but he had a plurality of 2,170,000 over Roosevelt, his closest rival. He received the news of his election at the cottage next to Hibben's house in Princeton. To a group of students who came to cheer him he spoke as follows: "I do not feel exuberant or cheerful. I feel exceedingly solemn. I have no inclination to jump up and crack my heels together. A weight of seriousness and responsibility seems to be pressing down upon me. I feel more like kneeling down and praying for strength to do what is expected of me." And to McCombs, the chairman of his campaign committee, he said: "Whether you did little or much, remember that God ordained that I should be the next President of the United States. Neither you nor any other mortal or mortals could have prevented it." Mr. Ray Stannard Baker recorded that later, when warned that he might be assassinated, he replied, "I am immortal until my time comes."

The reader who has followed the development of Wilson's relations with the deity will not be surprised that he believed God had chosen him to be President of the United States or that in office he felt himself to be the personal representative of the Almighty. And the reader will not be astonished that at the moment when he had achieved the ambition of his life he felt not "exuberant or cheerful" but "exceedingly solemn" with "a weight of seriousness and responsibility" pressing down upon him. Like the acceptance of *Congressional Government,* like his marriage and first professional successes, like the establishment of the preceptorial system, his election as President of the United States gave him only the feeling that he had not done enough. His Super-Ego was insatiable.

He was a very tired man. Before his election as President of the United States his tissues were worn out. He had avoided collapse while he was Governor of New Jersey; but he had to conserve his strength to the utmost, to watch the condition of his arteries, and to nurse his neuritis, sick stomach and aching head. When he entered the White House on March 4, 1913, he carried with him a stomach pump, which he was in the habit of using frequently to pump out the acid contents of his own stomach, and a quart can of headache tablets, which he continued to take until the White House physician, Admiral Cary T. Grayson, discovered that they were damaging his kidneys and took them away from him. He was worried about his finances. He had to borrow money to purchase himself and his family new clothing for the inauguration ceremonies, and when he was inaugurated he was five thousand dollars in debt. He felt that it would be desecration to begin his administration with the customary inaugural ball. He was God's anointed setting forth on his mission, and to dance was not in the best Presbyterian tradition. He abolished the inaugural ball.

XIV

THAT A MAN of fifty-six in the physical and mental condition of
Woodrow Wilson should have been able to do the work he did
during the six and a half years which separated his inauguration in
March 1913 from his collapse in September 1919 is remarkable.
He went through several crises during that period but never once
did he break down completely. Two factors seem to have contributed to the improvement in his health: the watchful care of his
White House physician, Admiral Cary T. Grayson, and an unusual
combination of psychic satisfactions.

Admiral Grayson supervised every detail of his personal life. He
worked out a strict diet for the President and made him discard the
stomach pump. He persuaded Wilson to play golf each morning if
possible, and to take a long automobile ride each afternoon, and
saw to it that the President had nine hours of uninterrupted sleep.
The President's entourage gave out the impression that he was
working hard for long hours; but in fact he rarely was at his desk
for more than four hours a day. In the evenings he never worked,
except in great political crises, but either went to the theater or
read poems and short stories to his wife and daughters. To read
aloud soothed his nerves as much as to see the vaudeville at Keith's
Theatre. The Reverend Joseph Ruggles Wilson had also found
satisfaction in reading aloud to his family in the evenings.

The President lived an extraordinarily isolated life. He saw little or nothing of the members of his Cabinet or of the leaders of his
party in the Congress. He did not take them into his confidence
and made them feel that they had no idea what was in his mind.
Whenever he had them at the White House for a meal, he enter-

tained them with a meagerness which they resented. He neither smoked nor drank, and to his guests he gave neither wine, cigarettes nor cigars. He had decided to save two thousand dollars a month while he was in the White House and he was doing so. To talk seriously at meals gave him indigestion. After a dispute with Tumulty or his son-in-law, McAdoo, at luncheon, which occasionally occurred, he might be tortured by indigestion and sick headache for two days. To spare his nerves and his physical strength he avoided personal contacts and depended largely on House and Tumulty for his knowledge of men and affairs. He refused to join the Chevy Chase Country Club, where he would have come in contact with the leaders of political and social life, and played his golf alone with Admiral Grayson at a remote little course in Virginia. Thus he was able to preserve sufficient physical strength to perform his executive duties.

In spite of Admiral Grayson's care, his psychic conflicts would doubtless have driven him to his customary "breakdowns" if fortune had not given him excellent outlets for his conflicting desires. The thin stream of libido which had been directed toward his mother continued to find perfect expression through his wife so long as she lived. His Super-Ego to be sure could never be satisfied by any achievement; but so long as he was President there was always before him some new achievement with which he could pacify it temporarily. Moreover his executive actions offered complete outlet for his identification with his father, and his activity toward his father, and a large degree of outlet for his reaction against his passivity to his father. There were many distinguished political opponents whom he could hate and attempt to destroy, and thus find outlet for whatever surplus of libido was stored in this reaction-formation. His love of House gave him a large outlet for his passivity to his father. Moreover the libido accumulated by his unconscious identification with Christ was able to find outlet through "service" of mankind. The reader will recall the line in his letter of complaint about Hibben: "Perhaps it is better to love men in the mass than to love them individually." He did "love

men in the mass" in the most Christian manner, and with few ex-
ceptions shunned or hated them individually. Finally, through
speech-making he was able to give outlet to both his activity and
passivity to his father, to obey his father and to be his father, the
God in the pulpit. Thus so long as his wife lived, so long as House
remained his friend and so long as his political success continued,
his psychic conflicts did not become acute. The combination of
Dr. Grayson's care and this favorable psychic constellation preserved him from breakdown.

In the selection of his Cabinet and his diplomatic representatives, Wilson was guided chiefly by House and Tumulty, and his
notable legislative program of the years 1912 to 1914 was largely
the program of House's book *Philip Dru: Administrator.* The
passage of this legislation, which included the Federal Reserve Act,
gave him no joy but only his customary feeling that he had not
done enough. He introduced one novelty into his administration
which was entirely Wilsonian in origin and had its roots in his
youthful preference for the practices of the House of Commons as
opposed to the methods of the Congress. He delivered his messages
to the Congress by word of mouth instead of in writing as had been
the custom since 1797. The Constitution of the United States did
not permit him to be Prime Minister in fact but, in so far as he was
able, he imitated his beloved Gladstone.

Before his inauguration Wilson had remarked to a friend, "It
would be the irony of fate if my administration should have to deal
chiefly with foreign affairs." He had been interested in domestic
politics for forty years and felt certain of his ability to solve domestic problems; but he had never been interested in international
politics and his ignorance of foreign relations was as comprehensive as his ignorance of foreign countries. He knew something
about Great Britain. Wilson's interest in domestic affairs was indeed so much greater than his interest in foreign affairs that, instead of compensating for his ignorance by the appointment of a
Secretary of State who was familiar with international politics, he
appointed William Jennings Bryan, who was as undefiled as him-

self by knowledge of the world, in order to obtain the support of Bryan for his program of domestic legislation. This appointment meant that he had decided to be his own Secretary of State; for he had no confidence in Bryan's judgment. His contempt for Bryan's intellectual equipment was, however, superficial rather than deep. Bryan might well have been a member of his own family. Bryan like himself was a Presbyterian Elder who found his supreme expression in preaching. Bryan like himself esteemed noble intentions and "high moral principles" more highly than facts. Moreover, those of Bryan's beliefs which Wilson thought ridiculous or dangerous were few compared to those of Bryan's beliefs with which he was in complete agreement. He, like Bryan, was convinced that "principles" plus a little knowledge of fact would lead to high achievements in international affairs.

The President's ignorance of the world outside the United States enabled him to employ foreign policy more freely than domestic policy for the expression of his unconscious desires. His domestic policies produced distinguished results and by the spring of 1914 the domestic program of *Philip Dru* had been largely embodied in legislation. The international program of *Philip Dru* remained unrealized, and House attempted to interest Wilson in a new international agreement for the development of backward countries and the preservation of European peace. Although Wilson was little interested in European affairs, he agreed to allow House to try to work out something of the sort.

As we have noted, Wilson's mental life had always been bounded by the United States and Great Britain, and in the White House he remained astonishingly ignorant of European politics, geography and racial distribution. Even after he had made his great speeches on international affairs his knowledge of the continent of Europe remained elementary. He learned enough facts to make his speeches but often did not understand the implications of his own words. On the *George Washington,* when he was on his way to the Peace Conference, he said that he intended to give Bohemia to Czechoslovakia. When he was asked what he intended to do with the three million Germans in Bohemia, he replied: "Three million Germans in Bohemia! That's curious! Masaryk never told me that!" At dinner in the White House in February 1916 there was a discussion of the Jewish race. Wilson insisted that there were at least one hundred million Jews in the world. When he was told that there were less than fifteen million, he sent for the World Almanac and even after seeing the figures could scarcely believe that he had been mistaken. He gave the southern Tyrol to Italy because he did not know there were Austrians of German blood south of the Brenner Pass.

In the spring of 1914, Wilson let House go abroad as his personal agent. House talked with the Kaiser on June 1, 1914, about the desirability of working out a general understanding between Germany, England, the United States and the other great powers. The Kaiser said he approved of House's project, and the Colonel, delighted, went to Paris and thence to England to see Sir Edward Grey, in whom he had an almost filial confidence.

Grey kept House waiting in London for a week before he saw him on June 17, 1914. Then, though he charmed House as usual, he did not give House any word to pass to the Kaiser. House remained in London trying to get from Grey some message for the Kaiser. On June 28, the Archduke Franz Ferdinand, heir apparent to the thrones of Austria and Hungary, was murdered by a Serb in Sarajevo. On July 3, House at last heard from Tyrrell that Grey wanted him to let the Kaiser know of the peaceable sentiments of the British in order that further negotiations might follow. House did not write his letter passing along this information to the Kaiser until July 7. When House's letter reached Berlin, the Kaiser had already left for his cruise in Norwegian waters. He did not receive House's letter until he was recalled to Berlin after the Austrian ultimatum to Serbia of July 23, 1914. Thus ended the first effort of House and Wilson to produce an international agreement for the preservation of peace. The war began. On August 4, 1914, Wilson proclaimed the neutrality of the United States.

XV

On August 6, 1914, Ellen Axson Wilson died. She had been a perfect wife to Woodrow Wilson: an admirable mother representative, a "center of quiet" for his life. For twenty-nine years the charge of libido lodged in his desires with regard to his mother had needed no other outlet. His friendships with women had all been unpassionate. The amount of his libido directed toward women was, to be sure, extremely small compared to the amount directed toward men, but an outlet for it was none the less an absolute necessity, and the loss of Ellen Axson shook the foundations of his character. He could not pull himself out of the depression caused by her death. Again and again he expressed his grief and hopelessness, saying that "he felt like a machine that had run down and there was nothing left in him worth while . . . that he looked forward to the remaining two years and a half of his Presidential term with dread, he did not see how he could go through with it . . . that he was broken in spirit by Mrs. Wilson's death and was not fit to be President because he did not think straight any longer, and had no heart in the things he was doing . . . that his life was unbearably lonely and sad since Mrs. Wilson's death and he could not help wishing someone would kill him . . . that he had himself so disciplined that he knew perfectly well that unless someone killed him he would go on to the end doing the best he could." Tears would come into his eyes when he spoke of not wanting to live longer and of not being fit to do the work he had in hand.

Grayson, Tumulty and House did their best to cheer him, but without success. He invited Tumulty to live at the White House;

but his greatest solace was the friendship of House, whom he addressed in his letters of that period as, "My dear, dear Friend" or Dearest Friend." Yet House's friendship was not enough. Wilson desperately needed a woman to care for him as his mother and Ellen Axson had cared for him. On December 12, 1914, he wrote to Mrs. Toy: "All the elasticity has gone out of me. I have not yet learned to throw off the incubus of my grief and live as I used to live, in thought and spirit, in spite of it. Even books have grown meaningless to me. I read detective stories to forget, as a man would get drunk!" By a curious slip of the pen, the words he actually used were words which showed that in his unconscious he had withdrawn himself from the male sex and had identified himself with the female sex. A woman, not a man writes, "I read detective stories to forget, as a man would get drunk." We may be sure that, until he found another mother representative, Wilson replaced his lost mother substitute by himself, just as he had replaced his cousin Hattie Woodrow by himself when he became Woodrow Wilson.

Wilson's acute depression continued through the Christmas holidays of 1914, and it was accentuated when in January 1915 he felt obliged to send House abroad. Count von Bernstorff, the German Ambassador, had assured Wilson that if House should go to Berlin he would find the German Government ready to make peace on reasonable terms. On January 25, 1915, House left Washington. That evening he recorded in his diary: "The President's eyes were moist when he said his last words of farewell. He said: 'Your unselfish and intelligent friendship has meant much to me,' and he expressed his gratitude again and again calling me his 'most trusted friend.' He declared I was the only one in all the world to whom he could open his entire mind . . . He insisted upon going to the station with me. He got out of the car and walked through the station and to the ticket office, and then to the train itself, refusing to leave until I entered the car."

After the departure of House, the solitary President, without a wife, without a friend, stalking through the White House by himself, grew so desperately lonely that his physician Cary Grayson, fearing a collapse, insisted on music and guests. Among the friends of Dr. Grayson's fiancée was a widow of forty-three named Mrs. Galt. In the month of April 1915, eight months after the death of Ellen Axson Wilson, she was invited to hear music at the White House. Wilson fell in love with her at once.

Mrs. Edith Bolling Galt was a simple, healthy, full-bosomed American woman of the upper middle class, the respectable relict of the owner of a jewelry store. She was plump, pretty and moderately rich, and she possessed abundant vitality; but she had neither intellectual nor physical vivacity. She was rather shy, and until Wilson fell in love with her she lived in quiet obscurity. It seems the part of courtesy to refrain from discussion of Wilson's reasons for choosing her; but we must note that he required a mother substitute in his life and that the personality of the mother substitute was a secondary consideration. In order to be able to fall in love again, he needed merely to be able to find some characteristic in some woman which might serve as an unconscious mental link to connect the prospective love-object to his mother. Let us content ourselves with noting that Edith Bolling Galt like Ellen Axson became a mother representative to Wilson and satisfied his need for a mother substitute. Again he refound "a center of quiet" for his life and a mother's breast on which to rest. His passivity to his mother drove him to try to reproduce the same attitude toward his second wife that he had enjoyed with his mother and his first wife. He even confided to Mrs. Galt that Joe Tumulty had advised him not to marry her! And he expected her thereafter to love Tumulty! One wonders, however, if at that moment he was not acting at the behest of an unconscious wish to make trouble between his mother and his little brother Joe.

Wilson was so engulfed by Mrs. Galt that he could not see enough of her, and his subordinates began to find it difficult to get his attention for public business. Ellen Axson Wilson faded swiftly into the background. This rapid turning from his dead wife to Mrs. Galt was, however, proof rather than disproof of the depth of his affection for the former. He could not live without a substitute for her. He found a substitute in Mrs. Galt, and from the depths of depression mounted rapidly to heights of exaltation.

XVI

THE FIFTY-EIGHT-YEAR-OLD President in love in the spring was suddenly confronted by a problem of the utmost gravity. House had discovered in Berlin no wish to make a reasonable peace, and on May 7, 1915, the British liner *Lusitania* was sunk without warning and one hundred and twenty-four American passengers were drowned. Hitherto Wilson had felt remote from the European conflict. That the United States should be drawn into it seemed most unlikely. His efforts to end the war had been the efforts of a comparatively disinterested outsider anxious to put an end to a holocaust which was destroying the civilized world. The sinking of the *Lusitania* compelled him to face for the first time a new question: Could he keep the United States out of the war?

Wilson sincerely hoped that he could keep the United States out of the war. He was not a pacifist. He had said to House that "he did not share the views of many of our present day statesmen that war was so much to be deprecated. He considered it as an economic proposition ruinous, but he thought there was no more glorious way to die than in battle." Moreover, personally he sympathized strongly with the Allies. His British ancestry, his worship of Burke, Bright, Bagehot and Gladstone, his love of Rydal, his devotion to the ideas and ideals of the British middle class, his ignorance of European life and languages and of the intricacies of European politics, made it inevitable that his sympathies should be with England. Yet this personal sympathy did not lead him to conclude in 1914 that he ought to bring the United States into the war to help England. He was acutely aware that while in America there were violently pro-Ally and pro-German groups, the vast majority of the American people wished to keep out of the war. He felt that he would not be justified in leading the United States into the war unless a majority of the American people desired war.

Wilson, in spite of his sympathy for England, had at that time no difficulty in distinguishing between the interests of England and those of the United States. House, on the other hand, often exhibited a curious inability to distinguish between Englishmen and Americans. Two days after the sinking of the *Lusitania,* House cabled to Wilson from London: "I believe an immediate demand should be made upon Germany for assurance that this shall not occur again. If she fails to give such assurance then I should inform her that our Government expected to take such measures as were necessary to ensure the safety of American citizens. If war follows it will not be a new war but an endeavor to end more speedily an old one."

Something in House's mind made him overlook the fact that it would be "a new war" for the United States, and that American lives would pay for the decreased loss of English lives. House habitually permitted Sir William Wiseman, head of the British Secret Service in the United States, to sit in his private office in New York and read the most secret documents of the American Government. House's father and mother had both been English.

Wilson's sympathy for England, his romantic feeling that death in battle was a glorious end and House's influence all tended to make him wish to lead the United States into the war. And these conscious motives were supported by unconscious powers. In his unconscious he had identified himself with the Hebrew Jehovah who delighted in smiting his enemies, and his Super-Ego was constantly demanding that he should become the ruler of the world. But on the other hand his feeling of responsibility to the American people was also supported by an unconscious force. A large portion of his passivity to his father was flowing into his unconscious identification with Christ and was finding outlet through loving "men in the mass." He wanted to serve mankind as the Prince of Peace. He read his Bible twice daily and was thoroughly familiar with the phrase: "By their fruits ye shall know them." He wanted to bring forth not the fruit of war but the fruit of peace. In the early days of 1915 his identification of himself with Christ was sufficiently powerful to counterbalance his belligerent inclinations.

The sinking of the *Lusitania* threw Wilson into a condition of uncertainty which lasted six days; then, following House's advice, he prepared and read to the Cabinet a note demanding from the German Government an official disavowal of the sinking of the *Lusitania,* reparation and a pledge that such acts would not be repeated. His note contained the threatening phrase: "The Imperial German Government will not expect the Government of the United States to omit any word or act . . ." But no sooner had Wilson taken this warlike stand than he began to vacillate.

Bryan, Secretary of State, was a pacifist. After the Cabinet meeting, at which Wilson's note had been approved, Bryan continued to plead with the President, urging that the American people did not want war and that it was not in keeping with Christian doctrine for America to threaten war. Bryan had negotiated treaties with thirty nations providing that disputes with the United States should be submitted to a commission of inquiry during the sessions of which, for a period of at least nine months, the disputants would not engage in hostilities. Germany alone of all great European powers had refused to sign such a treaty with the United States. Bryan persuaded Wilson to allow him to draft an instruction to James W. Gerard, the American Ambassador in Berlin, to be sent simultaneously with the *Lusitania* note, ordering Gerard to advise the German Government that the Government of the United States was willing to submit the *Lusitania* dispute to a commission of investigation on the principle of the Bryan treaties. Wilson thus decided to send simultaneously to Berlin a public note threatening war and a secret instruction offering to make it impossible for the

United States to go to war with Germany for at least nine months. The conflict in his mind could scarcely find better illustration. By this illogical action he found expression for both his desire for war and his desire for peace.

Bryan, in the White House with Wilson, wrote the instruction to Gerard and it was sent from the White House to the Department of State to be put in code and cabled to Berlin. No official of the American Government except Wilson and Bryan knew that it existed. Then Robert Lansing, Counsellor of the Department of State, was informed of its existence by the officials of the coding room, and at once took steps to prevent its dispatch. Lansing, Tumulty and all the members of the Cabinet (Bryan excepted), two of whom incidentally had been born British subjects, argued with Wilson that the instruction to Gerard should not be sent. Wilson yielded; the instruction was destroyed and the *Lusitania* note went to Germany without gloss.

On May 28, the German Government replied to Wilson that the *Lusitania* was an armed cruiser and transport and, as such, a vessel of war. Wilson on June 9, 1915, brushed aside the German argument as irrelevant and demanded assurances that such an act would not be repeated. Bryan, bitterly disappointed by the suppression of his instruction to Gerard and feeling that this note would lead inevitably to war, resigned. Wilson appointed Lansing Secretary of State.

The German Government delayed its reply to Wilson's second *Lusitania* note, and on August 19, 1915, Wilson's difficulties were increased by the sinking of the British liner *Arabic*, headed for New York. Two Americans were drowned. On August 21, Wilson wrote to House: "I greatly need your advice what to do in view of the sinking of the *Arabic*, if it turns out to be the simple case it seems . . . Two things are plain to me: 1. The people of this country count on me to keep them out of the war. 2. It would be a calamity to the world at large if we should be drawn actively into the conflict and so deprived of all disinterested influence over the settlement." House, in reply, advised Wilson to recall Gerard and to send Bernstorff home, and added that this meant war. Wilson refused to be pushed into war, and House noted in his diary: "I am surprised at the attitude he takes. He evidently will go to great lengths to avoid war."

On September 1, 1915, Wilson's patience was rewarded. Bernstorff wrote formally to Lansing: "Liners will not be sunk by our submarines without warning and without safety of the lives of non-combatants, provided that the liners do not try to escape or offer resistance . . ."

This note did not end Wilson's worries. The promise of the German Government to refrain from sinking without warning removed all immediate danger of war; but the refusal of the German Government to admit the illegality of such attacks made him fear that the attacks would be resumed as soon as the German Government should consider their resumption expedient. Moreover, he was greatly troubled by the strained relations between England and the United States. Resentment against the British blockade had become so intense that various members of the Cabinet suggested that, in order to compel the British Navy to stop interfering with legal American trade, an embargo should be placed on the shipment of munitions to the Allies. To these suggestions, Wilson in Cabinet meeting replied: "Gentlemen, the Allies are standing with their backs to the wall, fighting wild beasts. I will permit nothing to be done by our country to hinder or embarrass them in the prosecution of the war unless admitted rights are grossly violated."

The expression "wild beasts" indicates accurately Wilson's opinion of the Germans in the summer of 1915. He had been shocked by the invasion of Belgium, horrified by the sinking of the *Lusitania* and revolted by the imaginary Belgian atrocities vouched for by Lord Bryce. His personal knowledge of the German Army was insufficient to enable him to discount British propaganda. In the late summer of 1915 he saw himself being driven closer and closer to placing an embargo on the shipment of munitions to the English whom he loved and thus insuring the victory of the Germans whom he loathed.

Wilson did not know what to do. Moreover, he resented the interruption of his love-making by the European war. His "one track mind" was occupied by Mrs. Galt, and to turn from private to public affairs had become so distasteful to him that he found it difficult to attend to urgent matters of public interest. In so far as possible he allowed House to do his thinking for him while he attended to his own love-making. He was recklessly in love with the recklessness of the man of sixty who has felt old because passionate love has passed from his life and suddenly experiences the miracle of the rebirth of passion and feels young, exalted, full of power, God-like. House's control of Wilson's political actions was never so complete as during the autumn of 1915. Wilson, puzzled and bored by the whole war, asked House, "Shall we ever get out of this labyrinth?" The Colonel replied: "Only by adopting a positive policy," and developed a plan to get Wilson out of his perplexity by getting the United States into the war on the side of England.

XVII

COLONEL HOUSE proposed that Wilson, in the name of humanity, should summon all the belligerents to a peace conference; should state that the United States would support whichever side would accept peace terms designed to secure Europe from future aggression; and should announce that the United States would enter the war against either side which might reject the settlement to be proposed by Wilson.

The terms of peace which House wanted Wilson to lay down were based on the stated war aims of the Allies. House felt almost certain that the Central Powers would not accept those terms; and, therefore, that the United States would be drawn into war against the Central Powers.

To make sure that his plan might not under any circumstance bring the United States into war against the Allies, House proposed that, before any action by Wilson, he should inform the British Government that his proposal was designed to get the United States to fight for the avowed war aims of the Allies, and that the President would not act unless and until the British Government approved. The proposal was, therefore, in the words of Professor Charles Seymour, who edited *The Intimate Papers Of Colonel House* with the Colonel's personal collaboration, "practically to guarantee Allied victory with the assistance of the United States."

House's plan ran counter to Wilson's conviction that he should keep the United States out of the European conflict, and also to the traditional American policy of staying out of European wars. House recorded his first effort to persuade Wilson to adopt it, in the following words:

"I outlined very briefly a plan which has occurred to me and which seems of much value. I thought we had lost our opportunity to break with Germany, and it looked as if she had a better chance than ever of winning, and if she did win our turn would come next; and we were not only unprepared, but there would be no one to help us stand the first shock. Therefore, we should do something decisive now — something that would either end the war in a way to abolish militarism or that would bring us in with the Allies to help them do it. My suggestion is to ask the Allies, unofficially, to let me know whether or not it would be agreeable to them to have us demand that hostilities cease. We would put it upon the high ground that the neutral world was suffering along with the belligerents and that we had rights as well as they, and that peace parleys should begin upon the broad basis of both military and naval disarmament . . .

"If the Allies understood our purpose, we could be as severe in our language concerning them as we were with the Central Powers. The Allies, after some hesitation, could accept our offer or demand and, if the Central Powers accepted, we would then have accomplished a master stroke of diplomacy. If the Central Powers refused to acquiesce, we could then push our insistence to a point where diplomatic relations would first be broken off, and later the whole force of our Government — and perhaps the force of every neutral — might be brought against them.

"The President was startled by this plan. He seemed to acquiesce by silence. I had no time to push it further, for our entire conversation did not last longer than twenty minutes."

Wilson must have been startled by the words: "I thought we had lost our opportunity to break with Germany"; and he must have perceived that action along the lines that House proposed would almost certainly produce war between the United States and the Central Powers.

As a statesman, Sir Edward Grey, the British Foreign Secretary, was House's ideal, and Wilson liked to handle matters of the highest importance through secret communications between House and Grey. A passage in a letter from Sir Edward to the Colonel dated September 22, 1915, gave House an opportunity to move toward action. Grey wrote: "To me, the great object of securing the elimination of militarism and navalism is to get security for the future against aggressive war. How much are the United States prepared to do in this direction? Would the President propose that there should be a League of Nations binding themselves to side against any Power which broke a treaty; which broke certain rules of warfare on sea or land (such rules would, of course, have to be drawn up after this war); or which refused, in case of dispute, to adopt some other method of settlement than that of war?"

Thus for the first time, in a secret communication from the British Government to the American Government, appeared the words: League of Nations. The British Government hoped that it might be able to persuade the American Government to guarantee the terms it expected to be able to impose on the Central Powers at the end of the war.

House took Grey's letter to Wilson, and the President "agreed that House should draft an encouraging reply to Sir Edward as the first step toward offering American help if Germany refused the terms they had in mind, which coincided with the public war aims of the Allies." Those aims included the return of Alsace-Lorraine to France, the complete restoration of Belgium and Serbia, the cession of Constantinople to Russia and a league to guarantee the terms of the peace and to prevent aggressive war. The secret war aims of the Allies were quite different.

Colonel House conducted the prolonged negotiations which then followed; but he conducted them as Wilson's agent, and responsibility for them was entirely Wilson's. House held no official position. He was merely Wilson's "other self." Wilson was President of the United States: trustee for the American people. He decided that under the cloak of a noble humanitarian gesture he would lead the American people into the war to achieve the avowed war aims of the Allies. This decision was the more remarkable because he was in no doubt as to the wishes of the American people. As late as December 1915, after he had offered to bring the United States into the war by this circuitous route, he said to Brand Whitlock: "I am not justified in forcing my opinion upon the people of the United States and bringing them into a war which they do not understand."

Wilson's behavior during the eight months from October 1915 to May 1916 is difficult to analyze. His words and actions were so inconsistent that it is impossible to explain them as products of one rational idea; but by reason we may perhaps be able to explain their irrationality. Let us make the attempt.

Let us first recognize that Wilson faced a situation of great complexity. He loved England and loathed Germany. He feared that Germany might win the war, and that he might have to make the task of the Allies even more difficult than it was by compelling the partial abandonment of the British blockade. Moreover, he feared that the unrestricted submarine warfare might be recommenced, and he felt that the had committed himself and the United States so deeply by his *Lusitania* notes that he was in honor bound to reply to a resumption of unrestricted submarine warfare by breaking diplomatic relations with Germany and that such a break would lead to war. Thus he regarded it as possible or likely that he would in any event be compelled to lead the United States into the war against Germany. He feared that, if he should lead the United States into the war without previous agreement with the Allies as to the final terms of peace, he might find himself at the end of the war facing jingo governments in England, France and Russia which might wish to impose a Carthaginian peace on Germany that would not resemble the published war aims of the Allies. In that case he might be powerless to prevent the establishment of a peace which would not be peace but a continuation of war in a different form. House had instilled in Wilson complete confidence in Grey, and he believed that the aims which the British Government avowed were the real aims, at the moment, of England. Those considerations led him to the conclusion that it was better for him to lead America into the war at once on the basis of an agreement that the final peace should be made in accordance with the avowed war aims of the Allies rather than risk the possibility of being forced into the war at a later date and of finding in the end that the United States had been the cat's-paw of the jingoes of the Allied nations.

This intellectual justification of his action was based on so many hypotheses that it would certainly have possessed no force in itself if it had not had behind it powerful unconscious desires. It was, in fact, but another example of the ability of his unconscious to employ his reason to find excuses to justify actions it desired.

We noted when examining Wilson's behavior in the preparation of the first *Lusitania* note and the inconsistent supplementary instruction that his desires provoked by the war were in conflict. The *Lusitania* note gave release to his hostility to his father, the supplementary instruction to his passivity to his father. Those desires were still in conflict. On the one hand he wanted to express his conscious hatred of Germany and his unconscious desire to be Jehovah. On the other hand he wanted to express his wish to be the Prince of Peace. His problem was to find some course of action which would satisfy both these charges of libido and at the same time would be acceptable to his Super-Ego. House's scheme provided a magnificent outlet, supremely acceptable to his Super-Ego, for all his conflicting desires. If, by defeating Germany, he could dictate a permanent peace to the whole world, he would be a Prince of Peace indeed! House persuaded Wilson that this would be the result of his entering the war on the side of the Allies, after previous agreement with them as to the terms of peace, by arguments like those in his letter of November 10, 1915: ". . . It seems to me that we must throw the influence of this nation in behalf of a plan by which international obligations must be kept and in behalf of some plan by which the peace of the world may be maintained.

We should do this not only for the sake of civilization, but for our own welfare — for who may say when we may be involved in such a holocaust as is now devastating Europe? Must we not be a party to the making of new and more humane rules of warfare, and must we not lend our influence towards the freedom of both the land and sea? This is the part I think you are destined to play in this world tragedy, and it is the noblest part that has ever come to a son of man. This country will follow you along such a path, no matter what the cost may be."

Woodrow Wilson, who in his unconscious was God and Christ, could not resist such words as these. All his identifications with Divinity demanded that he should play "the noblest part that has ever come to a son of man." House convinced him that he could make himself the Saviour of the World. Thus the power of his identification with Christ was switched from the side of peace to the side of war. He decided to go forth to war for peace. Many times as a child with his father he had sung: "The Son of God goes forth to war a kingly crown to gain." To gain the kingly crown of the Prince of Peace became, in the autumn of 1915, the aim of Woodrow Wilson's life. His Super-Ego, his activity toward his father and his passivity to his father united their strength in this wish and it became overwhelmingly powerful. It was not difficult for his unconscious to drive his reason to find intellectual excuses for the action he so deeply wished to take.

Thenceforth, he had no doubt as to what he wanted to do; but, from time to time, he did have doubt that he would be able to do what he wanted to do. Whenever sufficient facts stared him in the face to make him realize that by going to war he would probably not achieve the peace of God of which he dreamed but a vicious peace, his identification of himself with Christ again made him abhor the idea of going to war and speak again as if he had never intended to go to war. He could make war only for peace.

On October 17, 1915, House and Wilson prepared together a letter to Sir Edward Grey which House signed, offering to bring the United States into the war to "bring about a peace along the lines you and I have so often discussed." Wilson "declared the proposal to be altogether right and he 'prayed' God it might bring results." Among the results he expected were the deaths of thousands of American boys and the destruction of billions of dollars' worth of American wealth; but his eyes were fixed on other probable results: he would become the dictator of the terms of peace, the arbiter of the world; he would lay down terms of peace so just that men would never have to die in war again; he would be the Prince of Peace who at the end of the war would come to judge both the quick and the dead.

He did not doubt that he could persuade the people of America to follow him on this crusade. He knew that many Americans had already been convinced by distinguished British propagandists that the war was a "war to end war," and his confidence in the power of his own oratory was enormous. He had once said: "I wish there were some great orator who could go about and make men drunk with this spirit of self-sacrifice." He had no doubt that he was a great orator and that he could make the American people drunk with a spirit of self-sacrifice. Later, when he brought America into the war, he proved that his confidence in his oratorical powers had not been misplaced. He did make America drunk with the spirit of self-sacrifice.

XVIII

THE MOMENTOUS LETTER to Grey having been dispatched, Wilson returned to his love-making. Mrs. Galt was at that moment more important to him than all the rest of the world. House, in New York eagerly awaiting Grey's reply, recorded in his 1915 diary:

"November 20 . . . The reports from Washington tell of a curious inertia everywhere. It is largely due, of course, to the President. He is so engrossed with his fiancée that he is neglecting business. I would go to Washington, but I know I would not be very welcome at this time, particularly if I attempted to stir him to action.

"One peculiar phase of the President's character develops itself more fully from time to time, that is, he 'dodges trouble.' Let me put up something to him that is disagreeable and I have great difficulty in getting him to meet it. I have no doubt that some of the trouble he had at Princeton was caused by this delay in meeting vexatious problems.

"Another phase of his character is his intense prejudice against people. He likes a few and is very loyal to them, but his prejudices are many and often unjust. He finds great difficulty in conferring with men against whom, for some reason, he has a prejudice and in whom he can find nothing good . . .

"November 27 . . . The President and I had a few minutes talk before dinner and during dinner as we were quite alone. Much to my surprise, he told me he had not read Sir Edward Grey's letter which I had sent him and which was of great importance. He brought it over with him so we might discuss it together . . ."

The letter from Sir Edward Grey, which the President had not found time to read because of the pressing claims of Mrs. Galt, was the answer to his offer to bring the United States into the war on the side of the Allies for the attainment of their avowed aims. Upon reading Grey's letter, Wilson was somewhat shocked to discover that Grey expressed only the mildest interest in his proposal. House had read the letter a few days before and, deeply disappointed, had recorded in his diary on November 25, 1915: ". . . the offer which I made in my letter — which was practically to ensure victory for the Allies — should have met a warmer reception. The British are in many ways dull."

Neither Wilson nor House suspected at that time that Grey was negotiating secret treaties partitioning the German and Turkish Empires, and that the secret war aims of the British coincided with their avowed war aims in only one point: the restoration of Belgium. The secret war aims of the British were the following: the destruction of the German Navy, the confiscation of the German merchant marine, the elimination of Germany as an economic rival, the extraction of all possible indemnities from Germany, the annexation of German East Africa and the Cameroons, the annexation of all German colonies in the Pacific south of the Equator, including the bird droppings of the island of Nauru, the control of Mesopotamia, Transjordania, Palestine and as much of Syria as they might be able to get away from the French, the extension of their sphere of influence in Persia, the recognition of their protectorates of Cyprus and Egypt, and a number of smaller items. All these secret war aims of the British were actually achieved in one form or another by the Treaty of Versailles; and Grey's letter to Wilson refusing the help of the United States for the achievement of the avowed war aims of England marks the beginning of the battle for and against the Treaty of Versailles. If Grey had accepted Wilson's offer, England might have got out of the conflict nothing more than those of her war aims which were respectable enough to mention publicly. She would have had to abandon the colossal gains with which she emerged from the war. Rather than abandon those gains the British Government preferred to fight without the aid of the United States. Wilson and House, trusting Grey implicitly and having no suspicion of the actual aims of England, concluded that Grey was just a bit dull and that House must go to London to explain to him personally the desirability of accepting their proposal.

On December 18, 1915, Wilson, ecstatically happy, was married to Mrs. Galt. On December 28, 1915, House left for England. Until February 22, 1916, he struggled to persuade Grey to allow the United States to enter the war on the basis of an agreement that peace should be made in accordance with the avowed war aims of the Allies, which included restoration of Belgium, the return of Alsace-Lorraine to France and the annexation of Constantinople by Russia. That Wilson should have offered to ask Americans to lay down their lives and pour out their wealth to get Constantinople for Russia indicates the power of the desires which were compelling his actions. Grey refused to commit himself in any way; but he made House believe that he would later accept the proposal. Grey and House drew up a memorandum recording House's offer and Grey's noncommittal replies, and House returned to Washington.

Wilson received House on March 6, 1916, with open arms. After a two-week honeymoon he had returned to the joys of early married life in the White House and he was in a state of exalted happiness. Again he possessed a mother representative, and he believed that House had arranged for him to be called to dictate peace to the world. All the main streams of his libido had found outlets wider and more splendid than any he had ever possessed. House communicated to Wilson his confidence that Grey would accept the project. "As House rose to leave he placed his hand on the Colonel's shoulder and said, 'It would be impossible to imagine a more difficult task than the one placed in your hands, but you have accomplished it in a way beyond my expectations.' When House intimated the pride he would feel if Wilson were only given the opportunity to realize the plan, the President responded, 'You should be proud of yourself and not of me, since you have done it all.' " Happy in the White House, the President of the United States awaited the permission of the British Secretary of State for Foreign Affairs to bring the United States into the war to achieve the avowed war aims of the Allies, and establish Woodrow Wilson as the Prince of Peace: *Arbiter mundi.*

XIX

No PERMISSION came from Grey, and on March 24, 1916, Wilson's happiness was shattered by a torpedo which blew off the entire forward end of the British Channel steamer *Sussex*. House advised sending Bernstorff home and preparing for immediate war. Wilson hesitated. His wish to dictate a perfect peace to the world had roots so deep that he could not abandon it. His supreme desire was to lead the United States into the war after an agreement with the Allies that he should be allowed to dictate the peace; but he still looked with horror on the prospect of leading the United States into a war which might end in an evil peace. He wanted to bring forth not war but peace, and an ultimate perfect peace was to him always the noble end which justified the means of war.

He delayed dealing with the *Sussex* case for nearly four weeks and in that interval struggled to persuade Grey to allow him to come into the war as the Prince of Peace. On April 6, 1916, he wrote personally on his own little typewriter the following cable to Grey: "Since it seems probable that this country must break with Germany on the submarine question unless the unexpected happens, and since, if this country should once become a belligerent, the war would undoubtedly be prolonged, I beg to suggest that if you had any thought of acting at an early date on the plan we agreed upon, you might wish now to consult with your allies with a view to acting immediately."

Nine years later, on March 14, 1925, looking back at these negotiations, Colonel House wrote: "I think the cable that Wilson and I jointly prepared for him to send Grey a mistake. We should have known that it would not bring the response we desired. I am not sure that we did not make a greater mistake in not going ahead and calling for a peace conference rather than leaving it to the Allies to be the judges."

Wilson's cable was, indeed, somewhat naïve. To the British Foreign Office it meant: Wilson admits that he must soon go to war with Germany; thus the defeat of Germany and the attainment of all our secret war aims is made certain; we shall be able to annex the German colonies and control a vast belt of Turkish territory extending from Egypt to Persia; we shall be able to destroy the German fleet, confiscate the German merchant marine and cripple the economic strength of Germany. Wilson now asks us to give up all these gains in return for — what? For the pleasure of making him dictator of the world. The reply which Wilson hoped to receive from Grey did not come.

Wilson, hoping that a word from Grey would save him from having to enter the war without guarantee as to the final terms of peace, delayed his note to Germany until April 18. Then, extremely unhappy, feeling that this note meant war but that the words he had used in his *Lusitania* notes left him no alternative, he wrote: "Unless the Imperial Government should not immediately declare and effect an abandonment of its present methods of submarine warfare against passenger and freight carrying vessels, the Government of the United States can have no choice but to sever diplomatic relations with the German Empire altogether." To Wilson's intense astonishment and relief, Germany on May 5, 1916, submitted.

On May 12, 1916, a telegram from Grey to House destroyed Wilson's belief that the Allies were about to invite him to dictate the peace. His feelings with regard to the war changed at once. He began to suspect that Grey was not the archangel House believed him to be; but he still hoped that he might persuade Grey to allow him to make war for peace. On May 16, 1916, he wrote to House that it was time to get down to "hard pan." America, he said, must either make a decided move for peace on some basis likely to be permanent, or else must insist on her rights against Great Britain as firmly as she had against Germany. To do nothing, he insisted was impossible. He asked House to prepare a stiff cable to Grey. House sent Grey various messages the gist of which was: either accept Wilson as dictator of the peace or look out for trouble. Wilson's hope emerged in his addresses of the following weeks. On May 20, 1916, he said: "I would like, therefore, to think the spirit of this occasion could be expressed if we imagined ourselves lifting some sacred emblem of counsel and of peace, of accommodation and righteous judgment before the nations of the world and reminding them of that passage in the Scripture, 'After the wind, after the earthquake, after the fire, the still small voice of humanity.' " On May 30, 1916, he said: "And this spirit is going out conquering and to conquer until, it may be, in the Providence of God, a new light is lifted up in America which shall throw the rays of liberty and justice far abroad upon every sea, and even upon the lands which now wallow in darkness and refuse to see the light." He was ready to lift up his light and let it shine even upon Germany. "Came He not into the world to save sinners?"

Grey refused to see the light.

Wilson finally began to feel that the Allies, not Germany, stood between him and achievement of his desire to be the Saviour of the World and became extremely angry with them. He ceased to talk about the war as if all right were on the side of the Allies and all wrong on the side of the Germans. On July 23, 1916, he wrote to House: "I am, I must admit, about at the end of my patience with Great Britain and the Allies. This black list business is the last straw . . . I am seriously considering asking Congress to authorize me to prohibit loans and restrict exportations to the Allies. It is becoming clear to me that there lies latent in this policy the wish to prevent our merchants getting a foothold in markets which Great Britain has hitherto controlled and all but dominated. Polk and I are compounding a very sharp note. I may feel obliged to make it as sharp and final as the one to Germany on the submarines. What is your own judgment? Can we any longer endure their intolerable course?"

From October 17, 1915, when he dispatched the letter to Grey which he believed would lead to his being called to make the peace, to March 26, 1916, when the torpedoing of the *Sussex* made it seem certain that he would be forced into the war without a previous agreement with the Allies that he should be allowed to dictate the peace, Wilson had been in a state of exalted happiness. He had a new wife and he had taken the world under his personal charge. When Lansing, Secretary of State, was so presumptuous as to wish to know before he read the newspapers what was the foreign policy of the United States, Wilson grew angry and declared that Lansing must understand that he, himself, was conducting foreign affairs and would do it in the way he thought best. He considered dismissing Lansing. As soon as the prospect of becoming the Prince of Peace began to fade he grew intensely nervous and unhappy, and indigestion and headaches began to harass him. He began to be irritated by all his associates, bored by his Cabinet, bored by the presidency. On May 3, 1916, "He declared he did not desire to be President any longer, and it would be a delightful relief if he could conscientiously retire." The only living being who still completely pleased him was Mrs. Wilson.

On June 16, 1916, he was renominated unanimously by the Democrats, and the slogan of his second campaign for the presidency was for the first time shouted by Governor Glynn of New York: "He kept us out of war!" Wilson, knowing that he had been doing his best for the previous eight months to get the American people into the war on his own terms, had such a bad conscience that he avoided in his personal campaign speeches all reference to the fact that he had kept the country out of war and all promises to keep the country out of war in the future. Nevertheless, he knew that he could not be elected without the votes of the Western states, which were overwhelmingly against war. Therefore he sanctioned the use of the slogan, "He kept us out of war!" by his party; and from thousands of posters and thousands of throats the idea was driven into the American people: Wilson kept us out of war and he will keep us out of war. The vote for Wilson was a vote for peace. If the people of America had known that he had been attempting to get them into the war, he would have been overwhelmingly defeated.

Throughout the presidential campaign, Wilson continued to be in a bad temper, and he loosed his nervous irritation impartially on his friends and enemies. Senator Lodge got wind of the instruction to Gerard which Wilson and Bryan had prepared to accompany the first *Lusitania* note. Lodge made a speech in Boston asserting that Wilson's strong note to Berlin had been tempered by a hint that it was not meant seriously, and that Germany had continued to violate American rights because she knew or believed that the United States would not, so long as Wilson was President, defend those rights. Wilson replied ". . . the statement made by Senator Lodge is untrue. No postscript or amendment of the *Lusitania* note was ever written or contemplated by me, except such changes that I myself inserted which strengthened and emphasized the protest. It was suggested, after the note was ready for transmission, that an intimation be conveyed to the German Government that a proposal for arbitration would be acceptable, and one member of the Cabinet spoke to me about it, but it was never discussed in Cabinet meeting and no threat of any resignation was ever made, for the very good reason that I rejected the suggestion after giving it such consideration as I thought every proposal deserved which touched so grave a matter. It was inconsistent with the purpose of the note. The public is in possession of everything that was said to the German Government."

The reader will recall that Wilson and Bryan had prepared the instruction together and had sent it to the coding room of the Department of State to be dispatched and delivered to the German Government at the same time as the *Lusitania* note. Every statement in Wilson's reply to Lodge is, in one interpretation, true. The denial as a whole is an extremely adroit evasion of the truth. Far more important than the fact that this is another illustration of Wilson's disinclination to let the truth stand in the way of his career is the fact that at this moment Wilson began to hate Senator Lodge with a violent hatred. We have previously noted that since Wilson's college days Lodge had stood in the relation of a father representative to him. When Lodge drove him to use this magnificent evasion of the truth he began to employ Lodge, as he had employed West, as an outlet for his reaction-formation against his passivity to his father. Thereafter his relations with Lodge were not controlled by reason but by a compulsion. He was compelled to try to defeat Lodge as he had been compelled to try to defeat West.

Wilson's mood had completely changed since the day in 1915 when he had described the Germans as "wild beasts." Because the Allies had refused to accept him as the Saviour of the World he had begun to feel that they were nearly as great enemies of God as the Germans. His wish to turn the war into a crusade which he might lead and his growing belief that the Allies might be as infidel as the Germans were remarkably juxtaposed in his speech of October 5, 1916, in which he said: "The singularity of the present war is that its origin and objects have never been disclosed . . . It will take a long inquiry of history to explain this war. But Europe ought not to misunderstand us. We are holding off not because we do not feel concerned, but because when we exert the force of this nation we want to know what we are exerting it for . . . When you are asked, 'Aren't you willing to fight?' reply, yes, you are waiting for something worth fighting for; you are not looking about for petty quarrels, but you are looking about for that sort of quarrel within whose intricacies are written all the texts of the rights of man, you are looking for some cause which will elevate your spirit, not depress it, some cause in which it seems a glory to shed human blood, if it be necessary, so that all the common compacts of liberty may be sealed with the blood of free men." This somewhat involved statement reduced to plain words means: The Allies are probably as selfish as the Germans. I do not wish to enter the war because of a "petty quarrel" with Germany over the use of her submarines. I desire supremely to lead a crusade for a perfect peace.

Two weeks after he had made this speech he received a communication from the German Government which informed him that if he did not soon make a move for peace, the unrestricted submarine warfare would probably be recommenced. His bad temper increased. Even House began to feel the weight of it. On November 2, 1916, House recorded in his diary: "The President arrived. McCormick and I met him and went with him to the Mayflower. We talked to him for an hour and a half and it was the most acrimonious debate I have had with him for a long while . . . He thought New York 'rotten to the core,' and should be wiped off the map . . . He thought both McCormick and I had 'New Yorkitis' and that the campaign should be run from elsewhere . . . However, before we left, the President put his arms around us both and expressed appreciation for what we were doing . . . He said: 'I do not believe the American people would wish to go to war no matter how many Americans were lost at sea.' He said he was sorry that this was true, but nevertheless it was his opinion."

Wilson became more and more indifferent as to the manner in which his campaign was conducted and, in spite of his Narcissism and his Super-Ego which of course demanded victory, seemed at times not to care whether he were elected or not. House recorded in his diary: "The President has left everything in our hands and has not telephoned, written a suggestion or given a word of advice although his fortunes are so wholly at stake." Wilson decided to resign the presidency immediately if Hughes should be elected, instead of serving the remaining four months of his constitutional term. On November 7, 1916, Wilson was re-elected President. He owed his election to the votes of the doubtful Western states, which were overwhelmingly against war.

In the summer and early autumn of 1916 the nervous, unhappy President was at odds with nearly everyone and everything in life. In the winter and early spring of 1916 he had been joyously happy. What had reduced him from happiness to discontent? There had been no alteration in his personal life. His second marriage was giving him the same sort of satisfaction that his first had given him. His wife pleased him completely; but just as Ellen Axson Wilson had been unable to keep him happy in the first year of their marriage, so Edith Bolling Galt Wilson was unable to keep him happy in the first year of their marriage. Satisfaction for the thin stream of his libido which was directed toward women could not compensate him for lack of satisfaction for the great streams of libido which had been directed toward his father. In the winter and early spring of 1916, when he had been so happy, he had believed that he was about to lead the United States into the war and became dictator of the peace. We have seen that this project offered a magnificent outlet for all the currents of libido directed toward his father. During the summer he had been forced to realize more clearly than ever that the people of America expected him to keep them out of the war and that the Allies would not permit him to dictate the peace. Thus he had been compelled to abandon the outlet for his desires directed toward his father which had given him such happiness. He had seen a vision of himself playing "the noblest part that has ever come to a son of man." All the main charges of his libido had united in an overwhelming desire to play that part. He could no longer be happy unless he could believe that he was about to become the Saviour of the World. If he could not lead the United States into war as a crusade for a peace to be dictated by himself, he did not much care whether he were President or not. And he was appalled by the specter which the German communication of October 18, 1916, raised before him. He felt that he might be compelled to drag the unwilling people of the United States into a "petty quarrel" which would result not only in the loss of thousands of American lives and billions of American wealth but also in the establishment of an evil peace. He had no exact idea of the secret war aims of the Allies; but the refusal of the Allies to accept the help of the United States for the achievement of their avowed war aims had convinced him that the secret aims of the Allies were no more noble than the aims of Germany. His desire to avoid a war that might result in an evil peace which would make new wars certain was almost as strong as his desire to lead a crusade for perfect peace. He wanted to bring forth not war but peace. His unconscious identification with Christ made it impossible for him to decide to go to war until he could believe that it was a war for peace.

XX

AFTER HE WAS re-elected Wilson decided that there was but one way out of his difficulties; he must demand that the war should stop in deference to the welfare of mankind, whether or not the British approved. He believed that such a moral demand would lead to negotiations and peace on the basis of the status quo ante bellum. House strongly opposed this course of action. Wilson's dependence on House was still very great. His contempt for Lansing had become intense and his distrust of Tumulty had driven him to ask his Secretary to leave the White House. He had not been able to resist Tumulty's tears and had retained him as his Secretary, but he was taking care to conceal his intentions from Tumulty as well as from Lansing. Aside from Mrs. Wilson and Dr. Grayson, House was the only human being he trusted.

On November 14, 1916, Wilson sent for House and they argued all day "over and over again the question of what was best to do," House "holding that for the moment nothing was necessary and we should sit tight and await further developments, the President holding that the submarine situation would not permit of delay and it was worthwhile to try mediation before breaking off with Germany." In his diary House recorded, "It was eleven o'clock before he proposed going to bed and I could see he was deeply disturbed." The next day House wrote, "I breakfasted alone. The President was unusually late which bespoke a bad night. I was sorry but it could not be helped. I dislike coming to the White House and upsetting him to the extent I often do . . . I told him that Lansing, Polk and others did not see any crisis in the U-boat controversy, and asked him to forget the entire matter for the present. This quieted him appreciably and put him in better spirits. He had been depressed . . ."

In spite of House's arguments, Wilson decided to appeal for peace; but House persuaded him to water down his appeal and to delay delivering it. The appeal was ready but Wilson was still hesitating about sending it when, on December 12, 1916, the German Government published a statement expressing Germany's willingness to enter a peace conference. Wilson, without consulting House, sent off his appeal with an explanation that it was not inspired by the German proposal. The note was signed by Secretary Lansing. In it Wilson showed clearly that he had come to regard the Allies and the Germans with almost equal suspicion. He wrote: "He takes the liberty of calling attention to the fact that the objects, which the statesmen of the belligerents on both sides have in mind in this war, are virtually the same, as stated in general terms to their own people and to the world."

Wilson's appeal brought no concrete result and he was intensely depressed by the failure of his effort. Yet so great was his horror of the path which he saw before him that he continued to struggle to achieve immediate peace in spite of House's efforts to persuade him to do nothing. House believed that Wilson should abandon hope of peace and prepare at once for war. Wilson refused to do anything to prepare the United States for war. He turned to the German Government, without the subservient intimacy but with the same hope with which he had turned to the British Government a year before. He tried to get a statement of reasonable peace terms from Germany; and he was ready, if Germany should put her specific terms in his hands and if they should be reasonable, to compel the Allies to accept them. He was so anxious to keep the United States out of war with Germany that he even considered making a "Bryan treaty" with Germany which would have made it impossible for the United States to go to war with Germany for a period of at least nine months, thus approaching the pacifist position which Bryan had urged him to take at the time of the sinking of the *Lusitania*. Wilson was, in fact, never so much of a pacifist as during the two months which preceded the declaration of unrestricted submarine warfare by Germany. Balked in his effort to become the Saviour of the World by way of war, he was determined to become a lesser Prince of Peace by refusing to go to war.

Count von Bernstorff called on House on December 27, 1916, and proposed that if the President approved he should cable his government suggesting it give its terms through him to go no further than the President and House. The President accepted this proposal with intense thankfulness. Bernstorff did his utmost to persuade his government to send him reasonable terms to present to the President and, through repeated conversations with House, led the President to believe that he probably would receive such terms.

Wilson began to believe the German Government was about to allow him to dictate the peace, as he had believed the year before that the British Government was about to allow him to do so. On January 4, 1917, when House urged him to prepare for war, he replied: "There will be no war. This country does not intend to become involved in this war. We are the only one of the great white nations that is free from war today, and it would be a crime against civilization for us to go in." He began to have most friendly feelings for Bernstorff, who was helping him wholeheartedly in his attempt to end the war, and to be very hostile to Lansing, whom he thought "was not in sympathy with his purpose to keep out of war." On January 11, he said to House: "Bernstorff is not nearly so dangerous to Lansing as he is to himself, for I came very near to asking for his resignation when he gave out the statement regarding the last note."

By January 19, 1917, he was so confident that Germany was about to tell him her terms, and that the terms would be reasonable, that he asked House to prepare in advance and put in code "a message to Balfour and Lloyd George . . . setting forth, as you get them in writing from Bernstorff, the terms and methods the Germans now indicate their willingness to accede to." On the same day, unknown to Wilson, Bernstorff received from the German Government not the reasonable terms of peace for which he and Wilson hoped but word that unrestricted submarine warfare would be recommenced on February 1, 1917.

Wilson, believing that peace, not war, lay just before him, delivered on January 22, 1917, one of the greatest speeches of his career, demanding "peace without victory." Bernstorff, on January 20, 1917, still struggling to avoid war between Germany and the United States but knowing that it was almost inevitable, had written to House: ". . . I am afraid the situation in Berlin is getting out of our hands. The exorbitant demands of our enemies and the insolent language of their note to the President seem to have infuriated public opinion in Germany to such an extent, that the result may be anything but favorable to our peace plans."

House sent this letter to Wilson. And Wilson on January 24, 1917, replied to House, "what is to be read between the lines of Sharp's message added to things such as you are learning from Hoover convinces me that if Germany really wants peace she can get it, and get it soon, *if she will but confide in me and let me have a chance.* What Bernstorff said to you the other day as trimmed and qualified by what he wrote afterwards amounts to nothing so far as negotiations between the belligerents are concerned. It occurs to me that it would be well for you to see Bernstorff again at once (not where your meeting can be noted, as the last one was, but at some place which is not under observation) and tell him that this is the time to accomplish something, if they really and truly want peace; that the indications that come to us are of a sort to lead us to believe that with something reasonable to suggest, as from them, I can bring things about; and that otherwise, with the preparations they are apparently making with regard to unrestrained attacks on merchantmen on the plea that they are armed for defense, there is a terrible likelihood that the relations between the United States and Germany may come to a breaking point and everything assume a different aspect. Feelings, exasperations are neither here nor there. Do they in fact want me to help? I am entitled to know because I genuinely want to help and have now put myself in a position to help without favor to either side . . . Again bless you for the encouragement and support you constantly give me. I feel very lonely sometimes and sometimes very low in my mind, in spite of myself."

It is impossible to withhold either sympathy or admiration from the Woodrow Wilson who wrote the above letter. In January 1917 he spoke, wrote and behaved like a great man; and it was in no way his fault that the deeply sincere efforts he was making at that time to bring about peace ended in war. That any man should conceive of himself as the Saviour of the World is perhaps absurd; but mankind would have been fortunate if at that moment Wilson's leadership had been accepted by the Great Powers.

House, replying to Wilson's letter of January 24, 1917, wrote on January 27: "I told him [Bernstorff] that Germany must give you something definite to work on, and immediately. I suggested that they state that they would be willing completely to evacuate both Belgium and France and that they would agree to *mutual* 'restoration, reparation, and indemnity.' "

If Wilson had received from the German Government terms drawn on the lines of the above suggestion, he would have used every power he possessed to bring about immediate peace on those terms. At that moment the Allies were so dependent on the United States for munitions and financial assistance that they could not have resisted a threat of embargo. There can be little doubt that Wilson would have been able to compel a "peace without victory." But the German Government did not want a peace without annexations and indemnities. Just as the British Government in 1915 and 1916 had preferred to fight for secret war aims without the help of the United States, so the German Government

in 1917, hoping for vast territorial gains and indemnities, preferred to bring the United States into the war as Germany's enemy.
On January 31, 1917, Count von Bernstorff, carrying out orders
from Berlin, wrote two letters: a letter to Secretary Lansing which
contained the declaration of unrestricted submarine warfare, and a
letter to Colonel House which contained Germany's terms of peace
— terms which would have made the Kaiser dictator of Europe.

XXI

WILSON WAS DUMBFOUNDED. He had hoped that without involving the United States in the war he was about to be able to arrange a just peace; he found that he was about to have to involve the United States in the war without guarantee that the peace would be just. He had come to believe that the aims of the Allies were as selfish as the aims of the Central Powers, and he felt that he was about to be forced to become the tool of the Allies. He would bring forth war without a perfect peace to hallow it. To his identification with Christ that was intolerable.

House recorded in his diary: "The President was sad and depressed, and I did not succeed at any time during the day in lifting him into a better frame of mine. He was deeply disappointed in the sudden and unwarranted action of the German Government. We had every reason to believe that within a month the belligerents would be talking peace. The President said he felt as if the world had suddenly reversed itself; that after going from east to west, it had begun to go from west to east, and that he could not get his balance.

"The question we discussed longest was whether it was better to give Bernstorff his passports immediately or wait until the Germans committed some overt act. When Lansing came, the discussion was renewed, and we all agreed that it was best to give him his passports at once, because by taking that course there was a possibility of bringing the Germans to their senses. . . . The President was insistent that he would not allow it to lead to war if it could possibly be avoided. He reiterated his belief that it would be a crime for this Government to involve itself in war to such an extent as to make it impossible to save Europe afterward. He spoke of Germany as 'a madman that should be curbed.' I asked if he thought it fair to the Allies to ask them to do the curbing without doing our share. He noticeably winced at this, but still held to his determination not to become involved if it were humanly possible to do otherwise."

On February 3, 1917, Wilson announced to the Congress that he had decided to break diplomatic relations with Germany but emphasized the pacific character of the policy he hoped to pursue. He could not bring himself to admit the fact, which nearly every other human being in America recognized, that war would inevitably follow. He still recoiled with horror from the fate he had so long tried to avoid. He did not object to war in principle but approved one kind of war and loathed another kind. He would have been overjoyed to lead the United States into a war which he felt sure was a crusade for peace; but he was unsure that the war would be a crusade for peace. Indeed, he was almost sure that the war would end in an evil peace. That thought he could not endure. He had to find some outlet for his desire to be the Prince of Peace.

An anger against Germany flooded him. Germany had forced him into the situation which his identification with Christ found intolerable. Mixed with this anger was a bitter resentment against the German Government. He felt that the rulers of Germany had played him for a fool by deceiving him as to their intentions in January 1917, and he vowed that he would never again take the word of the German Government. He especially blamed the German Government for the deception which had been practiced upon him, but he included in his hatred the entire governing class of Germany. That class became to him a hydra which was forcing him into the kind of war he had so long struggled to avoid. He continued to include in his "love of mankind" the German people, but the rulers of Germany were thenceforth, to him, devils. The distinction he invariably made between the German Government and the German people was first made in his own unconscious.

He began to feel extremely ill. He prayed for guidance. He could not sleep. His nervousness, headaches and indigestion increased. Until March 31, 1917, he held out against the tide of public opinion, which rose fast after the publication of Zimmerman's note to Mexico. In the early morning hours of April 1, 1917, he wrote his war message.

Mr. Frank Cobb's remarkable conversation with Wilson on that day shows clearly that when Wilson wrote his war message he was looking with helpless horror at the prospect of leading America into a war to make an evil peace. He felt that he was entering not the war he wanted but the war "the Allies thought they wanted, and that they would have their way in the very thing America had hoped against and struggled against." Nevertheless in the speech which he had prepared just before he talked with Cobb, he spoke as if he were entering the kind of war he wished to enter. Publicly he spoke as if he were leading the United States into a crusade for a perfect peace.

This looks like hypocrisy; but careful examination will show that it was not hypocrisy. Wilson's apparent hypocrisy was nearly always self-deception. He had an enormous ability to ignore facts and an enormous belief in words. His feeling for facts and phrases was the exact reverse of the feeling of a scientist. He could not bear to allow a beautiful phrase to be slain by a refractory fact. He delighted in allowing an unpleasant fact to be annihilated by a beautiful phrase. When he had invented a beautiful phrase, he began to believe in his phrase whatever the facts might be. At the end of March 1917 he found himself facing a dilemma neither horn of which he could bear to grasp. The facts told him that the war would end in an evil peace. So long as he stuck to the facts he had but two choices. He could take the position: the war will end in an evil peace but Germany's action compels us to enter it; or he could take the position: because the war will end in an evil peace I refuse to enter it in spite of Germany's provocations. He could not make himself accept either of these alternatives. On the one hand, he had announced so definitely and repeatedly the intention of the

United States to go to war, if Germany resumed sinking without warning, that to have refused to go to war would have made him and the United States an international jest. On the other hand, he could not force himself to say to the Congress: Germany has committed acts of war against us, therefore we shall have to declare war. I am sorry because it will cost us thousands of lives and billions of wealth and in the end there will be an outrageous peace which will condemn the world to another war worse than this one. His identification with Christ was so powerful that he could not ask for war except as a means to produce peace. He had to believe that somehow he would emerge from the war as the Saviour of the World. At the end of March 1917 he had to ask for a declaration of war. He could not ask about it except as a crusade for peace. He knew that it would not be a crusade for peace. The facts conflicted most terribly with his desire. And, in the manner which had become habitual to him, he escaped from his dilemma by ignoring the facts.

In his war message he expressed not his desire that the war should be a crusade but his belief that it was a crusade, and forgot the facts. But the facts were still vivid in his mind when Cobb talked to him, and to Cobb he expressed the facts. Thereafter he did his best to suppress the unpleasant facts, and in large measure he succeeded. The facts of the war became to him not the actual facts but facts which he invented to express his wishes. From time to time the actual facts rose out of suppression and he drove them back by renewed assertions of the imaginary facts which expressed his desires. He was persuaded by his own words. He began to believe utterly in his phrases. By his words he made many men in many lands believe that the war would end in a just peace, and he made all America "drunk with this spirit of self-sacrifice"; but no man was more deceived or intoxicated by his words than he himself.

From April 1, 1917, until his death there were in Wilson's mind two completely different sets of facts with regard to the war and the peace: the actual facts, suppressed in so far as possible, and the facts which his desires had invented. The divorce from reality which finally made him able to hail the Treaty of Versailles as "ninety-nine percent insurance against war" had its roots to be sure in his childhood; but it began to flower freely in the night when he wrote his war message and could not face the facts. He announced that the war was a crusade, knowing well in one locked chamber of his mind that the Crusaders would never reach the Holy Land but believing in the rest of his mind, because he desired to believe, that by the words he had learned at his father's knee he would lead all the armies past selfishness at last to the Holy Sepulcher of universal peace, where they would find — himself.

Wilson's uncertainty during the two months which separated the declaration of unrestricted submarine warfare on February 1, 1917, from his decision to go to war on April 1, 1917, seems to require a further brief word of comment. Even after he had written his war message his uncertainty persisted. Cobb's memorandum of his conversation with Wilson on April 1, 1917, contains the following passage: "I'd never seen him so worn down. He looked as if he hadn't slept and he said he hadn't. He said he probably was going before Congress the next day to ask a declaration of war, and he'd never been so uncertain about anything in his life as about that decision. For nights, he said, he'd been lying awake going over the whole situation. . . ." Wilson's identification of himself with Christ was unquestionably the chief psychic force which made it so difficult for him to make his decision; but an additional cause seems to have contributed to his excessive uncertainty. The scene in the Cabinet Room of the White House after Wilson had delivered his war message to Congress remains unexplained. Tumulty described it thus: "For a while he sat silent and pale in the Cabinet Room. At last he said: 'Think what it was they were applauding. My message today was a message of death for our young men. How strange it seems to applaud that. . . . While I have appeared to be indifferent to the criticism which has been my portion during these critical days, a few have tried to understand my purpose and have sympathized throughout with what I sought to do. . . . There is a fine old chap in Springfield, Massachusetts, editor of a great paper there who understood my position from the beginning and who has sympathized with me throughout this whole business. . . . I want to read you the letter I received from this fine old man.' As he read, the emotion he felt at the tender sympathy which the words conveyed gripped him. . . . 'That man understood me and sympathized.' As he said this, the President drew his handkerchief from his pocket, wiped away great tears that stood in his eyes, and then laying his head on the Cabinet table sobbed as if he had been a child."

Woodrow Wilson so long as his father lived had never made any important decision without asking his father's advice. And a portion of his uncertainty when he faced the supreme decision of his life seems to have sprung from the simple circumstance that he could not ask his father what he should do. He had to make his decision without his father's approval. Fresh from making it, he read a letter of "tender sympathy" from a "fine old man," then "laying his head on the Cabinet table sobbed as if he had been a child." Little Tommy Wilson still needed enormously the tender sympathy and approval of his "incomparable father."

XXII

THE POWER of Wilson's desire to lead a crusade which would end
in the establishment of himself as judge of the world was shown by
his volunteering to play that role in October 1915 and by his unhappiness in the months following May 1916, when he had become
convinced that England would not allow him to do so. As soon as
he had made himself believe that he might make the war a crusade
by saying that it was a crusade, he became calm, relatively happy
and strong. He carried great burdens during the war for a man
whose arteries were in precarious condition; and, although he continued to be troubled as usual by nervous indigestion and sick
headaches, he suffered no "breakdown." His Super-Ego, his Narcissism, his activity toward his father, his passivity to his father and
his reaction-formation against his passivity to his father were all
provided with supremely satisfactory outlets by the war. He was in
the act of accomplishing the impossible, he was the greatest man in
the world, he was killing men, he was the Saviour of the World and
he still had his wife and House to love.

He shrank from no measure which promised to make the en-
trance of the United States effective and decisive. He advocated
and obtained the passage of a conscription law. He organized new
governmental agencies to handle various war problems. He appointed as heads of these agencies the ablest men he could find
without distinction of party. In some cases his appointees were extremely efficient, in others extremely inefficient. He stood by them
all. He had neither the physical strength nor the desire to super-
vise the work of these new agencies or of the Departments. He had

taken foreign affairs into his own hands, and his personal interest lay less in the war than in the peace he hoped to make at the end of it. Senator Lodge, who had become Chairman of the Committee on Foreign Relations of the Senate, offered his cooperation in the field of foreign affairs. Wilson, who, as we have seen, had begun in 1916 to hate Lodge with an intense neurotic hatred, refused Lodge's offer of cooperation.

Balfour had replaced Grey as British Foreign Secretary. He came to America in April 1917 to inform Wilson that the condition of the Allies was desperate, that Russia was more than likely to withdraw from the war, that the morale of France was collapsing, that the financial condition of England threatened calamity and that the United States would have to carry a war burden enormously greater than either Wilson or anyone else in America had anticipated. He was prepared to reveal to Wilson some at least of the secret treaties of the Allies and to discuss war aims, assuming naturally that Wilson would insist on defining the precise aims for which he must ask the people of the United States to pour out a flood of blood and wealth.

Wilson wished to settle the question of war aims with Balfour definitely and at once. At that moment he might have written his own peace terms and might possibly have turned the war into the crusade for peace which he had proclaimed. The Allies were completely at his mercy. But House persuaded him not to demand a definition of war aims from Balfour by the argument that the discussion which would ensue would interfere with the prosecution of the war. Both Wilson and House overlooked the fact that all the warring powers had discussed their peace terms in detail while prosecuting the war with notable efficiency. House also inserted in Wilson's mind the picture of a Peace Conference at which England would loyally cooperate with the United States in establishing a just and lasting peace. And Wilson, always anxious to "dodge trouble," let slip this opportunity to avoid the terms of the Treaty of Versailles and secure the just peace of which he dreamed. Both the President and House seem to have misunderstood totally the sort of respect that the governments of Europe had for Wilson. For the President as wielder of the physical strength of America, they had the greatest respect; for Woodrow Wilson as a moral leader, they had no respect. So long as the physical assistance of the United States was vital to the Allies they had to defer to the President of the United States; but Woodrow Wilson was never able to make any European statesman "drunk with this spirit of self-sacrifice."

Balfour mentioned the existence of some of the secret treaties to Wilson and promised to send them to Wilson; but he never sent them and, having arranged for the utmost physical assistance from the United States, went home happy.

Although Wilson had failed to fight out the question of the secret treaties with Balfour, he expressed in all his public addresses absolute assurance that he would get a just and lasting peace at the end of the war, and again and again announced his friendship for the German people and his conviction that defeat would bring them not suffering but benefit. For example on June 14, 1917, he said: "We know now as clearly as we knew before we were ourselves engaged that we are not the enemies of the German people and that they are not our enemies. They did not originate or desire this hideous war or wish that we should be drawn into it; and we are vaguely conscious that we are fighting their cause, as they will some day see it, as well as our own . . . the great fact that stands out above all the rest is that this is a People's War, a war for freedom and justice and self-government amongst all the nations of the world, a war to make the world safe for the peoples who live upon it and have made it their own, the German people themselves included."

The indigestible fact of the existence of the secret treaties, however, lay in Wilson's mind and disturbed him. On July 21, 1917, he wrote to House: *"England and France have not the same views with regard to peace that we have by any means. When the war is* over we can force them to our way of thinking because by that time they will, among other things, be financially in our hands; but we cannot force them now, and any attempt to speak for them or to speak our common mind would bring on disagreements which would inevitably come to the surface in public and rob the whole thing of its effect. . . . Our real peace terms — those upon which we shall undoubtedly insist — are not now acceptable either to France or Italy (leaving Great Britain for the moment out of consideration).'

Wilson, with his curious habit of repeating to House the very thoughts which House had instilled in his mind, thus took the position definitely that he would ignore the secret treaties while the war was in progress because he did not want friction with the Allies; but asserted his determination to force the Allies to make a peace of reconciliation after victory by wielding the financial power of the United States. He felt sure that by using his economic weapons and his power to sway men by his words he could achieve the peace he desired. Again and again he promised publicly to the German people a peace of absolute justice.

It has often been asserted that Wilson was an arrant hypocrite, that he never intended to give the German people a decent peace, but that his pledges were merely weapons to destroy German morale, means to "build a fire behind the German Government." This is profoundly untrue. He realized fully that words of his which diminished the confidence of the German people in their government and made them believe that defeat would bring them a just and lasting peace would break down their will to fight and thus hasten Germany's collapse; but his intention to give the German people a fair peace was absolute. His deepest desires stood behind his wish to make such a peace. In his conversation with one of the authors of this volume after his exalted address of December 4, 1917, he expressed his true feelings: "Yes, and wasn't it horrible? All those Congressmen and Senators applauding every wretched little warlike thing I had to say, ignoring all the things for which I really care. I hate this war! I hate all war, and the only thing I care about on earth is the peace I am going to make at the end of it." As he said this, tears welled out of his eyes and ran down his cheeks. He believed utterly in his mission. He was the Son of God going forth to war to give the whole world perfect peace. He made his pledges to the German people with the utmost sincerity.

Once he had made those pledges and rejected the method of trying to make them good by immediate negotiations with the Allies, he felt in honor deeply bound to the German people and the American people and all other peoples of the world to make good his pledges by the means he had selected. He felt this obligation acutely and he was sure that he would have the courage to use his weapons, carry out his pledges and achieve a perfect peace. His confidence in his courage and his wisdom was absolute. On November 12, 1917, he said in an address: "What I am opposed to is not the feeling of the pacifists, but their stupidity. My heart is with them, but my mind has contempt for them. I want peace, but I know how to get it, and they do not."

On January 8, 1918, he delivered the address to the Congress in which he enumerated the Fourteen Points which became the basis for the armistice agreement and the Treaty of Versailles. To specify war aims even so unspecific as these was beyond his knowledge of Europe, and he based his points largely on recommendations from the House Inquiry, an organization of college professors which Wilson had asked House to form the previous September to prepare data for the Peace Conference.

By January 1918 Wilson believed fully that he could lift the war to the plane of a crusade for the principles of the Sermon on the Mount by the power of his words. His identification with Christ controlled his speeches. The extent to which this identification possessed him is illustrated by the fact that after reading George B. Herron's book in which he was likened to Jesus, he presented it to various friends, saying, "Herron is the only man who really understands me."

Ludendorff's successful attack of March 22, 1918, compelled Wilson to temper momentarily the Christian tenor of his speeches and to devote his attention to arousing war spirit in America, and it was not until September 1918 when the German armies were in full retreat that he was again able to speak freely as Christ.

House on September 2, 1918, wrote to Wilson asking him "to consider whether it would not be wise to try to commit the Allies to some of the things for which we are fighting?" and urged him to take the very course which he had persuaded him not to take when Balfour was in America in April 1917. Wilson, having made House's thoughts of April 1917 his own, refused to start negotiating with the Allies. Instead, on September 27, 1918, he spoke again as Christ, laying down four principles upon which peace must be made, the first of which was: "The impartial justice meted out must involve no discrimination between those to whom we wish to be just and those to whom we do not wish to be just. It must be a justice that plays no favorites and knows no standard but the equal rights of the several peoples concerned."

On September 29, 1918, Ludendorff, believing that his armies faced destruction, demanded that the German Government should ask for an immediate armistice. On October 5, 1918, the German Chancellor Prince Maximilian of Baden asked for an immediate armistice and accepted "as a basis for the peace negotiations, the programme laid down by the President of the United States in his Message to Congress of January 8, 1918, and in his subsequent pronouncements particularly in his address of September 27, 1918."

XXIII

WILSON SENT HOUSE to Paris to handle the armistice negotiations with the Allies. On October 19, 1918, when Clemenceau, Lloyd George and Sonnino faced House in Paris, they refused to make an armistice on the basis of the Fourteen Points. House threatened that the United States might make a separate peace. Wilson supported House by the following cablegram: "I feel it my solemn duty to authorize you to say that I cannot consent to take part in the negotiations of a peace which does not include the Freedom of the Seas, because we are pledged to fight not only Prussian militarism but militarism everywhere. Neither could I participate in a settlement which does not include a League of Nations because such a peace would result within a period of years in there being no guarantee except universal armaments, which would be disastrous. I hope I shall not be obliged to make this decision public."

Thus Wilson began his struggle with the Allies by supporting House's threat to make a separate peace, and added a personal threat to make public his disagreement with the leaders of the Allies if they should refuse to carry out the Fourteen Points. No words permissible in diplomatic negotiations could have shown more clearly his determination to fight for the peace he had promised to the world, or the strength of his desire to be the just judge of mankind. His identifications with the Trinity were in full control of him.

On November 14, 1918, he cabled to House with regard to the organization of the Peace Conference: "I assume also that I shall be selected to preside." House replied that since the Peace Conference was to be held in France, diplomatic usage made it necessary that Clemenceau should preside and that it might be unwise for Wilson to sit in the Peace Conference. Wilson was extremely displeased. He cabled to House on November 16, 1918: "It upsets every plan we had made. I am thrown into complete confusion by the change of programme. . . . I infer the French and British leaders desire to exclude me from the Conference for fear I might there lead the weaker nations against them. . . . I object very strongly to the fact that dignity must prevent our obtaining the results we have set our hearts to. . . ."

To lay down the law of God to the nations offered such a magnificant outlet for all Wilson's deepest desires that the mere suggestion that it might be wiser for him not to participate in the Conference threw him "into complete confusion." He wished to judge the world in person, in real presence, with undelegated authority, from the throne. He could not stay away from the Peace Conference.

Wilson, in the White House, contemplating the task before him, said to his Secretary: "Well, Tumulty, this trip will either be the greatest success or the supremest tragedy in all history; but I believe in a Divine Providence. If I did not have faith I should go crazy. If I thought that the direction of the affairs of this disordered world depended upon our finite intelligence, I should not know how to reason my way to sanity; but it is my faith that no body of men however they concert their power or their influence can defeat this great world enterprise, which after all is the enterprise of Divine mercy, peace and good will." Just as he had felt in 1912 that God had ordained that he should be the President of the United States, so he felt in 1918 that God had ordained that he should bring eternal peace to the world. He went to Paris as the delegate of God.

He intended to make the peace himself with the unobtrusive assistance of House; and, in spite of the fact that the Republicans had gained a majority in the Senate at the November election and that the treaty he was about to negotiate would require ratification by a two-thirds majority of the Senate, he refused the proposals of the Republicans that he should obtain their cooperation by taking with him two outstanding leaders of the Republican Party. As the agent of God he felt sure of his power to overcome any possible senatorial opposition.

He also refused to take with him any personal secretary. His mixed feelings with regard to Joe Tumulty, which had their root in the mingled emotions his baby brother Joe Wilson had aroused, produced this extraordinary phenomenon. He distrusted Tumulty so much that he would not take him to the Peace Conference. He loved Tumulty so much that he could not bear to hurt Tumulty's feelings by taking another secretary. He set out to remake the world with a personal staff consisting of his physician and two stenographers.

He took also the professors of the House Inquiry, who had read many books but were untrained in international negotiation. To these professors, during an audience on the steamship *George Washington,* in which he revealed how comprehensive was his ignorance of Europe, he said: "Tell me what is right and I'll fight for it; give me a guaranteed position." Beyond this he did nothing to organize his forces. He had no detailed plan of diplomatic campaign and no diplomatic organization. He had not bothered personally about the organization of the American delegation and, when he discovered on the *George Washington* that the Secretary and Assistant Secretaries of the American delegation, selected by Lansing, were men for whom he had personal contempt, he was furious. On arriving in Paris on December 14, 1918, he said to House that he intended to dismiss these secretaries and select others. House persuaded him not to take this drastic action. Then in so far as possible, Wilson avoided any contact with Lansing and the secretariat of the American delegation, thus cutting himself off from such assistance as his diplomatic service might have been able to give him.

House urged him to take a personal secretary at once. Wilson refused, saying, "It would break Tumulty's heart." House then offered Wilson the services of his own staff, the head of which was House's son-in-law, whom Wilson disliked. House's secretariat was housed in the Hotel Crillon; Wilson was in residence in the Murat Palace half a mile away. The result was that, while Wilson referred many matters to House during the Conference, he never employed House's secretariat as his own and personally did his own work without any secretary. He sat in the Murat Palace with his wife, his doctor and his two stenographers attending personally to thousands of unimportant matters which should never have been allowed to occupy his attention or his scant supply of physical strength. The confusion in his papers and his mind became appalling.

Nevertheless, he believed during his first weeks in Europe that he was about to give the world the perfect peace he had promised. He was received by all the peoples of Europe as a Saviour. To the adulation of France and England was added the adoration of Italy, where peasants were burning candles in front of his picture, and the desperate faith of Germany, where tired soldiers marching home passed through a sad arch of honor bearing the words:

> Seid willkommen, wackre Streiter,
> Gott und Wilson heifen weiter.

Wilson spent three happy weeks showing himself to adoring Europeans, and it is not remarkable that his confidence in himself and his mission should have increased. In Buckingham Palace, after dinner he made an address in which he referred regally to the citizens of the United States as "my people." In Milan he rose above all Presbyterian precedents and went to the opera on Sunday. There the screaming worship of the crowd passed into delirium. Wilson began to throw kisses to the crowd, the crowd threw kisses back to Wilson, and Wilson threw kisses back again to the crowd until delirium reached ecstasy. It is not remarkable that he returned from his travels convinced that the peoples of Europe would rise and follow him even against their own governments.

XXIV

HE RETURNED to Paris on January 7, 1919, eager to get to work. But no program for the Conference had been agreed upon. Wilson personally had rejected the logical French program because it made the League of Nations the last question to be considered by the Conference; and he wished the League of Nations to be established before the peace terms were discussed. He insisted on giving the guarantee of the United States for the peace before agreement on any term of the peace. He explained his preference for this procedure to House on December 14, 1918, saying that he intended "making the League of Nations the centre of the whole programme and letting everything revolve around that. Once that is a *fait accompli* nearly all the very serious difficulties will disappear."

The practical disadvantages of Wilson's plan of procedure were obvious. By guaranteeing the peace terms before he knew that they were fair and satisfactory and ought to be perpetuated, he risked the possibility that at the end of the Conference he would find that he had pledged the United States to maintain terms which were unfair and ought not to be perpetuated, and had thereby made certain the involvement of the American people in the future wars which might be expected to arise from unfair settlements. Moreover, by guaranteeing the peace in advance he handed to the statesmen of the Allies one of his strongest diplomatic cards. The ultimate hope of Lloyd George, Clemenceau and Orlando was to obtain the guarantee of the United States for the annexations they expected to make. The British had been attempting to get this guarantee by way of a League of Nations ever since Grey's 1915 letters to House. And on January 7, 1919, when House pointed out to Clemenceau, who was ready to accept a League but skeptical as to its value, that he could get the boundaries of France guaranteed by the United States by way of a League of Nations, Clemenceau became the advocate of a much stronger League than either the British or Wilson wanted. If Wilson had stuck to the point of view which he had repeatedly expressed in his address of January 22, 1917, and had reasserted in his letter to House of March 22, 1918, that a trustee for the American people could in honor ask them to guarantee the peace only "if the final territorial agreements of the Peace Conference are fair and satisfactory and *ought* to be perpetuated," the wish of the leaders of the Allies to obtain the guarantee of the United States would have been an influence in favor of fair terms. But with the guarantee of the United States given in advance they felt free to insist on their extreme terms.

The practical advantages of Wilson's plan of procedure were, to say the least, somewhat problematical. He believed that the establishment of the League of Nations by making "safety antedate the peace" would give the statesmen assembled in Paris such a feeling of security and brotherhood that he could lead them to treat all nations in the spirit of the Sermon on the Mount and that "all the very serious difficulties would disappear." Yet the conversion of Lloyd George, Clemenceau and Orlando was so doubtful that we must suspect that Wilson's reason was acting again in the service of his libido and that his real motives were in his unconscious.

The reader will perhaps recall his letter of July 21, 1917 to House, in which he wrote, *"England and France have not the same views with regard to peace that we have* by any means. When the war is over we can force them to our way of thinking because by that time they will, among other things, be financially in our hands . . ."* The war was over. All the Allies were financially in his hands. His stern cable at the time of the armistice negotiations had made it seem certain that when he reached Paris he would say to

Lloyd George, Clemenceau and Orlando: Gentlemen, I have come here to make peace on the basis of my Fourteen Points and on no other basis. Those points must be interpreted in a spirit of the most impartial justice, as I said on September 27 last. You pledged your word to make peace on that basis by your acceptance of the armistice agreement. If you attempt to break your word and evade your obligations under the armistice agreement, I will under no conditions bind the people of the United States to guarantee the peace you make and thus involve them in the future wars an evil peace will ensure. I will withdraw from the Conference, publicly denounce you as the enemies of permanent peace, cut off the financial and economic assistance of the United States which alone is enabling you to live, make a separate peace on just terms with Germany and leave you to face the peoples of your respective countries who want a just peace and a permanent peace whether you want it or not.

If he had followed that course he might possibly have obtained the "just and lasting peace" he had promised to the world. But at some time between the armistice negotiations and his arrival in Paris on December 14, 1918, he decided to fight for the peace he wanted not with these masculine weapons but with the weapons of femininity, not with force but with persuasion. He had tremendously powerful economic and financial weapons in his hands. All the Allied nations were living on supplies and credits from America. But to use those weapons involved a fight of precisely the sort he had never made and could not make in person, unless compelled to by his reaction-formation against his passivity to his father. He had never dared to have a fist fight in his life. All his fighting had been done with his mouth. When he had sent his strong cable to House, he had been in the White House far from the field of battle. Isolated in that comfortable citadel he could thunder like Jehovah; but when he personally approached battle with Clemenceau and Lloyd George, the deep underlying femininity of his nature began to control him and he discovered that he did not want to fight them with force. He wanted to preach sermons to them and convert them to righteousness by paraphrases of the Sermon on the Mount. As a statesman in Paris he was the true son of the Reverend Joseph Ruggles Wilson, overwhelmed by his passivity to his father.

His reason, in the service of his fear of a masculine fight and his unconscious desire to be Christ, invented the comforting theory that he could obtain all that he wished without a fight, that he could hand all his weapons to his enemies and convert them by that noble gesture into saints. He decided not to use his economic and financial weapons, not to withhold his guarantee of the peace until the terms of the peace had been drawn as he wished them to be drawn, but to continue to give colossal credits to the Allies and to establish the League of Nations and guarantee the peace before its terms were considered. His obedient reason told him that the statesmen assembled in Paris would then feel such a sense of security and brotherhood and such a love for his own noble nature that they would hearken to his appeals to treat all nations in the spirit of the Sermon on the Mount. He began to envisage the Peace Conference in a form which was both familiar and deeply congenial to him: the form of a brotherly debating club; the form of the Lightfoots and of the debating societies of Davidson, Princeton, the University of Virginia, Johns Hopkins and Wesleyan. He felt himself again about to draw up a constitution for a debating club to be called the League of Nations, and pictured himself taking the floor in a brotherly assembly at the Peace Conference to "lead the weaker nations" against the stronger powers. The professors of the Inquiry would tell him what was right and, in debate, he would fight for it. In that assemblage of brothers he would "make men drunk with this spirit of self-sacrifice," and overcome by his words all opposition and lead the world to lasting peace and himself to immortality. The prospect pleased him exceedingly. Not only did it enable him to "dodge trouble" but also to display to the rulers of the world those of his qualities of which he was proudest.

Unfortunately his hypothesis had nothing to do with the facts. His belief, that once the League was a *fait accompli* nearly all the serious difficulties would disappear, had no basis in reality, but only a source in his unconscious. The establishment of the League altered in no degree the characters of the statesmen assembled in Paris. It gave them indeed a final weapon to use against him. They soon came to realize that the League of Nations had become to Wilson a sacred thing, a part of himself, his title to immortality, his law; that he could not bring himself to withdraw his guarantee of the peace no matter what terms they demanded; and that they could themselves use the League as a weapon against him by telling him that he would lose the League unless he accepted their terms.

Wilson, having convinced himself that once the League of Nations was established all shadows would disappear in a sunrise of Christian love, put his entire energy into the work of drawing up a constitution for the League. He faced the military, economic and territorial problems of the Conference by turning his back to them, and it was not until January 24, 1919, that he was compelled to face an unpleasant reality. On that day, speaking for the British Empire, Lloyd George said that he opposed the return to Germany of any of her colonies. Point Five of Wilson's Fourteen Points, which the British Empire had accepted, read: "A free, open-minded, and absolutely impartial adjustment of all colonial claims, based upon a strict observance of the principle that in determining all such questions of sovereignty the interests of the populations concerned must have equal weight with the equitable claims of the Government whose title is to be determined." Wilson faced his first test. His reply was awaited with acute anxiety not merely because of the importance of the colonies but because his answer would indicate the manner in which he intended to battle for his Fourteen Points. "President Wilson said that he thought all were agreed to oppose the restoration of the German Colonies." Thus there was no battle. Wilson did not fight. With this sentence Germany lost her colonies and Wilson began his march down to the Treaty of Versailles.

Lloyd George, emboldened by Wilson's failure to fight, then

made a more audacious advance. "He would like the Conference to treat the territories as part of the Dominions which had captured them." This was too much for Wilson. He had made the great concession that the colonies should be taken away from Germany; but he could not bring himself to concede that they had already been annexed by the British Empire. He insisted that a moral veil called Mandate should be drawn over the face of each annexation.

This was the only concrete problem of peace terms which Wilson faced before his return to America on February 14, 1919. He conceded the main point without question and he refused to concede a point of minor importance because he felt that annexation could not be reconciled with words he had used in his speeches, and might endanger the League of Nations.

On February 14, 1919, just before his departure for America he read to a plenary session of the Peace Conference the Covenant of the League of Nations. He was a very happy man. He was sure that the Covenant meant lasting peace for the whole world. He concluded his speech with words which indicated clearly the effect he believed the Covenant would have on all mankind, Lloyd George and Clemenceau included: "Many terrible things have come out of this war, gentlemen, but some very beautiful things have come out of it. Wrong has been defeated, but the rest of the world has been more conscious than it ever was before of the majesty of right. People that were suspicious of one another can now live as friends and comrades in a single family, and desire to do so. The miasma of distrust, of intrigue is cleared away. Men are looking eye to eye and saying 'We are brothers and have a common purpose. We did not realize it before but we do realize it, and this is our covenant of fraternity and friendship.' " He believed that the mere existence of the piece of paper he held in his hands established the Brotherhood of Man. He had given peace to the world. All fear, hatred, greed and cruelty would vanish. The Covenant was a *fait accompli*.

XXV

ON THE EVENING of Wilson's departure for America, February 14, 1919, House recorded in his diary: "The President bade me a fervent goodbye, clasping my hand and placing his arm around me . . . He looked happy, as well indeed he should." That was the last time Woodrow Wilson ever placed his arm around Colonel House.

Floods of words have been devoted to explanations of the death of Wilson's love for House. The explanations vary astonishingly. On the one hand, Mrs. Wilson is depicted as a sort of female demon, "the woman in purple," who destroyed a beautiful friendship; on the other hand, House is depicted as a Judas who conspired to cut the League of Nations out of the treaty of peace while Wilson was in America. The explanations which lie between these extremes usually conclude feebly that the matter is a tragic mystery. Examination of the facts convinces us, however, that Mrs. Wilson was no female demon, that House was no Judas and that the matter is no mystery. We are also unfortunately convinced that we shall have to discuss the question at length, because Wilson's public actions and personal reactions during the remainder of his life cannot be understood unless his relationship to House is understood.

Let us begin by reminding the reader that Wilson was bound to House by both conscious and unconscious bonds. His dependence on House's advice was enormous and he was at least partially conscious of the benefits he received from House's services; but the foundation of Wilson's love for House was the fact that in his unconscious House represented little Tommy Wilson. By identifying himself with his father and House with himself, he was able to recreate in his unconscious his own relationship to his own "incomparable father," and, in the person of House, to receive from himself the love he wanted and could no longer get from his own father. Thus by the familiar method of double identification Wilson's passivity to his father found outlet through House. He had another important outlet for this desire, his unconscious identification with Jesus Christ; but a younger, smaller man to love was essential to his happiness.

Wilson's love for House, warm from its birth in 1911, was hottest in the six months which followed the death of his first wife. From August 1914 to January 1915 House was his chief love-object. In addition to his passivity to his father, which as usual was finding outlet by way of House, his passivity to his mother probably also then found outlet through his friend. We have noted that in the months which followed Ellen Axson Wilson's death Wilson replaced his lost mother substitute by identifying himself with his mother. House, representing little Tommy Wilson, must have received from Wilson during those months at least a portion of the love which Wilson wanted and could not get from his mother or a mother substitute. Thus, until House went abroad in January 1915, Wilson was able to re-create in some measure both his relationship to his father and his relationship to his mother by playing father and mother to the Colonel, and it is not surprising that his eyes were moist when he said farewell to his representative of himself.

As we have already noted, Wilson then became so desperately lonely that he approached nervous collapse, and his physician, Admiral Grayson, insisted that he should have music and guests at the White House. Among them was Mrs. Galt, with whom Wilson at once fell in love. He was deeply in love with her when House returned to America in June 1915; but his emotional dependence on his friend remained almost as great as before the Colonel's departure. He told House all about his love, continued to address

House in his letters as *My dear, dear Friend* or *Dearest Friend,* and asked House's advice as to when and how he should announce his engagement and get married.

Wilson married Mrs. Galt on December 18, 1915, and House left America ten days later to persuade the British Government to allow Wilson to dictate the peace. When House returned to Washington on March 6, 1916, Wilson, believing that House had arranged for him to be called to save mankind, received the Colonel with open arms. But he received House's report in the course of a two-hour automobile ride, with Mrs. Wilson seated in the middle of the back seat between him and his friend. She was a large woman to talk across.

In the late winter and early spring of 1916, when Wilson believed that he was about to be called to end the war, an enormous quantity of libido derived from his passivity to his father charged his unconscious identification with Jesus Christ. So large was this charge of libido that, when Wilson saw in May 1916 that he was not to be summoned to save the world, he could not withdraw it from his identification with Christ. He had to go on trying to become the same Saviour in the world of reality that he was in his unconscious. His unconscious identification with the Saviour seems to have become a fixation.

In the period when Wilson believed that House had prepared the way of the Lord and made his paths straight, his love for the Colonel was intense. Hope held out and disappointed is a potent factor in the unconscious. He who disappoints a hope betrays a hope. House had promised Wilson that he could play "the noblest part that has ever come to a son of man," that he could save mankind. House had originated the idea, conducted the negotiations and led Wilson to believe that the moment was close at hand when he might appear as the Prince of Peace. House was responsible for both his hope and his disappointment. He began to find House irritating and fell into an extraordinarily bad temper with everyone on earth except his wife.

Once before in his unconscious Wilson had regarded himself as the Only Begotten Son of God and had been disappointed. His brother Joe had burst into the world and destroyed his unique position. We have noted that a portion of Wilson's passivity to his father had reached his younger friends by way of his brother Joe, and that all those friends were not only representatives of little Tommy Wilson but also in some measure representatives of little Joe Wilson, the original betrayer. In the summer of 1916, when the expectations which House had aroused in Wilson were disappointed, the hostility, suspicion and sense of betrayal which had been fastened on the infant Joe seems to have been transferred in some measure to House. This substitution of House for the original disappointer and betrayer, though not very important in 1916, was doubtless the original factor in the eventual destruction of Wilson's love for House.

It was easy for Wilson in the summer of 1916 to diminish somewhat the quantity of his libido which found outlet by way of House. He had just enormously increased the quantity of his libido directed toward his unconscious identification with Jesus Christ. Both his love for House and his identification with the Saviour were outlets for the same great source of libido, his passivity to his father. Therefore, as his unconscious identification wich Christ increased, his need to love House decreased. His passivity to his father was, however, the most powerful of all his desires and he needed both to identify himself with Christ and to love a representative of little Tommy Wilson in order to give it adequate outlet. House remained his most valued representative of Tommy Wilson; but in the summer of 1916 he seems to have taken the important step of turning the major charge of libido produced by his passivity to his father away from House to his unconscious identification with Christ.

Wilson was encouraged to diminish the intensity of his love for House by the quiet influence of his wife. She did not dislike House but she was not fond of him. She was not altogether pleased by his control of her husband and resented the growing belief in

America that her husband's thoughts and actions originated in the brain of House. All his life Wilson was sensitive to the atmosphere created by his mother representative.

After his re-election in November 1916 Wilson wished again to offer mediation. House vigorously opposed any move to open this outlet toward which the main current of Wilson's passivity to his father was directed. Wilson had several arguments with House which so upset him that he could not sleep in the nights which followed them. In the end, against the advice of House, he decided to appeal for peace. Thus in the autumn of 1916 House stood in the way of the immense quantity of libido which charged Wilson's unconscious identification with Christ. He was no longer the forerunner of the Lord but was actually attempting to prevent Wilson from trying to become the Saviour. It is not difficult to imagine the effect on Wilson's unconscious. In the depths of his mind he must have felt that House was opposed to his being the Only Begotten Son of God, that House had become the same sort of enemy that his brother Joe had been. He decided, in spite of House's opposition, that he would be the Saviour. He issued his appeal for peace on December 18, 1916; and in January 1917, he ceased to address House in his letters as *Dearest Friend,* and reverted to *My dear House.* In the same month of January he spoke magnificently in his "peace without victory" address, and at the end of that month he wrote beneath the etching we have placed at the beginning of this book the extraordinary words: "May this autograph suggest to those who see it a good man and an honest lover of his fellowmen."

It is not difficult to observe what had happened in Wilson's unconscious. He had merely turned more of the libido which sprang from his passivity to his father away from House into his identification with Jesus Christ. House still remained the best substitute he had for little Tommy Wilson, and his minor outlet for his passivity to his father; but identification with Christ had become the main conduit for this great flood of libido and neither House nor any

other friend could resist it, and by opposing it could achieve only
the status, in Wilson's unconscious, of the friend of the Saviour
turned betrayer, the status of Judas Iscariot.

Thus the disappointment of the hope which House had aroused
in Wilson, the nurture of his irritation with the Colonel by Mrs.
Wilson, and House's opposition to his wish to move to make himself the Saviour, reduced House from *Dearest Friend* to *My dear
House*. House still represented little Tommy Wilson but an imperfect Tommy Wilson who had about him a distinct aroma of
little Joe Wilson, the original betrayer who had ended Wilson's
happy uniqueness as the Only Begotten Son of God his Father. A
few suits of the Colonel's continued to hang in a closet in the
White House, his shaving things continued to lie ready in an ad-
joining bathroom, the White House room known as "Colonel
House's room" continued to be kept vacant awaiting his arrival;
whenever Wilson had to make an address he called in House to
advise him as to what he should say, and he seldom made an important decision without asking House's advice; but he never again
loved House so intensely as in the years from 1912 to 1917.

Although Wilson's intellectual dependence on House continued
to be extraordinary throughout 1917 and 1918, two personal actions of the Colonel thoroughly displeased him. House, after obtaining Wilson's consent, established in the autumn of 1917 an organization of college professors called the Inquiry to collect data
for use at the Peace Conference. House chose as the head of the
Inquiry his own brother-in-law Sidney Edward Mezes, President of
the College of the City of New York. Wilson had disliked Mezes
ever since he had hoped that a brother-in-law of his might be
chosen as President of the College of the City of New York, and
House's brother-in-law had been chosen in preference to his own
brother-in-law. He considered the appointment of Mezes an act of
nepotism on the part of House and was not pleased. Then, when it
seemed desirable that someone should be appointed to sit at the
end of a private telephone wire in the Department of State to keep

the Colonel, in New York, in close touch with Washington, House again selected a member of his own family, his son-in-law Gordon Auchincloss, a young man who had no connection with the Department of State and had no experience in foreign affairs. Wilson disliked Auchincloss and repeatedly in the White House criticized the Colonel for "nepotism" in the cases of Mezes and Auchincloss. But he never made the criticism to House face to face, and House continued to be unaware of the extent to which his brother-in-law and son-in-law irked Wilson. Thus it is evident that in spite of their intimate intellectual collaboration in matters of international politics, Wilson had receded from his complete personal frankness with House. Mrs. Wilson had become his confidante.

It is, after all, only normal that a man should be to some extent reserved in conversation with even his most intimate friend; and it is clear that in Wilson's unconscious until the armistice House still represented little Tommy Wilson although he was no longer quite a perfect little Tommy Wilson. "Mr. House is my second personality. He is my independent self. His thoughts and mine are one." Those words which Wilson used in 1912 showed vividly the extent to which he regarded House as himself; but his sense of identity with the Colonel was revealed almost as vividly in October 1918 by his sending House to Europe to negotiate the armistice without giving him instructions of any kind. House noted in his diary: "As I was leaving he said, 'I have not given you any instructions because I feel you will know what to do.' I had been thinking of this before he spoke and wondered at the strange situation our relations had brought about. I am going on one of the most important missions anyone ever undertook, and yet there is no word of direction, advice or discussion between us."

House in Paris displeased both Wilson and Mrs. Wilson intensely by his suggestion that they should not come to Europe but should remain in Washington during the peace negotiations. Wilson wanted to go in person to judge the world. House had become a world figure by his handling of the armistice negotiations. If

Wilson had remained in the White House, House inevitably would have negotiated the peace. His delicate suggestion that Wilson should not come to Paris therefore appeared in Washington to be a suggestion that he himself should lay down the law of his father in the White House. It was no part of the plan of either Wilson or Mrs. Wilson that House should become the Saviour of the World. They went to Paris.

House, suffering from influenza, awaited their arrival with his son-in-law Auchincloss beside him. Wilson had refused to allow his son-in-law Sayre to go with him to the Conference although it was reasonable that Sayre, as a member of the Inquiry, should have been invited to go. Wilson's conscious dislike of nepotism, whatever its unconscious source, had become intense. He had issued orders that all wives of all men attached to the American peace delegation should be left in America. When he boarded the *George Washington,* he found on board not only House's brother-in-law Mezes but also Mrs. Mezes and House's very charming daughter, the wife of the son-in-law Auchincloss. Wilson became less enthusiastic than ever about House's tendency to favor his relatives. House had no suspicion of this fact and when Wilson, on arriving in Paris, furiously denounced the secretariat that Lansing had chosen, House generously offered him the services of Auchincloss! Wilson declined with thanks. But when Wilson went to London to visit the King, House attached Auchincloss to the presidential party to instruct Wilson in English etiquette, adding Sir William Wiseman to instruct Auchincloss! Wilson was infuriated by Auchincloss' admonitions. After Wilson had returned to Paris in January 1919, House, seeing clearly the confusion into which the President's papers and mind were falling because he had no secretary but quite blind to the depth of the President's dislike of Auchincloss, again urged Wilson to take a secretary: Auchincloss.

The entire matter of Auchincloss would have been unimportant if it had stopped with these rather comic attempts of House to persuade Wilson to enter into an intimate relationship with a man he disliked; but House's son-in-law, unfortunately, was in the habit of talking about Wilson in a most disparaging manner, referring to him as "little Woody" and spreading the impression that House and Auchincloss controlled Wilson's actions. Several other men in House's entourage were as indiscreet as Auchincloss in their remarks about the relative importance of House and Wilson. There were also among the Americans in Paris a number of old women of both sexes who collected droppings from the House secretariat and ran to insert the tittle-tattle in Mrs. Wilson's ear. Mrs. Wilson began to believe that House encouraged his subordinates to talk disparagingly about her husband in order to make himself appear the great man of America.

House, in point of fact, was as self-effacing as ever. In the meetings of the Committee on the League of Nations he subordinated himself to the point of not even playing second fiddle to Wilson; he merely turned the pages of the score for his master. So pleased was Wilson with his faithful servant that he invited House to take his place in the Council of Ten during his absence in America and asked House to work out with the representatives of the Allies the terms of a preliminary peace, and at the moment of his departure bade House a fervent goodbye, clasping his hand and placing an arm around him. It is clear that in spite of the diminution in the quantity of Wilson's passivity to his father which was finding outlet by way of House, his identification of House with little Tommy Wilson remained intact until after his departure for America on February 14, 1919.

Wilson's own words with regard to the course of action he wished House to pursue during his absence may be found in the minutes of the Supreme War Council of February 12, 1919, and in Colonel House's diary of February 14, 1919. At the morning meeting of the Supreme War Council of February 12, 1919, Wilson strongly supported a proposal of Balfour's that "the final naval and military terms of peace" should be drawn up as soon as possible and imposed on Germany. Clemenceau objected that the strictly

military terms would depend on the political, economic and financial terms. At the afternoon meeting of the Council, when the discussion was resumed, Wilson argued that Clemenceau's objection
could be overcome by reducing Germany's armed forces to the extreme conceivable limit: "the amount of armed force required by
Germany to maintain internal order and to keep down Bolshevism." No matter what the other terms of peace might be, it would
obviously be impracticable to reduce Germany's forces below this
limit.

Clemenceau, quick to see the advantage to France in the proposal of the President of the United States that Germany's armed
forces should be reduced to this extreme extent, but apparently
aware, as he had been in the morning, that a treaty of peace —
whether or not labeled "preliminary" — would make peace, and
still determined to include political, economic and financial terms,
said that he was prepared to accept Wilson's proposal; "before
doing so, however, he would like more precise information on certain points . . . Though the report of the experts might be received in a short time, he would not like to discuss a matter of such
importance in the absence of President Wilson."

Wilson replied "that M. Clemenceau had paid him an undeserved compliment. In technical matters most of the brains he
used were borrowed: the possessors of these brains were in Paris.
He would, therefore, go away with an easy mind if he thought that
his plan had been adopted in principle . . . If his plan were
agreed on in principle, he would be prepared to go away and leave
it to his colleagues to decide whether the programme drafted by
the technical advisers was the right one. He did not wish his absence to stop so important, essential and urgent a work as the preparation of a preliminary peace. He hoped to return by the 13th or
15th March, allowing himself only a week in America. But he did
not wish that during his unavoidable absence, such questions as the
territorial question and questions of compensation should be held
up. He had asked Colonel House to take his place while he was
away.

"M. Clemenceau said that he was completely satisfied."

He had every reason to be completely satisfied, since Wilson had proposed the elimination of the German Army and Navy, except for a minute force to preserve internal order, and had then opened the preliminary treaty to the inclusion of the territorial and financial terms which Clemenceau thought necessary.

Before the discussion closed, Wilson showed clearly that he had in mind, at least for a moment, an actual treaty of peace which would bring the armistice to an end by saying that he advocated a renewal of the armistice *sine die:* "The armistice would then be ended by the formulation of definite preliminary terms of peace on military conditions." Wilson added, however, "the question of the Kiel Canal and the question of the cables, included in the naval report, would have to be dissociated from the purely naval conditions to be imposed at the close of the Armistice. These matters concerned the ultimate peace."

It is impossible to avoid the conclusion that Wilson had in mind three distinct states of international relations: "armistice," "preliminary peace," "ultimate peace." And it is obvious that he had overlooked the fact that a treaty of peace, whether labeled preliminary or not, makes peace and must be ratified by the Senate of the United States in order to bind the United States. There is no such thing in international law as a state of preliminary peace. There is war, armistice or peace. The word "preliminary" alters no fact. A "preliminary peace treaty" with Germany containing military terms alone would have had to be ratified by the United States Senate and when ratified would have ended the state of war and restored peace. A subsequent treaty, containing additional terms, called final treaty, or "ultimate peace," would have been a treaty not between belligerents but between former belligerents. Thus the proposal which Wilson championed so vigorously involved making a treaty of peace which did not include the League of Nations. Wilson's dearest hope was to make the League of Nations an integral part of the treaty of peace; but on February 12, 1919, he argued in favor of making as soon as possible a treaty of peace, labeled preliminary to be sure but nevertheless a treaty of peace, which did not include the League, and on February 14 specified to House the subjects which should be included in this treaty.

House recorded in his diary: "February 14, 1919 . . . I outlined my plan of procedure during his absence: we could button up everything during the next four weeks. He seemed startled and even alarmed at this statement. I therefore explained that the plan was not to actually bring these matters to a final conclusion but to have them ready for him to do so when he returned . . .

"One of the main things we should do was to fix a programme regarding what was necessary to make a preliminary peace with Germany, as follows:

"1. A reduction of their army and navy to a peace footing.

"2. A delineation of the boundaries of Germany. This is to include the cession of the colonies.

"3. The amount of money to be paid for reparation and the length of time in which to pay it.

"4. An agreement as to the economic treatment of Germany.

"I asked him if he had anything to suggest in addition to these four articles. He thought they were sufficient."

It is clear that Wilson had not changed his opinion that it was desirable to include the League of Nations in the treaty of peace but believed the addition of the word "preliminary" to the words "treaty of peace" would produce the magic result of making a treaty of peace which would be a treaty of peace when he wished it to be one and not a treaty of peace when he did not wish it to be one. It would end the armistice, it would bind Germany, it would make "safety antedate the peace"; but it would not have to be ratified by the United States Senate and it would not be an "ultimate peace." Once again, Wilson had been led to an incredible conclusion by his confidence in the power of words to transform facts in accordance with his wishes.

House, Balfour, Clemenceau and everyone else in Paris naturally assumed that when Wilson said he wanted a preliminary treaty of peace and specified the terms which should be included in such a treaty, he meant he wanted a preliminary treaty of peace. But in point of fact he wanted nothing of the sort. He left France under the illusion that the treaty labeled "preliminary" which he had ordered would fall within his unlimited power to make an armistice, and it never occurred to him that such a treaty inevitably would come under his power to make a treaty with the advice and consent of the Senate, and that he had in fact ordered the preparation of a treaty of peace which did not include the League of Nations. He had, curiously enough, taken the exact course advocated by Senator Knox, a former Republican Secretary of State, who next to Lodge was his most formidable opponent; but he thought he had merely discovered another admirable method of making "safety antedate the peace," and after putting an arm around House, he left Paris, the Covenant in his pocket, convinced that he was immortal as the man who had at last brought peace to the earth.

XXVI

IN SPITE OF the triumph of Wilson's unconscious identification with the Saviour of the World, he was exceedingly nervous and exhausted. For five weeks in Paris he had worked harder than he had ever worked in his life. He was not used to hard work. Throughout his administration Admiral Grayson had protected him from exhaustion, but in Paris the defenses behind which he rested broke down. He had no secretary, and, if he did not do his own work, it was not done. He had to work. His eyes began to ache, his head began to throb and his stomach turned acid. When he boarded the *George Washington* he was close to physical and nervous collapse; and his mental condition may be judged from his self-deception in the matter of the preliminary treaty.

The tired President on the *George Washington* began to hear unpleasant stories about his friend House. He was told that House's son-in-law, Auchincloss, had said in the presence of Vance McCormick and various other persons, "the Colonel is well again, so now little Woody's batting average will begin to improve." In addition, he was told that House himself encouraged his secretaries to talk in this way. It was true that Auchincloss had made the remark; it was untrue that House encouraged such remarks. But Wilson was susceptible to tittle-tattle, especially if it were endorsed by a mother representative, and he could not treat the story with the contempt it deserved; his dislike of Auchincloss was too great, his unconscious attachment to House too deep and his conscious dependence on House too extensive. Moreover, the remark cut close to the truth. He had isolated himself from all advisers except

House. He had refused to have Tumulty at his side and had refused to use the secretariat of the American delegation. He had ignored Lansing and the other American Commissioners. The experts of the House Inquiry reported to him through Mezes, House's brother-in-law. House's secretariat, which, in default of a secretariat of his own, was the only secretariat at his disposal, was headed by House's son-in-law. His legal adviser was the law partner of House's son-in-law. House was his representative in the Council of Ten. So long as he felt that House was his "independent self," this dependence on House and House's satellites was agreeable to him. But, added to his emotional need for House, it made the maintenance of unclouded relations with House a necessity. The Auchincloss story was a slight cloud; but it threatened both the inadequate working arrangements he had established in Paris and the flow of his passivity to his father through the outlet of his love for House.

Wilson had the evidence gathered by his own eyes and ears to prove that House was still his quiet, self-effacing, subordinate friend, the perfect little Tommy Wilson; but, impressed by the story, he began to think that perhaps House behind his back was something quite different. He no doubt recalled that House had planned to "button up everything during the next four weeks," and he perhaps remembered that House had advised him not to come to Europe at all. In any event, his identification of House with himself as a child received a blow from the Auchincloss story. For the first time House began to resemble little Joe Wilson, the deceiver, rival and betrayer, more than little Tommy Wilson.

On February 24, 1919, Wilson landed in Boston and at once attacked his domestic opponents in an emotional address — an attempt to make America "drunk with this spirit of self-sacrifice." Many portions of his speech show that he had lost touch with reality. He spoke of the American soldiers as "fighting in dream," and estimated the power of his words thus: "I have had this sweet revenge. Speaking with perfect frankness in the name of the people of the United States I have uttered as the objects of this war ideals, and nothing but ideals, and the war has been won by that inspiration." His ideals had not merely won the war but had achieved further wonders. "And now these ideals have wrought this new magic that all the peoples of Europe are buoyed up and confident in the spirit of hope, because they believe that we are at the eve of a new age in the world, when nations will understand one another; when nations will support one another in every just cause; when nations will unite every moral and every physical strength to see that right shall prevail. If America were at this juncture to fail the world, what would come of it?"

America was not impressed by this speech. It did not ring true. Wilson seemed to be trying to wipe away facts by his words. American liberals felt that it was not America but Wilson who was about to fail the world, and American conservatives felt that Wilson was about to fail America.

Opposition to the Covenant in America sprang in part from personal dislike of Wilson — Lodge, for example, hated Wilson almost as bitterly as Wilson hated Lodge — but it drew its chief strength from the conviction that the terms of the treaty of peace would not lessen the probability of future wars and that the United States would be drawn into those wars by obligations undertaken in the Covenant. The opponents of the Covenant in 1919 took the exact position that Wilson had taken in his great "peace without victory" address to the United States Senate on January 22, 1917, in which he had stated that there was only one sort of peace that the people of America could join in guaranteeing: "The treaties and agreements which bring it to an end must embody terms which will create a peace that is worth guaranteeing and preserving, a peace that will win the approval of mankind, not merely a peace that will serve the several interests and immediate aims of the nations engaged." Wilson, attributing an almost magical healing power to the Covenant, had forgotten his convictions of the previous two years.

Wilson went to Washington and, following the advice of House, gave a dinner for the members of the Senate Committee on Foreign Relations and the House Committee on Foreign Affairs. The dinner did not produce the rapprochement for which House had hoped. Senators Lodge and Knox refused to open their mouths except to eat. Wilson turned his anger in part against House, blaming the Colonel for advising him to give the dinner.

The reader will recall that Wilson had avoided facing the concrete demands of the Allies while he was in Paris. In Washington, through cables from House, he became aware of the Allies' peace terms for the first time. House, in transmitting these demands, did not comment upon them belligerently. As soon as the aims of the Allies were revealed to the Colonel, particularly the aims of the British, upon whom he had counted to stand shoulder to shoulder with the Americans for a decent peace, he gave up hope that the peace might be the peace Wilson had promised to the world. On March 3, 1919, he wrote in his diary: "It is now evident that the peace will not be such a peace as I had hoped, or one which this terrible upheaval should have brought about . . . I dislike to sit and have forced upon us such a peace as we are facing. We will get something out of it in the way of a League of Nations, but even that is an imperfect instrument."

On March 4, 1919, Lodge announced in the Senate that thirty-seven Senators had pledged themselves to vote against ratification of the Covenant of the League of Nations. Wilson replied to Lodge the same evening by a defiance and a threat, saying, "When that treaty comes back, gentlemen on this side will find the Covenant not only in it, but so many threads of the treaty tied to the Covenant that you cannot dissect the Covenant from the treaty without destroying the whole vital structure." Thus his parting threat to Lodge before he left New York for France, exhausted, "worn and grey," was: "You'll take the treaty with my Covenant in it or you'll get no treaty at all."

Wilson made this threat because he knew that the people of the

United States wished to get back to peace as soon as possible, and he felt sure that they would prefer an immediate treaty with the League in it to indefinite delay in escaping from war restrictions. Thus by entwining the League and the treaty he hoped to make Lodge hated as the opponent of a speedy return to peace and to compel Lodge to accept the League. But he overlooked the fact that before leaving Paris he had ordered the preparation of a preliminary treaty, including military, naval, territorial, economic and financial terms which might strike from his hand the weapon he had chosen for his fight against Lodge. The Senate might ratify the preliminary treaty and thus make peace with Germany and might reject a subsequent "final" treaty which included the League of Nations. It is obvious that Wilson had not the slightest idea that the treaty of peace — labeled preliminary, for which he had argued — actually could restore peace. But in point of fact, when he made this threat in New York, House, loyally carrying out his orders, was working hard in Paris to get ready a treaty which would reduce Wilson's threat to wind. Wilson had created a dilemma for himself: either he would have to kill the preliminary treaty he had ordered or swallow his threat to Lodge.

His hatred of Lodge had become more violent than ever, and it seems important to note that he began to battle Lodge before he began to struggle with Lloyd George and Clemenceau. We have seen that Lodge had long been a father representative to him and that his reaction-formation against his passivity to his father had for several years found a minor outlet by way of hatred of Lodge. We have also seen that when the energy of that reaction-formation was turned against a father representative, as in the case of West, Wilson could fight with ruthless determination; but when, for one reason of another, the energy of that reaction-formation was not turned against a man whom he had to meet on terms of mental and moral equality, he was ill at ease and weak. Throughout 1919 the energy of his reaction-formation against his passivity to his father was turned against Lodge, and it was never turned against any European statesman, except briefly against President Poincaré. Wilson remained ruthless and unbending in his opposition to Lodge; but he was never ruthless and unbending to Clemenceau and Lloyd George.

His disinclination to face the leaders of the Allies with uncompromising hostility doubtless sprang in part from his ignorance of Europe. He was on unfamiliar ground and could be frightened by all sorts of ogres, like the bugaboo dangled so effectively before him that uncompromising opposition to Lloyd George and Clemenceau would throw all Europe into Bolshevism. When he battled Lodge he was at home, on familiar ground, sure of himself. But the basic reason for his rigidity when facing Lodge and his flaccidity when facing Lloyd George and Clemenceau seems to have been the simple fact that Lodge, not Clemenceau or Lloyd George, became established as the heir of West. His hatred of Lodge seems to have consumed all or nearly all the energy of his not over-abundant masculinity. He met the leaders of the Allies not with the weapons of masculinity but with the weapons of femininity: appeals, supplications, concessions, submissions.

Throughout the two weeks Wilson was in America he was extremely busy and gave only casual attention to House's cables from Paris. He knew that a struggle lay before him but it was not until the *George Washington* reached Brest on March 14, 1919, and House by word of mouth told him the facts that he realized the enormity of the demands of the Allies or the magnitude of the fight before him. As the train raced toward Paris, they talked. Wilson was profoundly shocked, not only by the facts but even more by House's attitude toward the facts.

He had returned to France as the Son of God going forth to battle for the Lord, his God, who in his unconscious was also himself. He still believed that God had chosen him to give the world a just and lasting peace, and hoped that by making "safety antedate the peace" he had made it possible for himself to lift the negotiations to the plane of the Sermon on the Mount. House told him that the establishment of the League had not in any degree altered the demands of the Allies and that their terms were vindictive. He added that no amount of argument or persuasion would alter the demands of Clemenceau and Lloyd George, and advised Wilson to face this fact and, since the world needed peace, to compromise at once, and make as soon as possible the evil peace he would in the end be obliged to make.

House believed so completely that compromise was inevitable and, indeed, desirable compared to open battle that on the very day of Wilson's arrival in France, March 14, 1919, he wrote in his diary: "My main drive now is for peace with Germany at the earliest possible moment." All Wilson's identifications with Divinity cried out against House's estimate of the situation and against House's advice. He could not admit that it was impossible for him to lift the negotiations in Paris to the plane of Christian ideals. Still less could he admit that after all his noble hopes and words and promises, after calling America to follow him on a crusade for lasting peace, after the sacrifice of thousands of American lives and billions of American wealth, he must confess himself to be not the Saviour of the World but the tool of the Allies. To agree with House was to admit that the specter which had made him so nervous and unhappy in the summer and autumn of 1916 and had stood by his shoulder when he was writing his war message had become a reality. To accept House's advice was to abandon his belief in his own mission, in his own likeness to the Son of God. That belief had become the core of his being, the central illusion which facts had to be made to fit. His identification with Christ was a fixation. As we have pointed out, Wilson had reduced House from *Dearest Friend* to *My dear House* in January 1917 because House had resisted the discharge of the libido lodged in that identification. And on the night of March 14, 1919, House not only advised him to abandon his career as the Saviour but utterly horrified him by a casual remark which was so shocking to him that he had to tell someone about it as soon as possible. He went to his stateroom, summoned a friend and told the friend, as if he were imparting a dreadful secret, that he had asked the Colonel if he had agreed that a preliminary treaty should be made which should not include the League of Nations, and that the Colonel could not deny having done so!

Inasmuch as Wilson had ordered House to make such a treaty, a denial by House would have been an announcement that he had willfully disobeyed Wilson's orders, and it is not remarkable that the question and reply made no impression whatever on House and left no record in his diary. On Wilson they made a terrible impression. For hours he tossed in his berth in the train, unable to sleep. He did not recall that he had overlooked the League of Nations when he had ordered House to prepare a preliminary treaty. House's casual reply to his question was to him, therefore, the confession of a traitor. House had agreed to cut the Covenant of the League out of the treaty of peace. House had robbed him of his weapon against Lodge. House had tried to rob him of his title to immortality! It is not difficult to observe what happened in his unconscious. There, he was Jesus Christ. And House had betrayed him. House could be no one else than Judas Iscariot.

Wilson's identification of House with little Tommy Wilson received its deathblow on the train to Paris. It did not die at once. Old identifications die slowly. The life ebbs out of them gradually with grief and hopes for recovery. Wilson continued to see House, as Jesus broke bread with Judas, knowing the dreadful character of his friend. But the friendship was dying, doomed, beyond help. "From this time onward there began to grow up a coldness between the two men . . ." recorded Baker in the book he wrote with Wilson's cooperation. The "coldness" was all on the side of Wilson. House did his best to remain Wilson's friend, as Hibben had done his best to remain Wilson's friend. But there was nothing to be done. The unconscious is a hard master. Two days after his conversation on the train with House, Wilson, again with awe, asked the friend in whom he had confided on the train if he did not feel that Colonel House had changed and was no longer the same man he had been before. In Wilson's unconscious, House had changed and was no longer the same man he had been before. He had been little Tommy Wilson. He had become Joe Wilson, Hibben, Judas.

Thus on March 14, 1919, Wilson's love for House began to turn to "coldness" and he was cut off, in the crucial month of his life, from the outlet which for eight years had carried so satisfactorily a considerable portion of his passivity to his father. His unconscious identification with the Beloved Son of the Almighty Father was his only other large outlet for his passivity to the Reverend Joseph Ruggles Wilson, and it is not remarkable that as his love for House waned his need to identify himself with Christ waxed apace. Thenceforth an enormous quantity of libido charged his identification with the Saviour. But his passivity to his father was the strongest of his desires, and it is impossible to believe that this single identification could give it adequate outlet. One is compelled to suspect that after March 14, 1919, a considerable quantity of his passivity to his father was without outlet, needing outlet, seeking outlet. Direct submission to a masculine opponent, with an attendant mother identification, offered possible outlet. The weeks which followed Wilson's turning away from House were the weeks in which he submitted to the leaders of the Allies.

XXVII

WILSON ACCEPTED with enthusiasm one piece of advice House gave him on the train: the suggestion that he should no longer attend meetings of the Council of Ten but should settle the terms of peace in secret conversations with Lloyd George and Clemenceau. In spite of Wilson's advocacy of "open covenants of peace, openly arrived at," on the afternoon of his arrival in Paris, March 14, 1919, he met Lloyd George and Clemenceau alone, in House's office in the Hotel Crillon. He met them determined to lift the negotiations to the plane of the Sermon on the Mount, determined to make no compromises, determined to convert the leaders of the Allies to righteousness or, if they would not be converted, to wield the weapons of Jehovah, to withdraw the financial support of the United States from England, France and Italy, to leave the conference and to denounce Lloyd George and Celmenceau as the enemies of mankind.

That Wilson, on March 14, 1919, was determined to use these masculine weapons rather than submit to an evil peace is certain. But there are many sorts of determination, and there is only one variety that may be relied on: a determination which draws strength from some great flow of libido, like Wilson's determination when facing West or Lodge. Determination which springs from the Super-Ego is often as powerless as the determination of the habitual drunkard to abandon drink. From all Wilson's words and acts during the Peace Conference it is clear that his determination to fight, under certain circumstances, did not spring from his reaction-formation against his passivity to his father. It sprang from his reluctance to betray the promises he had made to the peoples of the world, that is to say from his Super-Ego; and from his inability to admit that he was not the Saviour of the World, that is to say from his need to identify himself with Jesus Christ in order to preserve that outlet for his passivity to his father. But passivity to the father may also find deep satisfaction in complete submission to a masculine opponent. Thus, while on the one hand his passivity to his father demanded that he should not abandon his identification with Christ, on the other hand it demanded that he should submit. Its strength was divided. And it should not be forgotten that the Saviour with whom he had identified himself had saved the world by complete submission to the will of His Father. To reconcile the conflicting demands of his passivity to his father, and to solve all his other personal difficulties, Wilson needed only to discover some rationalization which would permit him both to compromise and to remain in his own belief the Saviour of the World. But when he talked with House he had not discovered such a rationalization, or at least had not been able to silence doubts as to its validity. Therefore, when he met Lloyd George and Clemenceau on March 14, 1919, he was determined, if need be, at some future date, to fight.

Rarely in human history has the future course of world events depended so greatly on one human being as it depended on Wilson in the month which followed his return to Paris. When he faced Clemenceau and Lloyd George in House's office in the Hotel Crillon on March 14, 1919, the fate of the world hung on his personal character. He began to battle for the peace he had promised to mankind by making the most extraordinary concession he had ever made. "In a moment of enthusiasm" he agreed to make a treaty of alliance guaranteeing that the United States would immediately go to war on the side of France in case France were attacked by Germany. He did this for the same reason that he had insisted on guaranteeing the peace before any of its terms were fixed, in order to make "safety antedate the peace" and thus ensure that the actual peace terms should be discussed in a spirit of brotherly love. The establishment of the League of Nations had not lifted Clemenceau to the plane of the Sermon on the Mount. He hoped to raise Clemenceau by the alliance. In his desperate desire to conduct the peace negotiations in an atmosphere of Christian love, and to avoid having to use the weapons of Jehovah, he forgot entirely the deep feeling of the American people and the Senate against "entangling alliances," and his own conviction that alliances with European powers were contrary to the interests of the American people. No word or act could show more clearly the extent to which he had adopted the weapons of femininity. His offer was the gesture of a woman who says: 'I submit utterly to your wishes, now be kind to me. Respond to my submission by an equal concession. But Clemenceau remained Clemenceau: an old man obsessed by the idea of obtaining security for France by force.

The next morning Wilson issued an amazing "pronouncement," behaving as if he had forgotten completely his words in the Council of Ten on February 12, and his orders to House on February 14, treating the preliminary treaty as if it were the product not of his own words but of an "intrigue" against him. In Mr. Baker's book, *Woodrow Wilson and World Settlement,* Wilson's action of March 15, 1919, is described thus: "But in the meantime he had acted with stunning audacity and directness. Saturday morning, March 15, about 11 o'clock, he called the writer on the telephone through a secret circuit which ran directly from his study in the Place des Etats-Unis to the Hotel Crillon. He asked me to deny the report, now everywhere current in Europe — and to some extent in America — that there would be a separate preliminary treaty of peace with the Germans excluding the League of Nations. 'I want you to say that we stand exactly where we stood on January 25 when the Peace Conference adopted the resolution making the Covenant an integral part of the general treaty of peace.'

"I therefore drew up a statement, took it up to the President and secured his approval and issued it immediately. It follows: —

March 15, 1919,

The President said to day that the decision made at the Peace Conference at its plenary session, January 25, 1919, to the effect that the establishment of a League of Nations should be made an integral part of the Treaty of Peace is of final force and that there is no basis whatever for the reports that a change in this decision was contemplated . . .

"This bold pronouncement fell like a veritable bombshell in Paris. It overturned in one swift stroke the most important action of the Conference during the President's absence. The obscure tendencies, the 'dark forces' which had been at work for the past month were brought up with a jerk . . . It was an extraordinarily able stroke. . . . [H]e had demolished in one bold stroke (March 15) the intrigue, hatched while he was away to sidetrack his whole programme with a preliminary treaty in which the League was to have no place."

Thus Mr. Baker described what he and Wilson thought happened on March 15. There is no doubt that Wilson as well as Baker thought this had happened. Baker at the time was in daily contact with Wilson. He issued the "bold pronouncement" at Wilson's request. Wilson did not read the final manuscript of *Woodrow Wilson and World Settlement,* but gave Baker all his documents and papers and explained to Baker his view of the matter. Moreover Wilson and Mrs. Wilson were so pleased by Baker's book that later they entrusted to him the task of preparing the official biography of Wilson. There is, therefore, no doubt that Baker wrote what Wilson thought.

In point of fact Wilson's "bombshell" of March 15 blew up an "intrigue" which existed only in Wilson's brain. He himself had argued for the negotiation of the preliminary treaty and had not ordered the inclusion of the League of Nations in it. Moreover there were no "obscure tendencies," no "dark forces." Clemenceau and Lloyd George were present, fighting for the same demands they had cherished since the beginning of the conference.

And to believe that Colonel House had participated, however obliquely, in an "intrigue . . . to sidetrack his whole pro- gramme" was to abandon reality for the land in which facts are embodiments of unconscious desires.

The actual effect of Wilson's "pronouncement" of March 15, 1919, was merely to inform the world that there would be no pre- liminary peace but that the weary soldiers would continue to stand under arms and the people of Germany and Austria continue to starve under the blockade until the final treaty was signed with the League in it. And Wilson reversed his position of February 12 and 14 so completely that on March 17, two days after his "bombshell," he insisted that peace should be made simultaneously with Ger- many, Austria-Hungary and Turkey. In his diary House wrote: "Since both Austria-Hungary and Turkey are being dismembered, this would delay peace for an interminable time."

On March 17, 1919, at a meeting of the Supreme War Council Wilson completed his annihilation of the preliminary treaty of peace for which he had argued at the meetings of the same Su- preme War Council on February 12, 1919. He said that he had as- sumed that this preliminary Convention would only be temporary until the complete treaty was prepared, and that it would have the character of a sort of exalted armistice, the terms being re-included in the formal treaty. If this preliminary Convention should have to be submitted to the Senate for a general discussion there, he knew from the usual slow process of legislatures that it would be several months before it could be ratified.

He did not mention the real cause of his opposition to the pre- liminary treaty, omitting to say that it would unquestionably have been ratified and that the weapon by which he hoped to force Lodge to swallow the League would have been stricken from his hands. Mr. Balfour then in his most polite manner uttered the epitaph of the preliminary treaty of which he had been father and Wilson mother: Mr. Balfour expressed the view that the state- ments made by President Wilson were most important and serious.

As he understood the situation, the policy accepted was that a preliminary peace should be made, each clause of which should be a part of the final act, so that by the settlement of the preliminary peace a great part of the final permanent peace would actually have been conquered. It now appeared, however, that the American Constitution made that full programme impracticable. Mr. Balfour made no comment on the mental clarity of the President of the United States. And Wilson did not observe that the entire misunderstanding with regard to the preliminary treaty had arisen because of the confusion in his own mind when he had advocated such a treaty. He did not apologize to House for his suspicions and take the Colonel again "to his bosom." On the contrary, he continued to believe that House, Balfour and Foch, behind his back, had agreed to sidetrack the League.

Thus Wilson's return to France was marked by two startling political actions and two equally startling emotional reactions: He offered an alliance to France and announced that there would be no preliminary treaty without the League of Nations. He began to feel that House had betrayed him and that the preliminary treaty which he himself had ordered was the product of an "intrigue, hatched while he was away to sidetrack his whole programme." It is difficult not to see in these actions and reactions evidence of the divorce from reality which was beginning to characterize Wilson's mental life. They were produced not by events in the world of fact but by an overwhelming inner need to find outlet for his passivity to his father through his unconscious identification of himself with the Saviour. He was rapidly nearing that psychic land from which few travelers return, the land in which facts are the products of wishes, in which friends betray and in which an asylum chair may be the throne of God.

XXVIII

AFTER MARCH 14, 1919, Wilson met Clemenceau and Lloyd George daily, alone, in secret conference; and, in the words of Mr. Baker, "set his teeth and struggled manfully by sheer logic and appeal to higher motives to move Clemenceau from his position, to convince him that these military devices would never secure to France what she really wanted and that there were better — not only more just but more practical — ways of securing the future of France." There is but one word in the above description which seems somewhat inaccurate: the word "manfully" should perhaps read "femininely."

Clemenceau listened. On March 20, House, whom Wilson was not keeping informed as to the discussions of the Three, asked Clemenceau how they had got on that afternoon. "Splendidly," said Clemenceau, "we disagreed about everything."

It is difficult to admire the strategy and tactics employed by the President of the United States in his struggle to achieve the peace he had promised to the world; but it is impossible not to sympathize with the tired, ill human being who, clinging to his belief that his Almighty Father had sent him to give the world a just and lasting peace, wasted his ebbing strength in exhortations addressed to Clemenceau and Lloyd George. Wilson, after all, stood for human decency. He stood weakly for human decency; but he stood where it is an honor to stand.

He was sixty-two years old, a very tired man, threatened by his hardened arteries, suffering not only from indigestion, headaches and neuritis but also from an enlarged prostate. His distrust of

House had cut him off from intimacy with the only close friend he had. He stood alone, by his own will to be sure, but alone. He went into his daily conferences with Clemenceau and Lloyd George without a single American to assist him or to record the conclusions reached. His need for an intimate who believed in his mission was intense. House, as we have seen, had ceased to believe. Wilson turned to the emotional George D. Herron, who had written of his likeness to Christ. Herron appealed to him to withdraw from the Conference rather than compromise.

Clemenceau remained immovable. Lloyd Geroge on the other hand moved with a quicksilver celerity that made it impossible for Wilson, who had no secretary to record Lloyd George's promises, to know where he stood. On March 26, House told Wilson "that Lloyd George was saying that in spite of the fact that he had promised yesterday his willingness to have the Covenant go into the peace treaty that he had made no such promise. The President said: 'Then he lies, for he not only agreed but he agreed in the presence of Orlando and Clemenceau, who will bear witness.' " Poor Tommy Wilson, who all his life had revered British statesmen and despised the French, found himself at the crisis of his life despising Lloyd George and respecting Clemenceau.

By March 27, Wilson, still appealing and exhorting, was nearing nervous collapse. Clemenceau demanded a thirty-year occupation of the Rhineland and the annexation of the Saar. Wilson, in a burst of irritation, replied that the French were bringing up territorial questions that had nothing to do with the war aims of anybody, that no one had heard of their intention to annex the Saar Valley until after the armistice had been signed. Clemenceau returned an angry answer: "You are pro-German. You are seeking to destroy France." "That is untrue and you know it is untrue," said Wilson. Clemenceau then said that if France did not receive the Saar he would not sign the treaty of peace. Wilson replied: "Then if France does not get what she wishes, she will refuse to act with us. In that event do you wish me to return home?" "I do not wish you to go home but I intend to do so myself," said Clemenceau, and put on his hat and stalked from the house.

Mr. Baker's description of what followed runs thus: "The President, bitterly offended, went for a long drive in the Bois during the noon intermission, and at the beginning of the afternoon session he stood up before the other Three and in a great appeal — Admiral Grayson, who heard it, said it was one of the most powerful speeches the President ever made — set forth again his vision of the peace.

"After it was over M. Clemenceau was much affected, and he shook the President's hand and said: 'You are a good man, Mr. President, and you are a great man.'

"But though the President could touch Clemenceau's emotions he could not make him yield. 'A kind of feminine mind' was the President's characterization of his difficult opponent."

Wilson's opinion that Clemenceau had "a kind of feminine mind" throws more light on Wilson than on Clemenceau. Nothing less feminine than Clemenceau's refusal to be swept off his feet by Wilson's oratory could be imagined, and it is difficult to imagine anything more feminine than Wilson's response to Clemenceau's behavior of the morning. Clemenceau had stepped over the bonds of courtesy. He had insulted Wilson, and few men would have refused thereafter to employ the masculine weapons which Wilson had in his hands. But Wilson "in a great appeal . . . set forth again his vision of the peace." Thus Wilson's retaliation was the product of unadulterated femininity, and his remark that Clemenceau had a "kind of feminine mind" was clearly an attempt to persuade himself that his own behavior was not feminine by transferring his own attitude to Clemenceau. As always he could not bear to look frankly at the femininity in his own nature. Clemenceau's compliment was no doubt genuine. Four days later, describing Wilson, he said: "He thinks he is another Jesus Christ come upon the earth to reform men." Clemenceau probably knew nothing about psychoanalysis, but Wilson's unconscious identification of himself with the Saviour had become so obvious that it compelled even those who had never studied the deeper psychic strata to recognize its existence.

Wilson was impressed by Clemenceau's compliment. He felt that he might still be able to convert Clemenceau by his words and get the peace he had promised without open battle. On the evening of March 27, Mr. Baker suggested that he should issue an open statement denouncing the "obstructionist groups" which were making "claims for strategic frontiers and national aggrandizement," stating that "in pressing what they believe to be their own immediate interests they lose sight entirely of the fact that they are surely sowing seeds of future wars." Wilson refused to issue such a statement. The following evening Mr. Baker again urged him to attack openly. Wilson, still hanging back and hoping, replied, "The time has not come, we cannot risk breaking up the Peace Conference — yet."

By that time it was obvious to everyone in touch with the negotiations, except Wilson, that unless he was ready to accept the terms of Lloyd George and Clemenceau he would have to use the masculine weapons he had so long refused to use. Herron, who still believed utterly in Wilson's likeness to Christ, appealed to Wilson to withdraw from the Conference. "The President was greatly moved by Herron's appeal, and walked up and down the floor exclaiming: 'My God, I can never go through with it.' "

That unfortunately was the exact truth. At the moment when the fate of the world hung on his personal character he could not find in his body the courage to fight. His only source of masculine courage, his reaction-formation against his passivity to his father, was turned not against the leaders of the Allies but against Lodge. Yet at the same time he could not frankly compromise. All his identifications with the Divinity refused to allow him to admit that he had been nothing but the cat's-paw of the Allies. He hung on, hoping and praying to God his Father that he might still win by talking like Christ.

Mr. Baker recorded: "On April 2 the President was at the end of the tether. I find in my notes for that day:

"He (the President) said that it could not go on many days longer; that if some decision could not be reached by the middle of next week, he might have to make a positive break . . .

"I spoke of the feeling of unrest in the world, the new revolts in Germany and Hungary, and of the blame for the delay that was everywhere being charged, unjustly, against him.

" 'I know that,' he said, 'I know that.' He paused. 'But we've got to make peace on the principles laid down and accepted, or not make it at all.' "

Wilson had been avoiding, so far as possible, personal contact with House. But on the evening of April 2, 1919, he telephoned to House, and House recorded in his diary: "We went over the situation from start to finish . . . He declared the old man was stubborn and that he could not get him to come to a decision. What he really means is that he cannot get Clemenceau to come to his way of thinking . . . The President asked if I thought Lloyd George was sincere with him . . . The general impression is that George is playing him for a rupture with the French . . . I asked him if he had anyone at the Council of Four meetings who was taking notes. Professor Mantoux is there to do the interpreting for Signor Orlando. The President admitted that he thought Mantoux did not like him. He said, 'indeed, I am not sure that anybody does.' "

There is a genuine pathos in the words, "indeed, I am not sure that anybody does." They were spoken by the President of the United States, who three months before had been received by France, England and Italy with a love and worship so intense that he seemed to the world and to himself a King of Kings. And in fact he still had more men ready to answer his call and follow him to battle than any man has had before or since. He was still the leader of all the idealists of the world. They were perplexed and worried because he had not called them to battle, but they had not lost faith in him. He had lost faith in himself. The conflict between his determination to fight the battle which faced him and his fear to fight it had made him little Tommy Wilson again: Little Tommy Wilson, weak, sickly, with his spectacles, headaches and sour stomach, who did not dare to play with the rough boys in the Augusta streets, who felt out of life, alone and without a friend.

The day after this conversation with House, he collapsed in a complete nervous and physical breakdown. "He was seized with violent paroxysms of coughing, which were so severe and frequent that it interfered with his breathing. He had a fever of 103 and a profuse diarrhea . . . his condition looked very serious." Through the early morning hours of April 4, 1919, Wilson writhed in his bed, vomiting, coughing, giving out profuse diarrhea and bloody urine, pain shooting from his swollen prostate and the neuritis in his left shoulder, fighting for breath, his face haggard, its left side and his left eye twitching. But the torment in his body at that moment was perhaps less terrible to him than the torment in his mind. He faced alternatives both of which were horrible to him. He could break his promises and become the tool of the Allies, not the Prince of Peace, or he could hold to his promises, withdraw the financial support of the United States from Europe, denounce Clemenceau and Lloyd George, return to Washington and leave Europe to — what? and himself to — what?

He shrank from the possible consequences of wielding his masculine weapons with a fear that was overwhelming. He had exaggerated the danger of fighting and minimized the chance of fighting successfully. One threat to leave France to face Germany alone might have brought Clemenceau to compromise; one crack of his financial whip might have brought Lloyd George to heel. But the sick man in his bed had begun again to see the world with the eyes of little Tommy Wilson, and he saw a nightmare picture of the possible consequences of his actions. He feared that his withdrawal would result in an immediate renewal of war in Europe, that starving French armies would march over the bodies of starving Germans, Austrians, Hungarians and Russians and dictate in the end a peace far worse than the peace he faced; he feared that such events might produce a revolutionary movement so vast that the whole continent of Europe would succumb to Bolshevism, and above all else he could not contemplate that. He hated and feared Communists far more deeply than he hated and feared militarists. He had no spark of radicalism in his body. He was the "Christian statesman" sent to bring light to the capitalist world by paraphrases of the Sermon on the Mount. His vision of a perfect world was the vision of "The New Freedom" — a vision of prosperous small towns like the towns he had lived in most of his life. Communist revolution in either France or England was in fact beyond the bounds of possibility; but it was present in Wilson's fears. Again and again in those days and nights when the future of the world hung on his decision he repeated: "Europe is on fire and I can't add fuel to the flames!"

And what would be the effect of fighting on his own life? He saw himself reviled from one end of the capitalist world to the other, and that was his only world. Already the press of Paris and London was attacking him with a bitterness that hurt him extremely. He knew that, while he would be hailed as a prophet by the liberals and idealists of America, the mass of the nation would turn against him. He would be called "pro-German," as Clemenceau had called him. He would be accused of "wanting to let the Hun off." He would be called a Bolshevik. The propaganda he had loosed on America through his friend George Creel had had its effect. The American people had been whipped into a hatred of Germany and Russia. The dowagers were mewing for blood. If he should seem to favor Germany and aid Communism, the American people would turn that hatred against him. He would be hated by the whole world, except for a few American and British liberals, for whose good opinion he did care, and the Socialists and Communists of Europe, whose approval he could not bear to have, with whom he could not bear to identify himself in any way. And worst of all he would have to withdraw the United States from the

League of Nations. The League would be established; but without him. He would have to deprive himself of his title to immortality.

Thus the alternative of withdrawing from the Conference was unbearable to him; but his other alternative was equally unbearable. As deep an emotion as he had ever felt was his feeling that if he led the United States into war he must lead it into a war for peace. Nearly all the energy of his enormously powerful passivity to his father was charging his unconscious identification with Christ. To compromise, to quit, was to acknowledge that he was not the Prince of Peace. Moreover, he would break his word, he would make his pledges a jest. He would make ideals and idealists a joke. He would destroy the whole liberal movement in America of which he was the leader. He would be denounced by the very men whose good opinion he most valued. What would Herron, the man "who really understood him," say? What would all the young men who had believed in him think of him? What would he think of himself? He would stand before the world not as the Son of God who had gone forth to war to gain a kingly crown and had gained it; but as the Son of God who went forth to war and quit when he saw the Cross.

XXIX

THROUGH THE DAY and night of April 4, 1919, Wilson tossed in his bed unable to choose between the alternatives which were equally horrible to him. But he had to choose. He could not run off to Rydal to recover with a dear friend beside him and Wansfell "like some great nourishing breast" before him. The work of the Peace Conference had to go on.

On April 5, 1919, Wilson was still bedridden. Clemenceau, Lloyd George and Orlando met in Wilson's study, and Colonel House ran back and forth through the door in the book case which separated Wilson's bedroom from his study to keep him informed as to the progress of their negotiations. Reparations were under discussion. Wilson had already yielded to the demand of the British that pensions and separation allowances should be included in the reparations bill. He had also ordered the American experts to cease fighting for his original contention that a definite sum for Germany to pay must be named in the treaty, but he was under the illusion that he would not have to make further compromises and that Lloyd George would support him in insisting that the total reparations payments should be limited to the amount Germany could pay in thirty years.

To House's surprise, and to Wilson's when House came through the door in the book case and reported, Lloyd George opposed any limitation either of years or of amount to be paid. House, in despair, believing that it was better to have "an immediate peace and the world brought to order . . . than . . . a better peace and delay," submitted to Lloyd George and Clemenceau and suggested a form of words as a "reparations compromise" which was in reality surrender of the entire American position: "The schedule of payments to be made by the Enemy States shall be set forth by this Commission, taking into account, in the fixation of the time for payment, their capacity for payment."

House himself was so outraged by the demands of Clemenceau and Lloyd George that he advised Wilson to accept this "compromise" but to break up the Conference rather than make further concessions. In his diary the Colonel recorded: "I suggested that in the event there was no agreement by the end of next week (April 12), he draw up a statement of what the United States is willing to sign in the way of a peace treaty, and give the Allies notice that unless they can come near our way of thinking we would go home immediately and let them make whatever peace seems to them best. My suggestion was to do this gently and in the mildest possible tone, but firmly."

Thus on Saturday, April 5, 1919, even House, who had been the chief advocate of compromise, advised Wilson to fight. And from America Wilson received the same advice. Just before Wilson's breakdown, Admiral Grayson, his physician and friend, had sent a cable to Tumulty saying, "Am still confident President will win. Encountering difficulties; situation serious. President is the hope of the world more than ever, and with his courage, wisdom and force he will lead the way. Have you any suggestion as to publicity or otherwise." On April 5, 1919, Tumulty replied: "In my opinion the President must in some dramatic way clear the air of doubts and misunderstandings and despair which now pervade the whole world situation. He must take hold of the situation with both hands and shake it out of its present indecision, or political sabotage and scheming will triumph. Only a bold stroke by the President will save Europe and perhaps the world. That stroke must be made regardless of the cries and admonitions of his friendly advisers. He has tried to settle the issue in secret; only publicity of a dramatic kind now can save the situation. The occasion calls for that audacity which has helped him to win in every fight."

Wilson, still in bed, received Tumulty's telegram. And on April 6, Sunday, an appropriate day for him to decide to take his father's place in the pulpit and lay down the law of God to a congregation which was mankind, he sent for the American Commissioners. Colonel House recorded in his diary: "It was determined that if nothing happened within the next few days, the President would say to the Prime Ministers that unless peace was made according to their promises, which were to conform to the principles of the Fourteen Points, he would either have to go home or he would insist upon having the conferences in the open; in other words, to have Plenary Sessions with all the delegates of the smaller Powers sitting in."

Thus, on the afternoon of April 6, 1919, Wilson decided that unless Clemenceau and Lloyd George within a few days actually agreed to terms of peace which accorded with their pledges to make peace on the basis of the Fourteen Points, he would either go home or would insist on their making their proposals in the open so that he could combat them in the open and turn the opinion of the world against them. This decision was characteristic. It enabled him to "dodge trouble" for a few more days, and it expressed again the comforting hope that he might at last raise the Peace Conference to the level of the university debating societies which he had dominated by his moral earnestness and his phrases. Again he was able to think of the Peace Conference as he had thought of it on November 16, 1918, when he cabled House: "I infer the French and British leaders desire to exclude me from the Conference for fear I might there lead the weaker nations against them." Again he was able to hope that he would not have to use the masculine weapons he had put aside but would be able to indulge his preference for that very feminine weapon, the mouth.

Nevertheless the decision was important since it indicated that he was prepared to fight after some days, with one weapon or another, rather than to compromise further. But no sooner had he made this decision than he robbed it of immediate importance by accepting House's reparations "compromise." House recorded in his diary on that same Sunday: "I took up with the President the question of Reparations which the experts have been working on today, and got him in agreement with the plan, with slight modifications which they had worked out." Thus, since the reparations "compromise" was a complete abandonment of the American position, Wilson immediately followed his decision not to compromise further by a compromise so monstrous that it was surrender rather than compromise. It is clear that he was still caught by his conflicting desires and fears, that he wanted to go on saying and believing that he would not compromise and, at the same time by compromising, avoid the fight he feared.

Later in the evening of that same Sunday, April 6, 1919, he seemed to have come to a real decision to fight. He was seated in his bed, dressed in an old white sweater, and Mrs. Wilson was seated by his bedside knitting, when Admiral Grayson brought in Bernard M. Baruch, whose intimacy with the Wilsons had begun to increase as House's decreased. Wilson said that he had come to the end of his tether in argument with the English, French and Italians and had to put pressure on them somehow. Baruch suggested that he squeeze them financially, by stopping the credits from the United States upon which they were living. Wilson sent a cablegram to the Secretary of the Treasury ordering him not to give any new credits to England, France and Italy. He then emphasized his determination to fight by asking Grayson to have a cablegram sent ordering the *George Washington* to return to Brest as soon as possible. He had not decided to return to America at once but to have the ship ready so that he could return to America at once unless Lloyd George and Clemenceau should commence to respect their pledges to make peace on the basis of the Fourteen Points. Thus, on the evening of April 6, 1919, Wilson prepared to fight, and Admiral Grayson at least was convinced that he would fight rather than make any further compromise. When Clemenceau, referring to Wilson's purpose in ordering the *George Washington,* said, "It is a bluff, isn't it?" Grayson replied with entire sincerity, "He hasn't a bluffing corpuscle in his body."

Admiral Grayson, incidentally, on that same Sunday, April 6, 1919, at the request of one of the authors of this volume attempted to obtain a decision from Wilson on the Soviet Government's proposal for peace, which was to expire on April 10. Wilson, whose "one track mind" was fully occupied by Germany, said that he had turned over the question to House to handle and refused to bother personally about peace in and with Russia.

Lenin had offered to make an immediate armistice on all fronts, and to accord de facto recognition to the anti-Communist governments which had been set up in the following areas of the territory of the former Russian Empire: (1) Finland, (2) Murmansk-Archangel, (3) Esthonia, (4) Latvia, (5) Lithuania, (6) Poland, (7) the western part of White Russia, (8) Rumania, including Bessarabia, (9) more than half the Ukraine, (10) the Crimea, (11) the Caucasus, (12) Georgia, (13) Armenia, (14) Azerbaidjan, (15) the whole of the Urals, (16) all Siberia.

Thus Lenin had offered to confine Communist rule to Moscow and a small adjacent area, plus the city now known as Leningrad. As a Communist, Lenin naturally expected to expand the area of Communist rule whenever he could safely, regardless of any promises he might have made. Yet by reducing the Communist state to an area not much larger than that ruled by the first Russian dictator to call himself Czar — Ivan the Terrible — Lenin had offered the West a unique opportunity to prevent Communist conquest by force of adjacent areas. Incidentally, Lenin had also offered to recognize Soviet responsibility for the debts of the Russian Empire.

The consequences of Wilson's refusal to turn his mind to the question of Russia were considerable. We do not yet know, indeed, how immense the consequences may be. It is not impossible that Wilson's refusal to burden his "one track mind" with Russia may well, in the end, turn out to be the most important single decision that he made in Paris.

The next day, Monday, April 7, 1919, the telegram ordering the *George Washington* was dispatched, and House took Wilson's place at the meeting of the Prime Ministers which was held in Lloyd George's apartment. The representatives of the Allies so disgusted House by their haggling that the Colonel grew angry and left the meeting. The definite break seemed to have come at last. House recorded in his diary: "I crossed the street to tell the President about the meeting and he thoroughly approved what I had done. We wasted the entire afternoon accomplishing nothing . . . The President was thoroughly discouraged when we talked the matter over and wondered what the outcome was to be."

After House had left, Ray Stannard Baker talked with Wilson: "I went up to see President Wilson at 6:30 — the first time since he fell ill — and had a long talk. I found him fully dressed, in his study, looking thin and pale . . .

"He has reached the point where he will give no further . . . 'Then Italy will not get Fiume?' I asked. 'Absolutely not — as long as I am here,' he said sharply. 'Nor France the Saar?' 'No' . . . I asked him what I could say to the correspondents and he told me to tell them to read again our agreements with the other Allies and with Germany and to assure them that he would not surrender on these principles . . . I told the President the effect of his announcement regarding the *George Washington*. 'The time has come to bring this thing to a head,' he said. 'House was just here and told me that Clemenceau and Klotz had talked away another day . . . I will not discuss anything with them any more. We agreed among ourselves and we agreed with Germany upon certain general principles. The whole course of the conference has been made up of a series of attempts, especially by France, to break down this agreement, to get territory, and to impose crushing indemnities. The only real interest of France in Poland is in weakening Germany by giving Poland territory to which she has no right.' "

Mr. Baker also recorded in regard to this conversation with Wilson, "We talked about the shifty attitude of Lloyd George; it was even said that Lloyd George was preparing, at this crisis, to issue a statement throwing the blame for the delay upon him [Wilson]. I shall never forget the utter sadness of the President's response as he stood there by his desk, his face gaunt from his recent illness. 'Well,' he said, 'I suppose I shall have to stand alone.' "

In the face of these words it is difficult to believe that Wilson had any other idea on the evening of April 7, 1919, than to fight rather than to compromise further. But we have seen how often he had approached the idea of fighting and how often he had at the last moment compromised. And we may be shocked but not surprised to note that, on the afternoon of April 8, 1919, less than twenty-four hours after he had made these statements to Mr. Baker, he met the Prime Ministers for the first time after his illness and yielded to their demands, accepting the reparations settlement which wrecked the economic life of Europe. House recorded in his diary: "Much to my delight they came to a tentative settlement of the question of Reparations. The President yielded more than I thought he would, but not more, I think, than the occasion required."

Thenceforth Wilson's descent into the Treaty of Versailles was rapid. It was accelerated by the telegram which Tumulty sent him on April 9, 1919: "The ordering of the *George Washington* to return to France looked upon here as an act of impatience and petulance on the President's part and not accepted here in good grace by either friends or foes. It is considered as an evidence that the President intends to leave the Conference if his views are not accepted . . . A withdrawal at this time would be a desertion." Moreover, the Secretary of the Treasury cabled to him that credits covering the needs of the Allies until July had already been granted. On April 9, Wilson compromised on the Saar, and never again did he threaten to fight for the peace he had set out to give the world.

Before we attempt to analyze Wilson's moral collapse it seems advisable to note another alteration in his relationship to House. After their conversation of March 14 on the train, Wilson diminished his personal contact with House to the minimum demanded by the work in hand. But when he fell ill on April 3, he had to appoint someone to take his place in the Council of Four and, since he distrusted Lansing even more than he distrusted House, he chose the Colonel. For a few days it seemed possible that their relations might again become intimate. But among House's friends in Paris was an English journalist named Wickham Steed, who was acting as political correspondent in Paris for the London *Times* and writing editorials for the Paris *Daily Mail*. House had discovered that by treating Steed as if he were a gentleman he could control Steed's articles. He was boasting to Mrs. Wilson that Steed would write anything he wished, when Mrs. Wilson picked up a clipping from the *Times* of Monday, April 7, 1919, and handed it to the Colonel saying, "I suppose you asked him to write this." The clipping read:

THE MILLS OF PEACE...
(From our Political Correspondent)

Paris, April 6

Colonel House's Services

. . . Insofar as there is a real improvement in the prospects of the Conference, it is believed to be attributable chiefly to its practical statesmanship of Colonel House, who, in view of President Wilson's indisposition, has once again placed his *savoir faire* and conciliatory temperament at the disposal of the chief peacemakers.

Colonel House is one of the very few Delegates who have "made good" during the Conference. It is, indeed, probable that peace would have been made successfully weeks ago but for the unfortunate illness which overtook him at the very outset of the Conference. When he recovered the Council of Ten had already got into bad habits . . . Little could be done to mend matters until Mr. Lloyd George returned to England and the President to America. During their absence Colonel House, who has never found a difficulty in working with his colleagues, because he is a selfless man with no personal axe to grind, brought matters rapidly forward. The delay that has occurred since the return of President Wilson and Mr. Lloyd George has been due chiefly to the upset of the good work done during their absence, and to the abandonment of sound methods in favor of "genial improvisations" . . .

If there is now a chance that the Conference may be hauled back from the brink of failure on to relatively safe ground, it is mainly due to the efforts of Colonel House and to the salutary effect of the feeling that the Allied peoples are becoming seriously alarmed at the secret manipulations of their chief representatives.

House was flabbergasted. He stood speechless facing Mrs. Wilson. Then word came that the President was waiting for him. He hurried to the President, saying he would explain later. He never returned to explain. No explanation was possible. Steed had completed the circle of personal misunderstanding which Auchincloss had begun. Mrs. Wilson was convinced that House had inspired both Auchincloss and Steed. Thereafter she hated House and felt sure that he was a traitor to her husband, interested only in taking the credit for Wilson's achievements and leaving Wilson the blame for mistakes. Personal relations between the Wilson and House families grew distant.

Wilson was less bitter than Mrs. Wilson toward House. He distrusted House but he did not hate the Colonel. His identification of House with little Tommy Wilson though dying was not quite dead. He continued to employ House as an assistant just as he had continued to employ Tumulty as an assistant after losing confidence in him; but he was careful to keep House from knowing too much about his thoughts and actions, just as he had been careful to keep Tumulty at a distance. In the first days of April, Lloyd George had introduced Sir Maurice Hankey into the meetings of the Four to take minutes. Hankey had sent House minutes of the meetings in which House had represented Wilson. The British then suggested to Wilson that in order to keep the American peace delegation in touch with the negotiations Hankey should furnish House daily with minutes of the meetings of the Four. Wilson replied that minutes of the meetings of the Four should not be furnished to House nor to any other American except himself. Thereafter no American knew what agreements the President of the United States was making. Lloyd George had Hankey to assist him, Clemenceau had Mantoux, Wilson had no one. But at least Wilson demonstrated that he, not House, was the ruler of the United States. Alone, in the month of April 1919, he agreed to the transformation of the Fourteen Points into the Treaty of Versailles.

XXX

THE READER has probably been bored by our detailed examination of Wilson's words and actions in the months of February, March and April 1919. But we feel that we need not apologize for the closeness of our scrutiny. In so far as any human being is ever important, Wilson in those months was important.

The whole stream of human life may be deflected by the character of a single individual. If Miltiades had fled from Marathon or Charles Martel had turned tail at Poitiers, Western civilization would have developed differently. And all life would have been a different thing if Christ had recanted when He stood before Pilate. When Wilson quit in Paris, the stream of Western civilization was turned into a channel not pleasant to contemplate.

The psychological consequences of his moral collapse were perhaps as serious as the political and economic consequences. Mankind needs heroes, and just as the hero who is faithful to his trust raises the whole level of human life, so the hero who betrays his trust lowers the level of human life. Wilson preached magnificently, promised superbly, then fled. To talk and run is not in the best American tradition nor in the finest line of European development, and the Western world will not find it easy to wipe from memory the tragic-comic figure of its hero, the President who talked and ran. Our attempt to determine the exact cause and moment of Wilson's surrender, therefore, seems to us to need no defense. It was an important surrender.

If Wilson were alive and would submit to psychoanalysis it might be possible to discover exactly why and when he abandoned the fight he had promised to make. Actually, with evidence before us, we can do no more than to indicate a possibility. It is clear that the crisis began with Wilson's breakdown of April 3, and that it was over ten days later. Since he seemed to be utterly determined to fight on the evening of April 7 and surrendered in the important matter of reparations the next afternoon and never again fought (except over the side issue of Fiume), the conclusion seems obvious that at some time in the night of April 7 or the morning of April 8 he decided to quit. But he had told House on April 6 that he would accept the reparations "compromise," so that his surrender of April 8 was one which he had been prepared to make; he may have made it with the firm resolve never to surrender again, and his final decision to compromise to the bitter end may have come when he received Tumulty's telegram of April 9, which concluded: "A withdrawal at this time would be a desertion." He may, indeed, never have made any decision but merely disintegrated.

On the other hand, after his conversation of April 6 with House he had become much more belligerent. He had ordered the *George Washington* and ordered credits to the Allies stopped, and throughout the day of April 7, he had seemed so utterly determined to fight that even House was astonished by the completeness of his surrender on the afternoon of April 8. Thus it is difficult to escape the impression that there had been a considerable alteration in his attitude between the evening of April 7 and the afternoon of April 8. In the absence of Wilson it is impossible to fix the moment of his collapse; but one is left with the impression that his final decision not to fight for the treaty he had promised to the world was probably made in the night of April 7. And one is tempted to imagine that he lay awake that night, facing the fear of a masculine fight which lurked in the soul of little Tommy Wilson, who had never fought a fist fight in his life, and decided to quit. That may have happened. But Wilson was not given to facing unpleasant realities, and none of his future excuses or actions indicate that he consciously recognized the truth about himself. On the contrary they indicate that he repressed the truth into his unconscious, and consciously persuaded himself that by compromising he would achieve all and more than all he might achieve by fighting.

We noted that in order to solve the inner conflict which was torturing him Wilson needed only to discover some rationalization which would permit him both to surrender and to remain in his own belief the Saviour of the World. We find that he discovered not merely one such rationalization but three! In the month which followed his compromise of April 8, 1919, he repeated over and over again three excuses. His great excuse was, of course, the League of Nations. Each time he made a compromise which was irreconcilable with his pledge to the world that the peace would be made on the basis of the Fourteen Points, he would say in the evening to his associates: "I would never have done that if I had not been sure that the League of Nations would revise that decision." He persuaded himself that the League would alter all the unjust provisions of the treaty. When he was asked how the League could alter the treaty since the League was no Parliament of Man but on the contrary each member of the Council of the League had an absolute veto, he replied that it was true that the present League could not alter the treaty; but that the League would be altered and made stronger until it would become strong enough to alter the treaty, and that it would then alter the treaty. Thus he relieved himself of any moral obligation to fight. The moment he achieved the belief that the terms of the treaty were mere temporary expedients which would be rewritten by a permanent League, he could believe that nothing really mattered except the existence of the League. This he supremely wished to believe because the League was, he thought, his title to immortality. He closed his eyes to the fact that the League might be temporary and the terms permanent — until altered by war. In his eagerness to be the Father of the League, he totally forgot his point of view of the previous year:

that he could ask the American people to enter a League to guarantee the terms of the treaty only if the treaty should be so just that it would make new wars most improbable. He needed a rationalization so badly that he was able to blind himself to the fact that the League was essentially an organ to guarantee the permanence of the terms of the Treaty of Versailles, and he was able to believe that the League was essentially an organ to revise the very terms which it was designed to perpetuate! By the use of this rationalization he was able both to surrender and to believe that he was still the Saviour of the World.

His second excuse was and is astonishing. He was always able to find some principle to cover the nakedness of behavior which might be shocking to ordinary human decency; nevertheless it is astounding to find that he made the Treaty of Versailles as a matter of principle. He invented a magnificent sophism: He told his friends that since he had come to Europe to establish the principle of international cooperation he must support this principle and cooperate with Lloyd George and Clemenceau even at the cost of compromises which were difficult to reconcile with the Fourteen Points. He was able to fix his eyes so firmly on the words "international cooperation" that he could ignore the fact that his compromises, made in the name of the principle of international cooperation, would make international cooperation impossible. He labored for international cooperation by establishing the reparations settlement and the Polish Corridor! He applied his principle not to reality but to his conscience with such success that again he felt relieved from his obligation to fight. Indeed, it became a matter of principle not to fight! Once again, as so often in his life, a beautiful phrase had come to his rescue and slain a vicious fact that threatened his peace of mind.

His final excuse was Bolshevism. Again and again he painted word pictures of what would happen if he should fight and withdraw from the Peace Conference rather than compromise. He described the French Army marching into Germany, obliterating whole cities by chemical warfare, killing women and children, conquering all Europe and then being submerged by a Communist revolution. Again and again he repeated: "Europe is on fire and I can't add fuel to the flames." Thus he was finally able to convince himself that he had suppressed his personal masculine wish to fight in order to spare Europe from the dreadful consequences which would have followed his release of his masculinity. It became self-sacrificing of him not to fight. By this somewhat circuitous route he managed to bring further support to his conviction that he had sacrificed himself for the welfare of humanity, and therefore resembled Christ.

Wilson seems to have accepted these rationalizations fully and finally in the second week of April 1919. He wanted to believe in their validity, therefore he believed. Thus, most satisfactorily to him, he escaped from the inner conflict which tortured him. But all his excuses were based on the ignoring of facts, and facts are not easy to ignore. A man may repress knowledge of an unpleasant fact into his unconscious; but it remains there struggling to escape into consciousness and he is compelled to repress not only his memory of it but of all closely associated facts in order to continue to forget it. His mental integrity becomes impaired, and he moves steadily away from the fact making greater and greater denials that the fact exists. The man who faces facts, however unpleasant they may be, preserves his mental integrity. The facts which Wilson had to face were, to be sure, most unpleasant: He had called his countrymen to follow him on a crusade and they had followed him with courage and conspicuous self-abnegation; he had promised them and the enemy and, indeed, all mankind a peace of absolute justice based upon his Fourteen Points; he had preached like a prophet who was ready to face death for his principles; and he had quit. If, having quit, instead of inventing soothing rationalizations, Wilson had been able to say to himself, I broke my promises because I was afraid to fight, he would not have disintegrated mentally as he disintegrated after April 1919. His mental life from April to September 1919, when he collapsed completely and permanently, was a wild flight from fact. This mental disintegration is an additional indication that in the second week of April 1919 he could not face his femininity and fear but merely embraced with finality the rationalizations which enabled him to avoid looking at the truth. At the crisis of his life he was in fact overwhelmed once more by his passivity to his father and by fear. But he seems never to have let his knowledge of this fact rise into his consciousness. It seems clear that when he decided to allow the Fourteen Points to be transformed into the Treaty of Versailles he was conscious of only the most noble motives. He betrayed the trust of the world as a matter of principle.

XXXI

ONCE WILSON had decided to compromise to the bitter end rather than fight and had rescued his identification with the Saviour by convincing himself that the League of Nations would alter any unjust provisions he might allow in the treaty and preserve peace eternally, he made his compromises with astonishing celerity. On April 7, he had threatened to break up the Conference; one week later, April 14, the treaty was so far advanced that the German Government was invited to send delegates to Versailles to receive it.

Wilson's speed in compromising was accelerated not only by his rationalization that the terms of the treaty were relatively unimportant so long as the League existed but also by his need to ask for amendments to the Covenant of the League. It had become clear that, unless the Monroe Doctrine should be specifically exempted from review by the League, the Senate of the United States would not ratify the treaty. Wilson, therefore, had to ask for a Monroe Doctrine amendment to the Covenant. At last the British and French had him in the position of asking for something. They made it clear that he would not get the Monroe Doctrine amendment unless he should promise the British to limit the American fleet and agree to the peace terms of both Britain and France. On April 8, he accepted the reparations terms of Lloyd George and Clemenceau; on April 9 and 10, he compromised in the matter of the Saar and the American fleet; on April 11, he got his Monroe Doctrine amendment; on April 15 he accepted Clemenceau's demands with regard to the occupation of the Rhine.

As we have seen, Wilson had insisted on establishing the League of Nations and giving America's guarantee for the treaty before any term of the treaty was settled in the hope that he might lift the negotiations to the plane of the Sermon on the Mount and avoid fighting; and then, when he feared to fight in April, had adopted the League as his moral justification. Lloyd George and Clemenceau finally realized that Wilson could not bear to do without the League no matter what was in the treaty; and, when he objected to terms which could not be reconciled with the Fourteen Points, Lloyd George would politely remind him that further resistance would "put an end to the League of Nations," and Wilson would begin to "flutter."

Lloyd George was able to use this threat with effect merely because of Wilson's inner psychic need to preserve his identification with Christ by means of his rationalization that the League would alter all the evil terms of the treaty. The interests of the people of the United States did not demand that they should guarantee an evil peace. Wilson personally, however, needed not only a League but also a special sort of League in order to save the faint aroma of reason which clung to his rationalization. It was highly improbable, almost impossible, but nevertheless conceivable that the tail might wag the dog, that the League of Nations might grow into a Parliament of Man and revise the treaty and make peace. But it was inconceivable that a League in which the United States was not represented should become strong enough to achieve this unprecedented accomplishment, and equally inconceivable that if the already weak League should be further weakened by amendments and reservations it could grow into a powerful super-state which might alter boundaries and servitudes at will. Wilson therefore had to get a League which would both satisfy the Senate of the United States and not be altogether feeble, or abandon the rationalization which made it possible for him to believe that he had indeed saved the world. His actions during the remainder of his life were largely controlled by his need to get such a League.

Only once did he check, momentarily, his headlong descent to the Treaty of Versailles. On April 23, he issued his manifesto on Fiume, appealing to the people of Italy to support him against their own premier, Orlando. He issued this appeal after long, fruitless negotiations which were unimportant except in so far as they gave the final *coup de grâce* to his love for House. The Italians had refused to accept the proposal of the committee of American "experts" with regard to Fiume, and House had set up another committee, of which his brother-in-law Mezes was the head, which worked out a conciliatory proposal. Wilson, who was on the lookout for actions of the Colonel's which could be interpreted as betrayals, considered that the setting up of the Mezes committee was an attempt by House to stab him in the back. In the words of Mr. Baker, "It is unquestionable that the attitude of Colonel House in dividing the expert counsel of the Commission and in favoring concessions to Italy, although he constantly urged that it was necessary to do so to 'save the League,' widened the breach that already existed between him and President Wilson."

Wilson was averse to compromising with Italy not only because he had yielded so often to France and England that it was becoming difficult for him to reconcile the growing treaty with the Fourteen Points but also because he was profoundly ashamed that in a moment of pure ignorance he had promised all the Tyrol south of the Brenner Pass with its two hundred and fifty thousand German-speaking Austrian inhabitants to Italy. He was determined that Italy should get no more undeserved annexations out of him. He issued his manifesto. Orlando went back to Italy and said to the Italian people: Choose between Wilson and me. The pictures of Wilson before which the Italian peasants had been burning candles suddenly disappeared and his face appeared in cartoons surmounted by a German helmet. Wilson, upset by the unexpected response from the adorers to whom he had thrown kisses in Milan, was told that his manifesto had failed because Mezes and House had indicated to the Italians that he was merely bluffing. That was the end. His love for House expired. His identification of House with little Tommy Wilson existed no longer. The Colonel became to the President a composite paranoid figure: Joe Wilson, Hibben, Iscariot.

To record the details of the compromises Wilson made in the remainder of the month of April 1919 seems unnecessary. His reaction to the demands of the Allies became stereotyped: surrender, regret, self-justification. His behavior on the evening of April 30, 1919, after he had surrendered the Chinese province of Shantung to Japan was typical. Mr. Baker recorded: "I saw the President at 6:30 as usual and he went over the whole ground (of the Japanese settlement) with me at length. He said he had been unable to sleep the night before for thinking of it. Anything he might do was wrong. He said the settlement was the best that could be had out of a dirty past . . . The only hope was to keep the world together, get the League of Nations with Japan in it and then try to secure justice for the Chinese . . . He knew his decision would be unpopular in America, that the Chinese would be bitterly disappointed, that the Japanese would feel triumphant, that he would be accused of violating his own principles, but nevertheless, he *must* work for world order and organization against anarchy and a return to the old militarism." Therefore he worked against "a return to the old militarism" by relinquishing a Chinese province to old Japanese militarists.

The Treaty of Versailles was delivered to the Germans on May 7. The President of the National Assembly at Weimar, upon reading it, remarked, "it is incomprehensible that a man who had promised the world a peace of justice, upon which a society of nations would be founded has been able to assist in framing this project dictated by hate." The first German official comment on the treaty was made on May 10, 1919. It stated that a first perusal of the treaty revealed that "on essential points the basis of the Peace of Right, agreed upon between the belligerents, has been abandoned," that some of the demands were such as "no nation could endure" and that "many of them could not possibly be carried out."

This statement infuriated Wilson. He was striving to forget that he had made a peace which could not be reconciled with his Fourteen Points; and he could not bear to have anyone tell him that he had broken his word. To be reminded of the truth must have raised the scourgings of his Super-Ego to an unbearable severity. Mr. Baker wrote: "It had an especially unfortunate effect upon President Wilson, . . . who was simply rendered indignant by this blanket indictment. He knew well enough what had been done, knew that settlements had been agreed to which did not conform to his standards and did not satisfy him, for the sake of giving the chaotic world immediate peace and to secure a powerful new organization to guarantee it. Unsupported accusation only inspired him to general denial and plunged the whole discussion into an atmosphere of passionate controversy." The Germans had said what he knew to be true; what he could not, therefore, bear to hear. He had a marvelous ability to ignore facts and to believe what he wanted to believe, but it must have been difficult for him to preserve his confidence in his own likeness to the Saviour in the face of the German statement. He managed to do so, however, by clinging to his belief that the League would reform the treaty. And thenceforth he ignored in so far as possible all criticisms of the treaty. On May 12, House recorded in his diary: "The Associated Press gave me a copy of President Ebert's tirade against the President and his Fourteen Points. I asked the President if he desired to answer it. He said: No, and did not even want to read it, for the American people were satisfied with the peace and he did not care whether Germany was or not."

This statement of Wilson's seems to mark important progress in his flight from reality. Both assertions in it were untrue. It is obvious that he refused to read the German criticisms not because he cared nothing about them but because he cared so much about them that he could not face reading them. His inordinately pow-

erful Super-Ego still demanded that he should be the just Judge of
the World. And he was after all the same man who had insisted
that the Allies should accept as a part of the armistice agreement
his commandment of September 27, 1918: "First, the impartial
justice meted out must involve no discrimination between those to
whom we wish to be just and those to whom we do not wish to be
just. It must be a justice that plays no favorites and knows no
standard but the equal rights of the several peoples concerned."
He had, to be sure, altered considerably in the intervening
months but there was at least a historical continuity between the
Wilson of September 27, 1918, and the Wilson of May 12, 1919.
He had not lost his sense of identity. And no man who had talked
as he had talked and possessed his Super-Ego could have read the
German comments on the treaty without a sense of personal shame
— repressed perhaps but burning. He had after all let down the
world, and his sense of guilt must have been enormous; and every
time his attention was called to his monumental betrayal his sense
of guilt must have threatened to burst through from his unconscious into consciousness. Obviously he had to keep his eyes
averted in so far as possible from the truth about himself.

Unfortunately for Wilson's mental equilibrium his statement
that "the American people were satisfied with the peace" was also
untrue. Most Americans, to be sure, knew almost nothing about
international affairs and nothing whatever about the terms of the
Treaty of Versailles. Moreover they had been whipped by propaganda into an exaggerated hatred of Germany so that the severity
of the treaty was congenial to them. But most Americans were also
opposed to "European entanglements"; and since the League, an
integral part of the treaty, was regarded as entangling the United
States somehow in European squabbles, there was a strong feeling
against ratification even among the Americans who did not object
to the terms of the treaty and were ready to attack as "pro-German
and Boshevik" anyone who spoke the truth about the terms.

In addition, the few Americans who knew enough about international affairs to be able to visualize the political and economic consequences of the peace were heartily opposed to the treaty because of the viciousness of its terms. Even among the members of the American delegation in Paris, from Mr. Lansing downward, criticism of the treaty was widespread and violent. The reparations clauses were expected to condemn Europe to economic collapse, the political clauses to sow the seeds of new wars and the League clauses to make probable the involvement of the United States in such wars. This criticism for the most part was made behind closed doors, since many members of the American delegation felt themselves to be participants in the crime, accessories before the fact, and others were unready to take the step of resigning, which was a prerequisite to public criticism, and to face being denounced as "pro-German and Bolshevik." On May 17, 1919, however, one of the authors of this volume resigned from the American delegation and inaugurated a public attack on the treaty by the publication of the following letter to Wilson:

May 17, 1919

My dear Mr. President:

I have submitted today to the Secretary of State my resignation as an assistant in the Department of State, attaché to the American commission to negotiate peace. I was one of the millions who trusted confidently and implicitly in your leadership and believed that you would take nothing less than "a permanent peace" based upon "unselfish and unbiased justice." But our Government has consented now to deliver the suffering peoples of the world to new oppressions, subjections, and dismemberments — a new century of war. And I can convince myself no longer that effective labor for "a new world order" is possible as a servant of this Government.

Russia, "the acid test of good will," for me as for you, has not even been understood. Unjust decisions of the Conference in regard to Shantung, the Tyrol, Thrace, Hungary, East Prussia, Danzig, the Saar Valley, and the abandonment of the principle of the freedom of the seas, make new international conflicts certain. It is my conviction that the present League of Nations will be powerless to prevent these wars, and that the United States will be involved in them by the obligations undertaken in the covenant of the league and in the special understanding with France. Therefore the duty of the Government of the United States to its own people and to mankind is to refuse to sign or ratify this unjust treaty, to refuse to guarantee its settlements by entering the League of Nations, to refuse to entangle the United States further by the understanding with France.

That you personally opposed most of the unjust settlements, and that you accepted them only under great pressure, is well known. Nevertheless, it is my conviction that if you had made your fight in the open, instead of behind closed doors, you would have carried with you the public opinion of the world, which was yours; you would have been able to resist the pressure and might have established the "new international order based upon broad and universal principles of right and justice" of which you used to speak. I am sorry that you did not fight our fight to the finish and that you had so little faith in the millions of men, like myself, in every nation who had faith in you.

Very sincerely yours,
William C. Bullitt

To the Honorable Woodrow Wilson,
     President of the United States.

The repercussion of this letter was great, out of all proportion to the importance of the person who had written it. It was of course denounced as "pro-German" and "Bolshevik" by those who so enjoyed their hatred of Germany and Russia that they were unwilling to be recalled to reality; but it produced a world-wide wave of assent and thanks from those familiar with the realities of international relations. This reaction was especially strong in England. Wilson did not reply to the letter; but a week later he was compelled to face the point of view it expressed not only by General Smuts' letter of May 22, 1919, to Lloyd George denouncing the treaty but by Lloyd George himself!

Lloyd George, who had proudly carried the treaty to London, returned to Paris in a state of mind which Wilson described as "a perfect funk." In spite of the fact that he had garnered for the British Empire a new imperial domain in Africa, Asia Minor and the Eastern seas and had destroyed the economic, naval and military power of Germany, he had been harshly criticized by his associates in the government for allowing France to become too strong. It was pointed out to him that he had destroyed the balance of power in Europe and had made France England's chief potential enemy. He returned to Paris determined to modify the treaty at the expense of France and Poland, the ally of France, while clinging to all the gains of England. He attempted to persuade Wilson to join in his attack on the terms which favored France, but succeeded only in arousing Wilson's contempt and anger: contempt because the British conversion to virtue for others was in fact contemptible, anger because Lloyd George was actually venturing to suggest that the son of the Reverend Joseph Ruggles Wilson had presented to Germany terms which did not accord with his Fourteen Points. Wilson could never bear to admit in public that any terms of the treaty conflicted with the Fourteen Points. He might have welcomed Lloyd George's pretended conversion, demanded a revision of the entire treaty and the relinquishment of Britain's spoils as well as the gains of France, except for the fact that to have taken that course would have been to admit that he had done wrong, that he had prepared an evil treaty, that he had not been the perfect, just and righteous Judge of the World. It was at best difficult for him to repress his knowledge of the viciousness of the treaty, and Lloyd George's proposals threatened his entire belief in his own righteousness. He could not ask for general revision of the treaty he had sanctioned. Angry and contemptuous, Wilson pointed out that the terms of the treaty were what they were only because Lloyd George had sided with Clemenceau against him. He refused to bring pressure to bear on Clemenceau but said that he would assent to any modifications in the direction of clemency which Lloyd George could persuade Clemenceau to accept.

A fear that Germany would not sign the treaty began to spread in Paris, and Wilson's refusal to work with Lloyd George for last-minute modifications aroused widespread criticism. On May 30, 1919, House, no longer the beloved disciple, recorded in his diary: "The feeling has become fairly general that the President's actions do not square with his speeches. There is a bon mot going the round in Paris and London, 'Wilson talks like Jesus Christ and acts like Lloyd George.' I seldom or never have a chance to talk with him seriously and, for the moment, he is practically out from under my influence. When we meet, it it to settle some pressing problem and not to take inventory of things in general or plan for the future. This is what we used to do. If I could have the President in quiet, I am certain I could get him to square his actions with his words. The President does not truly feel as I do, although I have always been able to appeal to his intellectual liberalism."

On June 3, 1919, Wilson called a meeting of the American delegation and made the following remarks on Lloyd George's conversion to virtue for others: "Well, I don't want to seem to be unreasonable but my feeling is this . . . that the time to consider all these questions was when we were writing the treaty, and it makes me a little tired for people to come and say now that they are afraid the Germans won't sign, and their fear is based upon things that they insisted upon at the time of the writing of the treaty; that makes me very sick.

"And that is the thing that happened. These people that overrode our judgment and wrote things into the treaty that are now the stumbling blocks, are falling over themselves to remove those stumbling blocks. Now, if they ought not to have been there, I say remove them, but I say do not remove them merely for the fact of having the treaty signed . . .

"Though we did not keep them from putting irrational things in the treaty, we got very serious modifications out of them. If we had written the treaty the way they wanted it, the Germans would have gone home the minute they read it.

"Well, the Lord be with us."

Lloyd George began to talk like a cheap edition of Wilson, saying that the time had come to decide whether the peace should be a "hell peace" or a "heaven peace"; but Clemenceau remained immovable and merely suggested to Lloyd George that the gains of the British Empire were immeasurably greater than the gains of France and that he would be more impressive if he were ready to return the German colonies and to make his charitable gifts not solely at the expense of France. Yet for the first time during the Conference British interests and human decency were on the same side of a question; and Lloyd George continued to make the most of this unusual coincidence. The extent to which his evangelism was produced by the first and not the second of these motives was, however, clearly shown on June 9 in the Council of Four when the Americans proposed that the reparations terms should be altered and a definite sum fixed in the treaty, and Lloyd George definitely refused to consider any abatement of his unlimited claims. The British Prime Minister, who wished to turn the "hell peace" into a "heaven peace," was unwilling to abandon one molecule of the British pound of flesh. Thus the tragedy of the Peace Conference was lightened in its last days by the comic though somewhat nauseating spectacle of the little Welsh Shylock, his pound of flesh safely in his pocket, preaching unselfishness — for others.

XXXII

WILSON at the Peace Conference had never attempted to use his hands to pick pockets while using his mouth to utter the words of Christ, and his contempt for Lloyd George and the British policy of preach and grab grew violent in June 1919. All the illusions about the nobility of British statesmen which he had cherished since his childhood were shattered. He began to have most friendly feelings for Clemenceau, who spoke the truth and did not smear the demands of France with British moral marmalade. He was tired of the whole dirty business and anxious only to get the treaty signed as soon as possible, so that he could return to America and get it ratified by the Senate and the League established. The more criticisms of the treaty that were made by Lloyd George and others, the more desperately Wilson clung to his rationalization that the League would later alter anything which needed to be altered in the treaty.

Wilson was exhausted and ill, and more nervous and sour-tempered than he had ever been in his life. On June 10, he refused to sit again for the portrait that Sir William Orpen was painting of him because Orpen had drawn his ears as large and protuberant as they actually were, and he was persuaded to sit again only by the promise that the ears should be reduced to less grotesque dimensions. They were. Reluctantly he took his long delayed trip to Belgium, returning to Paris on June 20. On that day he, Clemenceau and Lloyd George authorized Foch to advance against Germany on the evening of June 23, unless the German Government should agree to sign. On the evening of June 23, the German Government submitted.

The German submission produced no elation in Wilson. His hatred and loathing of nearly all mankind, which must have been at bottom a hatred and loathing of himself, had reached a fantastic pitch. He was overflowing with bile. And the hatred which he had not dared to loose against either Clemenceau or Lloyd George burst against Poincaré, President of the French Republic, who on the occasion of Wilson's arrival in France had made him feel inferior by speaking better without notes than he had been able to speak with notes. He refused to attend the farewell dinner which Poincaré wished to give him before his departure for America. Jusserand, French Ambassador to the United States, called personally to straighten out the matter. Wilson refused to see Jusserand, although Jusserand sent word that he had a personal message from the President of France. On June 24, House recorded in his diary: "The matter has become so serious that Poincaré called a meeting of the Council of State . . . He [Wilson] has made every sort of foolish excuse to Jusserand, such as 'I am leaving immediately after the peace is signed and would not have time to partake of a dinner, since the train is to leave at 9 o'clock in the evening.' Jusserand sent word that French officials were running the French trains and that the President's special train would not leave until after the dinner was over.

"The President came to the Crillon around 12 o'clock and we had it out . . . He said he had no notion of eating with Poincaré, that he would choke if he sat at the table with him . . . I called his attention to the fact that Poincaré was representing the French people and that he, the President, had been the guest of the nation for nearly six months. He said it made no difference, that he would not eat with him; that Poincaré . . . had tried to make trouble by sending a message to the Italian people . . . He went on to say that he had not come to the Crillon to discuss such an unimportant matter as eating with 'that fellow Poincaré' . . . I went back to the Poincaré invitation and was not surprised to find signs of weakening. He insisted, though, he had not received a regular invitation; that Jusserand had merely called and asked him what time would be convenient . . . Both White and I told him that this was the only form in which an invitation could be brought to him. He insisted then that Poincaré was merely trying to get himself out of a hole and that he did not intend to help him. He said, 'why does he not come to me direct instead of sending House, Lansing, White and Jusserand to help him out?' Both White and I tried to explain that what Poincaré had done was entirely regular and the only way it could be done. I suggested if he wished a regular invitation I would see that he got it in short order. This stirred him, and he expressed a hope that none of us would take further action, that if we did, it would be a reflection upon his attitude, and would show that we considered he was in the wrong."

The following day House recorded in his diary: "He completely capitulated as far as the Poincaré dinner was concerned. When he left the Crillon yesterday he sent a note to Jusserand naming to-morrow, Thursday, as the time he would be glad to accept an invitation for dinner . . . The episode was a revelation to everyone excepting myself of something in his character which had not been seen before. It accounted to them for his many enemies. Although he finally goes to the dinner, Poincaré will never forgive his having forced upon him such an unpleasant situation."

This incident, though intrinsically unimportant, seems a most significant indication of Wilson's state of mind at the close of the Peace Conference. It is clear that the "something in his character" which surprised the peace Commissioners was his reaction-formation against his passivity to his father. He had been afraid to loose the charge of libido that it contained against Clemenceau and Lloyd George in spite of the extreme provocation they had given him. And he had submitted temporarily to Lodge by amending the Covenant in the hope of making it acceptable to Lodge. Thus the libido insulated in his reaction-formation against his passivity to his father had been without outlet and had reached such a pitch of intensity that it had to break out against someone. It broke out against Poincaré not only because Poincaré was a President but also because Poincaré had spoken better than he had spoken and was therefore an excellent substitute for the Reverend Joseph Ruggles Wilson. Then in the end Wilson submitted to Poincaré, and the charge of mingled libido and Death Instinct was again without outlet and remained repressed, awaiting Lodge.

On June 28, 1919, the day the Treaty of Versailles was signed, House talked with Wilson for the last time in his life, and the next day recorded in his diary: "My last conversation with the President was not reassuring. I urged him to meet the Senate in a conciliatory spirit; if he treated them with the same consideration he had used with his foreign colleagues here, all would be well. In reply he said, 'House, I have found one can never get anything in this life that is worth while without fighting for it!' " In order to find outlet for his reaction-formation against his passivity to his father he had to meet Lodge with uncompromising hatred. But he also had to obtain ratification of the treaty by the Senate in order to maintain the rationalization which preserved his identification with Christ. There was an incompatibility between these necessities. The great streams of libido which sprang from his infantile desires with regard to his father were, indeed, once again in conflict. Because of his reaction-formation against his passivity to his father it was impossible for him, by compromising with Lodge, to obtain the ratification of the treaty which his passivity to his father demanded. His psychic needs left but one course of action open to him: he had to obtain ratification by crushing Lodge.

Wilson, on the day the treaty was signed, commended it to the American people: "The treaty of peace has been signed. If it is ratified and acted upon in full and sincere execution of its terms it will furnish the charter for a new order of affairs in the world . . . It ends once for all an old and intolerable order under which small groups of selfish men could use the peoples of great empires to serve their own ambition for power and dominion . . . There is ground here for deep satisfaction, universal reassurance and confident hope."

House, the day after the treaty was signed, wrote in his diary: "To those who are saying that the Treaty is bad and should never have been made and that it will involve Europe in infinite difficulties in its enforcement, I feel like admitting it . . . We have had to deal with a situation pregnant with difficulties and one which could be met only by an unselfish and idealistic spirit, which was almost wholly absent and which was too much to expect of men come together at such a time and for such a purpose. And yet, I wish we had taken the other road, even if it were less smooth, both now and afterward, than the one we took. We would at least have gone in the right direction and if those who follow us had made it impossible to go the full length of the journey planned, the responsibility would have rested with them and not with us."

Wilson had escaped from the feeling of guilt which was weighing upon House by clinging firmly to the belief that the League would alter any imperfections in the treaty and the cognate belief that the imperfections were slight. He returned to America, and on the wings of his wishes soared away from the ugly facts until they fell below the horizon of his mind and he was able to declare that the treaty was almost perfect, "a ninety-nine percent insurance against war."

XXXIII

WILSON'S PROGRESS to mental and physical collapse in the three months which separated his signature of the Treaty of Versailles on June 28, 1919, from his breakdown of September 26, 1919, may be followed by the perusal of his public utterances. Let us glance at them, remembering that he was still in the grip of the conflict which had harassed him all his life: the conflict between his passivity to his father and his aggressive activity against his father, and that his mental equilibrium depended on his ability to beat Lodge into submission and to repress his knowledge of the truth about the Peace Conference.

He presented the treaty to the Senate for ratification on July 10, 1919, and his address, considering his precarious physical and mental condition, was surprisingly reasonable. He soared away from the facts in certain passages, saying for example, "Convenient, indeed indispensable, as statesmen found the newly planned League of Nations to be for the execution of present plans of peace and reparation, they saw it in a new aspect before their work was finished. They saw it as the main object of the peace, as the only thing that could complete it or make it worthwhile. They saw it as the hope of the world, and that hope they did not dare to disappoint. Shall we or any other free people hesitate to accept this great duty? Dare we reject it and break the heart of the world?" But after this flight he returned to the vicinity of the earth, no doubt on deference to criticisms of the Shantung settlement, and said, "It was impossible to accommodate the interests of so great a body of nations . . . without many minor compromises. The treaty, as a result, is not exactly what we would have written. But results were worked out which on the whole bear test. I think that it will be found that the compromises which were accepted as inevitable nowhere cut to the heart of any principle. The work of the Conference squares, as a whole, with the principles agreed upon as the basis of the peace as well as with the practical possibilities of the international situations which had to be faced and dealt with as facts."

For the next month he fretted, waiting for the Senate to act; but the Senate did not act and the treaty was as far from ratification as ever when he invited the members of the Senate Committee on Foreign Relations to meet him at the White House on August 19, 1919, for a conversation on the treaty. He began the conversation by a statement intended to turn against Lodge the desire of the nation to return to peace. He attributed the stagnation of American trade to the failure of the Senate to ratify the treaty, thus wielding the weapon to preserve which he had destroyed the "preliminary treaty." Then, in answering questions, he revealed an extraordinary mental disintegration. His argument with regard to Article X of the Covenant of the League, "fairly stated in syllogistic form would read thus:

"1. Certain moral obligations are imposed by Article X.

"2. Legal obligations are less binding than moral obligations.

"Hence, objection to Article X is unsound because its obligations are not legal, and therefore not binding."

But even more surprising than this logic was his testimony with regard to the secret treaties of the Allies. He testified that he knew nothing about them before reaching Paris for the Peace Conference, saying, "The whole series of understandings were disclosed to me for the first time then." He further stated that he was not informed of the Treaty of London. Senator Johnson recited the list of the treaties, including the Treaty of London, the agreement with Rumania and the various treaties dividing Asia Minor, and asked: "Did you have any knowledge prior to the Conference?" To which Wilson replied: "No, Sir, I can confidently answer that 'No' in regard to myself."

The fact is established that Wilson was informed of the existence of the secret treaties in 1917, when Balfour came to America, if not before. And one is left with no alternative but to conclude that Wilson either was lying or actually had forgotten when he answered Senator Johnson. The first denial "The whole series . . ." is curiously reminiscent of his denial of the "supplementary" *Lusitania* note; but he had little to gain from denying knowledge of the treaties and much to lose by being caught lying, and he was almost sure to be caught; so that it is difficult to believe that he deliberately lied. On the other hand, it is difficult to believe that he had forgotten that he wanted to fight out the matter of the secret treaties with Balfour in April 1917 and had been persuaded not to make the fight by House or that he had seen the texts later published by the Soviet Government. But one recalls that the terms of the secret treaties were the terms of the Treaty of Versailles and that he was striving to repress his knowledge of the terms of the Treaty of Versailles in order to preserve his identification with Christ and to escape the scourgings of his Super-Ego. To realize that he had incorporated many terms of the secret treaties in the treaty which he had presented to the world as the embodiment of his Fourteen Points would have been unendurable to him. It seems probable, therefore, that he was not lying, but that his repression of his knowledge that the Treaty of Versailles embodied the terms of the secret treaties had merely annexed an adjacent bit of territory. This repression of the fact that the existence of the secret treaties had been disclosed to him was no doubt strengthened by his unconscious wish to believe himself the victim of a conspiracy — Jesus Christ betrayed.

After this meeting with the Senators his physical condition grew worse; he suffered daily headaches and became intensely nervous. He decided, in spite of the objections of his physician, his wife and his Secretary, to tour America appealing to the people to support him in his fight for the treaty — his fight against Lodge. One recalls that he had toured America once before appealing for support in a fight against a father representative. Lodge was, after all, only the successor of West; and Wilson's attitude toward the second of these father substitutes was a reproduction of his attitude toward the first.

Tumulty argued against the trip. Wilson replied: "I know that I am at the end of my tether, but my friends on the Hill say that the trip is necessary to save the treaty and I am willing to make whatever personal sacrifice is required, for if the treaty should be defeated, God only knows what would happen to the world as a result of it. In the presence of the great tragedy which now faces the world, no decent man can count his own personal fortunes in the reckoning. Even though, in my condition, it might mean the giving up of my life, I will gladly make the sacrifice to save the treaty."

Admiral Grayson, his physician, warned Wilson that his speaking tour might result in a fatal collapse. For three weeks he kept Wilson from going. Finally Wilson said to him: "I hope it won't have any bad effects but even if it does, I must go. The soldiers in the trenches did not turn back because of the danger and I cannot turn back from my task of making the League of Nations an established fact." Thus in August he decided to lay down his life if necessary to save the same treaty which in April he had almost decided to lay down his life, if necessary, to destroy. It is obvious that the important thing to Wilson was not the purpose for which he might lay down his life but only that he should lay it down or believe that he might lay it down for some purpose which would enable him to preserve the belief in his unconscious that he was Christ. He had to reassure himself that he was the Saviour. His passivity to his father and his Super-Ego would not let him rest, and his knowledge of what he had done in Paris was not easy to keep repressed. On September 3, 1919, he took the train in Washington for the West, and one may be sure that in his unconscious when he boarded the train he was mounting an ass to ride into Jerusalem.

XXXIV

WILSON'S TRIP to the West in September 1919 was the supreme expression of the neurosis which controlled his life.

His first speech, made on September 4 at Columbus, Ohio, showed that he had left fact and reality behind for the land in which facts are merely the embodiment of wishes. He forgot that his mother was an immigrant from England and his father's parents immigrants from Ulster and said, "I have been bred and am proud to have been bred, of the old revolutionary stock which set this government up . . ." He described the Treaty of Versailles as "This incomparable consummation of the hopes of mankind." Later the same day at Richmond, Indiana, he said, "It is the first treaty ever made by great powers that was not made in their own favor." The treaty was a new Holy Writ. Neither England, France nor Italy had written a term in selfishness. They had annexed the German colonies, dismembered Austria, Hungary and Turkey, severed East Prussia from the body of Germany, disemboweled the Tyrol, confiscated the German merchant marine and all the German private property upon which they could lay hands, and placed a burden of tribute upon Germany without limit of time or amount; but not in their own favor!

The next day at St. Louis Wilson described his opponents as "contemptible quitters," whose "ignorance" and "aberrations" amazed him. He asked the question, "What was the old formula of Pan-Germanism?" And himself answered, "From Bremen to Bagdad, wasn't it? Well, look at the map. What lies between Bremen and Bagdad? After you get past the German territory, there is Poland. There is Bohemia which we have made into Czecho-

Slovakia. There is Hungary, which is divided from Austria and does not share Austria's strength. There is Rumania. There is Jugo-Slavia. There is broken Turkey; and then Persia and Bagdad." The ignorance of geography revealed by these sentences is so astounding, especially in view of the fact that Wilson had been studying maps for months in Paris, that it seems further evidence that he was striving to forget and succeeding in forgetting the map he had arranged.

In his evening speech at St. Louis on September 5, 1919, he stated: "The real reason that the war we have just finished took place was that Germany was afraid her commercial rivals were getting the better of her." Less than twenty-four hours later at Des Moines, Iowa, September 6, 1919, he stated: "The businessmen of Germany did not want the war that we have passed through. The bankers and manufacturers and the merchants knew that it was unspeakable folly. Why? Because Germany by her industrial genius was beginning to dominate the world economically, and all she had to do was to wait." That one mind could produce these two statements within twenty-four hours indicates merely that the mind was falling more and more under control of the unconscious, in which contradictions may exist happily side by side since desire, not reason, is omnipotent. He added, "The formula of Pan-Germanism, you remember, was Bremen to Bagdad — Bremen on the North Sea to Bagdad in *Persia*." And he concluded this speech with the following description of the Treaty of Versailles: "I want to say that this is an unparalleled achievement of thoughtful civilization. To my dying day I shall esteem it the crowning privilege of my life to have been permitted to put my name to a document like that."

Wilson could not have made a statement so perverted as this except as a defense against unbearable scourgings of conscience. It is clear that he was in the hands of an inquisition conducted by his Super-Ego. To escape from his inner torture he was ready to believe or to say anything. By this date, September 6, 1919, his need to forget what he had done in Paris had driven him close to psychosis. Facts had become anything he wished to believe. In the week which followed, it became clear that he wished to believe that he had got in Paris precisely the treaty he had set out to get, that he had fulfilled all his pledges, that the Treaty of Versailles was almost perfect. In Spokane, Washington, on September 12, he declared for the first time but not the last, "this is a ninety-nine percent insurance against war."

The next day, September 13, 1919, Wilson began to suffer from violent headaches which continued without interruption until his collapse on the train on September 26. He was suffering in addition from indigestion, neuritis and the nervous irritability which habitually preceded his nervous collapses. His face was gray and the left side of it and the eye twitched.

Sunday, September 14, he rested and prayed. On September 15, in Portland, Oregon, he opened his address with the statement: "There is nothing I respect so much as a fact," and went on to make a speech which contained not facts but awesome predictions and figures of speech; covenanters on tombstones, poison, paralysis, tears, murder and dragons' teeth. He concluded: "I am glad for one to have lived to see this day. I have lived to see a day in which, after saturating myself most of my life in the history and traditions of America, I seem suddenly to see the culmination of American hope and history — all the orators seeing their dreams realized, if their spirits are looking on; all the men who spoke the noblest sentiments for America heartened with the sight of a great nation responding to and acting upon those dreams and saying, 'At last, the world knows America as the saviour of the world!' " It is difficult to avoid the impression that at that moment poor little Tommy Wilson's need for the approval of his "incomparable father" produced the fantasy that the Reverend Joseph Ruggles Wilson was leaning over the gold bar of Heaven and saying, "At last the world knows as I have always known that my Tommy is the Saviour of the World."

In San Francisco, on September 17, poor Wilson lifted Clemenceau, Lloyd George and Orlando to the plane of the Sermon on the

Mount, thus accomplishing at least in his own mind the miracle which he had so long and vainly striven to accomplish in Paris. He described the Peace Conference in the following words: "An illumination of profound understanding of human affairs shines upon the deliberations of that conference that never shone upon the deliberations of any other international conference in history . . . I was glad after I inaugurated it that I drew together the little body that was called the Big Four . . . it was a very simple council of friends. The intimacies of that little room were the centre of the whole peace conference, and they were the intimacies of men who believed in the same things and sought the same objects. The hearts of men like Clemenceau and Lloyd George and Orlando beat with the people of the world as well as with the people of their own countries. They have the same fundamental sympathies that we have and they know that there is only one way to work out peace and that is to work it out right."

At the end of his address he said: "My fellow citizens, I believe in Divine Providence. If I did not I would go crazy. If I thought the direction of the disordered affairs of this world depended upon our finite intelligence I should not know how to reason my way to sanity, and I do not believe that there is any body of men however they concert their power or their influence, that can defeat this great enterprise, which is the enterprise of divine mercy and peace and good will." It was God's treaty given to mankind by God's son Woodrow.

Thus by September 17 the Treaty of Versailles had become divine, and the next day the American Army became a heavenly host: "That is the glory that is going to attach to the memories of that great American Army, that it made conquest of the armies of Germany not only, but made conquest of peace for the world. Greater armies than sought the Holy Grail, greater armies than sought to redeem the Holy Sepulchre, greater armies than fought under that visionary and wonderful girl Joan of Arc, greater than the armies of the American Revolution that sought to redeem us from the unjust rule of Britain, greater ever than the armies of our

Civil War which saved the Union, will be this noble army of Americans who saved the world!"

In the following days poor Wilson drew closer and closer to the table of sacrifice, saying for example at Los Angeles, on September 20, 1919: "The hardest thing that I had to do . . . was to continue to wear civilian clothes during the war, not to don a uniform, not to risk something besides reputation — risk life and everything. We knew that an altar had been erected upon which that sacrifice could be made more gloriously than upon any other altar that had ever been lifted among mankind, and we desired to offer ourselves as a sacrifice for humanity. And that is what we shall do, my fellow citizens." Mankind would at last be saved by the blood of Woodrow Wilson.

The perfection of the treaty steadily increased until on September 24, at Cheyenne, Wyoming, it became humanity's masterpiece: "That treaty is a unique document. It is the most remarkable document, I venture to say, in human history, because in it is recorded a complete reversal of the processes of government which had gone on throughout practically the whole history of mankind . . . we said that it must be a people's peace. It is a people's peace. I challenge any man to find a contradiction to that statement in the terms of the great document with which I returned from Paris. It is so much of a people's peace that in every portion of its settlement every thought of aggrandizement, of territorial or political aggrandizement on the part of the Great Powers was brushed aside, brushed aside by their own representatives . . . They did not claim a single piece of territory."

It is clear that when Wilson made these statements he was not consciously lying. He had started by repressing his knowledge of what he had done in Paris and in the customary manner the repressed area had annexed adjacent territory until it had become impossible for him to remember what he or anyone else had done in Paris. He was very close to psychosis.

The next evening, September 25, 1919, at Pueblo, Colorado, poor little Tommy Wilson, who had learned to talk like God by listening to his "incomparable father," talked like God for the last time. The facts in his address were fantastically distorted: "Not one foot of territory is demanded by the conquerors, not one single item of submission to their authority is demanded by them."

Yet the peroration, which was the peroration of his own life, was beautiful. He asked the question: "What of our pledges to the men that lie dead in France?" And answered, "These men were crusaders. They were not going forth to prove the might of the United States. They were going forth to prove the might of justice and right, and all the world accepted them as crusaders, and their transcendent achievement has made all the world believe in America as it believes in no other nation organized in the modern world. There seems to me to stand between us and the rejection or qualification of this treaty the serried ranks of those boys in khaki, not only those boys who came home, but those dear ghosts that still deploy upon the fields of France.

"My friends, on last Decoration Day I went to a beautiful hillside near Paris, where was located the cemetery of Suresnes, a cemetery given over to the burial of the American dead. Behind me on the slopes was rank upon rank of living American soldiers, and lying before me upon the levels of the plain was rank upon rank of departed American soldiers. Right by the side of the stand where I spoke there was a little group of French women who had adopted those graves, had made themselves mothers of those dear ghosts by putting flowers every day upon those graves, taking them as their own sons, their own beloved, because they had died in the same cause — France was free and the world was free because America had come! I wish some men in public life who are now opposing the settlement for which these men died could visit such a spot as that. I wish that the thought that comes out of those graves could penetrate their consciousness. I wish that they could feel the moral obligation that rests upon us not to go back on those boys, but to see the thing through, to see it through to the end and make good their redemption of the world. For nothing less depends upon this decision, nothing less than the liberation and salvation of the world." Wilson wept. He really believed that he had brought back from Paris the peace of God for which the American boys had died. But this belief was built above the gaping pit of his sense of guilt, the burning hole of fact in his unconscious.

That night on the train he collapsed. It was obvious to Admiral Grayson that if he should continue the tour he would die. He told Wilson that. Wilson said he preferred to continue the tour. Grayson awakened Tumulty. Wilson, tears running down his face, pleaded with Grayson and Tumulty to let the trip go on, saying, "Don't you see that if you cancel this trip Senator Lodge and his friends will say that I am a quitter and that the Western trip was a failure, and the treaty will be lost?" He did not say, but we may say for him, don't you see that if you cancel this trip I will not die for mankind, I will not be Christ, I will not conquer my father, I will not be God. They canceled the trip. Wilson returned to the White House. Three days later, at four o'clock in the morning, he fell on the floor of his bathroom, his left side paralyzed by thrombosis in the right side of his brain.

The reader will recall that in the year 1906 Wilson's Super-Ego and his conflicting desires with regard to his father drove him to a campaign of feverish speech-making which culminated in the bursting of a blood vessel in his left eye, and that the same desires were involved in his feverish speech-making of 1908, which also culminated in a collapse. The same desire drove him in 1919 to the campaign of speech-making which culminated in his thrombosis. After 1908 his father fixation had become complete. And the similarity of his actions in 1906, 1908 and 1919 is so striking that it is difficult to avoid the impression that he was acting in obedience to a *Wiederholungszwang,* a compulsion to repeat, when he set out in 1919 for the West. At least it is clear that he was driven to destruction by the old conflict he had never been able to solve, the conflict between his activity toward his father and his passivity to his father. He had never solved the major dilemma of the Oedipus complex, and in the end he was destroyed by the same "incomparable father" who created him.

XXXV

WILSON LIVED four years and four months after his collapse of September 1919. But we can draw no conclusions as to his character before his collapse from his behavior after it, since it is impossible to say how much the physical disorder in his brain affected his psychic life. His behavior in any given instance may have been produced by this organic affection rather than by psychic causes. The thrombosis was, to be sure, in the right side of his brain in an area which controlled motor functions, so that it produced paralysis of his left side and, superficially at least, seemed to leave his reason intact. But a neurotic's reason is merely the tool of his unconscious, and physical maladies of the brain invariably produce psychic repercussions. Wilson's thrombosis produced obvious alterations in his character and, while it may not be without interest to follow the physical entity called Woodrow Wilson to the grave, we must recognize that, as a character, the Thomas Woodrow Wilson we have studied died on the twenty-fifth of September 1919.

The Woodrow Wilson who lived on was a pathetic invalid, a querulous old man full of rage and tears, hatred and self-pity. He was so ill that he was allowed to receive only such information as his wife thought would be good for him. This fact increases our reluctance to draw any conclusions from his behavior after his collapse. His behavior in any given instance may have been produced by misinformation or lack of information. He was no longer an independent human being but a carefully coddled invalid. He remained, in title, President of the United States until March 4, 1921; but during the last eighteen months of his administration

Mrs. Wilson was in large measure the chief executive of the United States. From the point of view of this psychological study, the last four years of Wilson's life are, therefore, of minor interest; but it seems worth while to glance at them before we bring to an end this attempt to understand his character.

In November 1919, when he was still dangerously ill and entirely dependent on Mrs. Wilson for information, he had to decide whether or not he should accept Lodge's reservations to the Covenant of the League of Nations and thus obtain immediate ratification of the Treaty of Versailles. Wilson refused absolutely to accept the Lodge reservations, and the following statement was issued in his name: "In my opinion the resolution in that form does not provide for ratification but rather for nullification of the Treaty. I sincerely hope that the friends and supporters of the Treaty will vote against the Lodge Resolution." Enough Democrats, at Wilson's behest, joined the thirteen Republican "irreconcilables" to defeat a resolution of ratification which included the Lodge reservations. Those reservations did not greatly alter the obligations of the United States under the Covenant and would have been accepted by all parties to the treaty, so that if Wilson had been ready to compromise with Lodge, the United States would have ratified the Treaty of Versailles and would have become a member of the League. Since Wilson believed, or at least had said that he believed, that "the liberation and salvation of the world" depended on the ratification of the treaty, it is remarkable that he never showed the slightest sign of compromising with Lodge. In the early spring of 1920, Senator Hitchcock appealed to Wilson to make some concession to Lodge, saying, "Mr. President, perhaps the time has come to extend to Lodge and his followers the olive branch in the interests of an equitable settlement." Wilson, in bed, closed his eyes, then replied in a deadly voice: "Let Lodge extend the olive branch!"

The treaty, reintroduced with the Lodge reservations attached, was again defeated at the behest of Wilson. Wilson had already taken the position that "the clear and single way out" was "to give the next election the form of a great and solemn referendum" on the League of Nations. He believed that the American people would support the treaty and crush Lodge. But the Democratic candidate was defeated by seven million votes, and Harding, one of the Republican "irreconcilables," was elected President. "They have disgraced us in the eyes of the world," said Wilson to Tumulty; but he went on believing that somehow the treaty would be ratified. "You can't fight God!" he cried to his visitors. The treaty was God's treaty. Woodrow Wilson had written it.

In sharp contrast to this belief stands his remark quoted by Professor William E. Dodd, "I ought not to have signed; but what could I do?" He seems to have realized at times that the treaty was in truth a sentence of death for European civilization. And similar contradictions are to be found in his remarks about individuals. Edward Bok quotes him as saying to Mrs. Wilson in 1920, "I told you, Edith, House was all right." But in speaking to an intimate he said of House: "To think that that man for whom I have done everything, to whom I told my inmost thoughts, should betray me." Wilson then wept.

These remarks seem authentic, and the contradiction they involve seems to be evidence merely of a disturbed mental condition. Wilson seems to have thought one thing one day and another thing the next about many things and many people. The single consistent traits in his character during his last years were his self-pity, his admiration for his dead father and his hatred of nearly all men on earth. His illness seems to have thrown back a considerable portion of his libido from love-objects to his original Narcissism. He had never managed to get his libido far away from himself, even his passionately loved friends were loved only because they were representatives of himself, and his illness seems to have concentrated all his love on his own body. He never found another friend to replace House, as he had found House to replace Hibben. He loved and pitied himself. He adored his dead father in Heaven. He loosed his hatred of that same father on many men. He refused to see Lord Grey. He refused to see Colonel House. He refused to pardon the aged Socialist leader, Debs, and closed his official career with a refusal to pardon another old man. He publicly made the faithful Tumulty appear a liar and a false friend and refused to see him again. He dismissed his physician, Admiral Grayson, when Grayson defended Tumulty; but thereafter could not sleep, phoned for Grayson to return and, weeping, embraced him.

In his last days he helped Ray Stannard Baker with the preparation of his apologia and talked from time to time with new friends, since he had no old ones left. As he drew closer to death he talked less and less about his days as President of the United States and more and more about his days as President of Princeton. Again and again he refought his fight with West and grew emotional over the "treachery" of Hibben, forgetting his fight with Lodge and the "treachery" of House. Again and again he retold the old, old stories about his "incomparable father."

On Sunday, February 3, 1924, he died in his sleep.

INDEX

INDEX

Adams, Dr. Herbert B., 26, 27
Allies, 159, 244; U.S. alignment with, 164–166, 171–173; and Wilson's dictating the peace, 169–170, 174, 177, 179, 181–182, 183, 197, 215; secret war aims and treaties of, 173–174, 177, 184, 188, 198–199, 208, 282–283; armistice negotiations with, 203, 220; economic dependence of, 208–210, 235, 246, 252, 255, 260; leaders of, 229, 231, 234–235, 241–247; Wilson as tool of, 232, 246; and reparations question, 249–250; Wilson rationalizes submission to, 262–264
Annin, Robert Edward, vii
Arabic (British liner), 162
Auchincloss, Gordon, 219, 220–221, 226–227, 257
Austria-Hungary, 239
Axson, Ellen Louise, 8, 22, 24–25, 56, 57, 156, 183; as mother representative, 25–26, 91–92, 95–97, 143, 151–152; death of, 26, 92, 155, 214; Wilson's correspondence with, 27–28, 29–30, 56, 93–94, 97, 111, 138; marries Wilson (*1885*), 95; and Tumulty, 143; Wilson's reaction to death of, 143, 155–157
Axson, Stockton, 108

Bagehot, Walter, 19, 21, 26, 27, 31, 87, 107, 159
Baker, Ray Stannard, vi, 295; on Wilson's relationship with his father, 6, 58, 65; on Wilson's state of mind (*1905–1906*), 114–115, 118; on Wilson-Yates relationship, 119; on Wilson's feelings of immortality, 148; on Wilson-House friendship, 233, 267; on Clemenceau-Wilson "alliance," 237–238; on Council of Four meetings, 241, 244, 245, 254–255; on Wilson's disappointment with German reaction to Peace Treaty, 269
Balfour, Arthur James, 188, 221, 224; and secret treaties of Allies, 198–199, 283; and preliminary treaty, 239–240
Baruch, Bernard M., 148; at Paris Peace Conference, 252
Bellamy, John, 17
Bernstorff, Johann-Heinrich von, Count, 156, 163, 176, 187–190, 191
Bohemia, 153–154
Bok, Edward, 294
Bolshevism, 222, 231, 247; and Lenin's armistice offer, 253; as rationalization for Wilson, 262–263
Bones, James, 24
Bones, Jessie Woodrow, 11, 14, 24, 57
Brenner Pass, 154
Bridges, Robert, 17, 20, 96; on Wilson's passion for speech, 21
Bright, John, 18, 19, 82, 84, 87, 107, 159
Brooke, Francis J., 15–16, 20, 73–74, 88; and Wilson's "religious conversion," 15, 73–74, 77; as father representative, 75–76; as love-object, 79
Brougham, Henry Peter, 21